Vancouver Eats

Joanne Sasvari

Vancouver Eats

SIGNATURE RECIPES FROM THE CITY'S BEST RESTAURANTS

Figure.1
Vancouver / Berkeley

18 19 20 21 22   5 4 3 2 1

Cataloguing data is available from Library and Archives Canada
ISBN 978-1-77327-036-4 (hbk)

Design: Jessica Sullivan
Photography: Kevin Clark
Art direction: Naomi MacDougall, Jessica Sullivan
Prop styling: Naomi MacDougall, Issha Marie, Jessica Sullivan
Props: Issha Marie

Editing by Michelle Meade
Copy editing by Grace Yaginuma
Proofreading by Lucy Kenward
Indexing by Iva Cheung

Printed and bound in China by C&C Offset Printing Co., Ltd.
Distributed in the U.S. by Publishers Group West

Figure 1 Publishing Inc.
Vancouver BC Canada
www.figure1publishing.com

Dedicated to all
the growers, fishers,
ranchers and producers
who keep us so
deliciously well fed.
None of this is
possible without you.

Contents

Introduction

VANCOUVER IS A seriously foodie city. You don't have to spend much time here before someone will ask you the questions that are on all our minds: Where should we eat? And what should we order once we get there? Sometimes it seems that food is all we talk about—at least when we're not talking about real-estate prices—and dining is what we do when we're not busy jogging around the Seawall or doing SUP yoga in English Bay.

We're lucky to have incredible local bounty right on our doorstep—a wild ocean full of salmon, Dungeness crab and sweet, buttery spot prawns; dark forests that shelter savoury wild mushrooms; the Fraser Valley farms where it seems that just about everything grows, from berries to honeybees to Berkshire pigs; and just over the mountains, the Okanagan Valley, one of the world's great unsung wine regions. All those incredible ingredients inspire our chefs; farm to table is just how they roll in Vancouver. After all, why would you source food from anywhere else when it's so good right here at home?

It's also more sustainable to cook that way, and ethical dining is always on the table here. This is the home of Greenpeace, *Adbusters* and David Suzuki, not to mention Ocean Wise, the sustainable seafood program that sprang from the Vancouver Aquarium. We tend to raise an eyebrow at restaurants that don't serve Ocean Wise seafood (politely, of course—we're still Vancouverites). We love our veggies as much as we love our bacon, and woe betide the chef who doesn't know how to create vegan dishes that are every bit as delicious as their braised short ribs and roasted bone marrow. We expect our food to be organic and raised with compassion, though we really don't want to pay more for it. Did we mention the real-estate prices?

But mostly we want things to be local. It's not just the fuel miles, though that matters. We want to know that a farmer in a nearby suburb is going to benefit from our food dollars, and not some faceless corporation. Besides, it just tastes better that way.

Funnily enough, as obsessed as we are with all things local, Vancouver has become one of the world's most global dining cities. We can thank our location here on the edge of the continent, caught right smack between East and West. Waves of newcomers have brought their most delicious dishes to our tables. European immigrants imported French techniques, Italian pasta, German smokehouses, and English chowders and fish 'n' chips; meanwhile, from all over Asia arrived an almost infinite array of noodles, sushi, curries, soups, dumplings and all the bright, fragrant sweet-salty-sour-and-hot flavour combinations that make our mouths water so. Now we're seeing a new influx of culinary traditions coming from the south, from Mexico and Peru, Venezuela and Argentina: chilies and cilantro, sweet corn and tangy ceviche, and behind it all, the savoury sizzle of the traditional barbecue known as *asado*.

Sure, other cities have international tables, too. That's not unique. What is special to Vancouver is that all of it is on the same table at the same time. Fusion is just what we do. It's a whole new style of cooking, one so fresh that it hasn't yet been fully defined. But we know it when we taste it. Oh, we think as we bite into a tortilla filled with local spot prawns and yuzu-flavoured crème fraîche, now *that* tastes like Vancouver.

Some people might fuss about authenticity, but we're a bit more relaxed about it. As chef after chef told us, the point is to make a tasty dish. If it tastes good, who cares where it came from? Good point, we think. Besides, it's an attitude that fits with our casual approach, not just to food, but life itself. This is not a city of hushed dining rooms filled with white-tablecloth-covered tables. It's one where you're likely to slurp sherry from a

marrow bone, suck crabmeat from spindly legs, bite the heads off flash-fried prawns and lick the best gosh-darned barbecue sauce ever off your fingers.

We like our libations, too. The city's cocktail culture is among the most progressive in the world; Vancouver bartenders not only mix mean drinks, they also tend to kick butt at global competitions. The craft beer scene is fizzing, and more and more distilleries are coming on line all the time. Half the city, it seems, has sommelier training, which means you have to work pretty hard to get a bad glass of wine with your meal.

People rave about Vancouver's physical beauty, the mountains and beaches, the blue waters that surround us, the lush parks and blooming gardens, the glittering towers and gracious homes. But what's really remarkable is the people who live here, and all the delicious things they've brought to the table. We've gathered up just a few of those things in the following pages, pages that we hope will become spattered and worn as you make your favourites again and again and again.

In fact, we've assembled more than a hundred recipes from the city's best restaurants. That way you can make your favourite dishes at home where no one will notice if you lick the plate. Go ahead. We won't judge.

The Restaurants

The Recipes

Mains

RICARDO VALVERDE

Ancora Waterfront Dining and Patio

DISTRACTED BY THE VIEW outside the floor-to-ceiling windows? Don't blame you. Here on the Seawall overlooking Granville Island, it's easy to while away the hours just watching the joggers and shoppers, the cheery little Aquabuses in False Creek, and the sun set beyond the Burrard Bridge. But tear your eyes away from the scenery for just a moment. Ancora is one coolly elegant, chandelier-lit space, almost as beautiful as the food from Ricardo Valverde's kitchen.

The Lima-born chef combines elements of his South American heritage with Japanese traditions and B.C. ingredients to create a vibrantly new cuisine. "We're trying to break boundaries with the food. We give people the West Coast ingredients and West Coast flavours, but we put a Peruvian twist on it. That's what makes it special," he says.

Consider it a culinary adventure that travels around the Pacific Rim and back home again. Chili and citrus dance through Valverde's updated South American classics, including the ceviche and *causa* that feature in the Glacier, a fresh take on the been-there-done-that seafood tower that's a sprawling spread of oysters, tartare, crab, mussels, escabeche and poached prawns. Meanwhile, at the raw bar, legendary sushi chef Yoshi Tabo has inspired the team that deftly slices up hamachi and toro, while award-winning wine director Andrea Vescovi pours notable world wines from a remarkable cellar.

"Being a chef in Vancouver allows me to showcase the things I want to do," Valverde says. "There's a unique consumer here willing to try new flavours and new concepts."

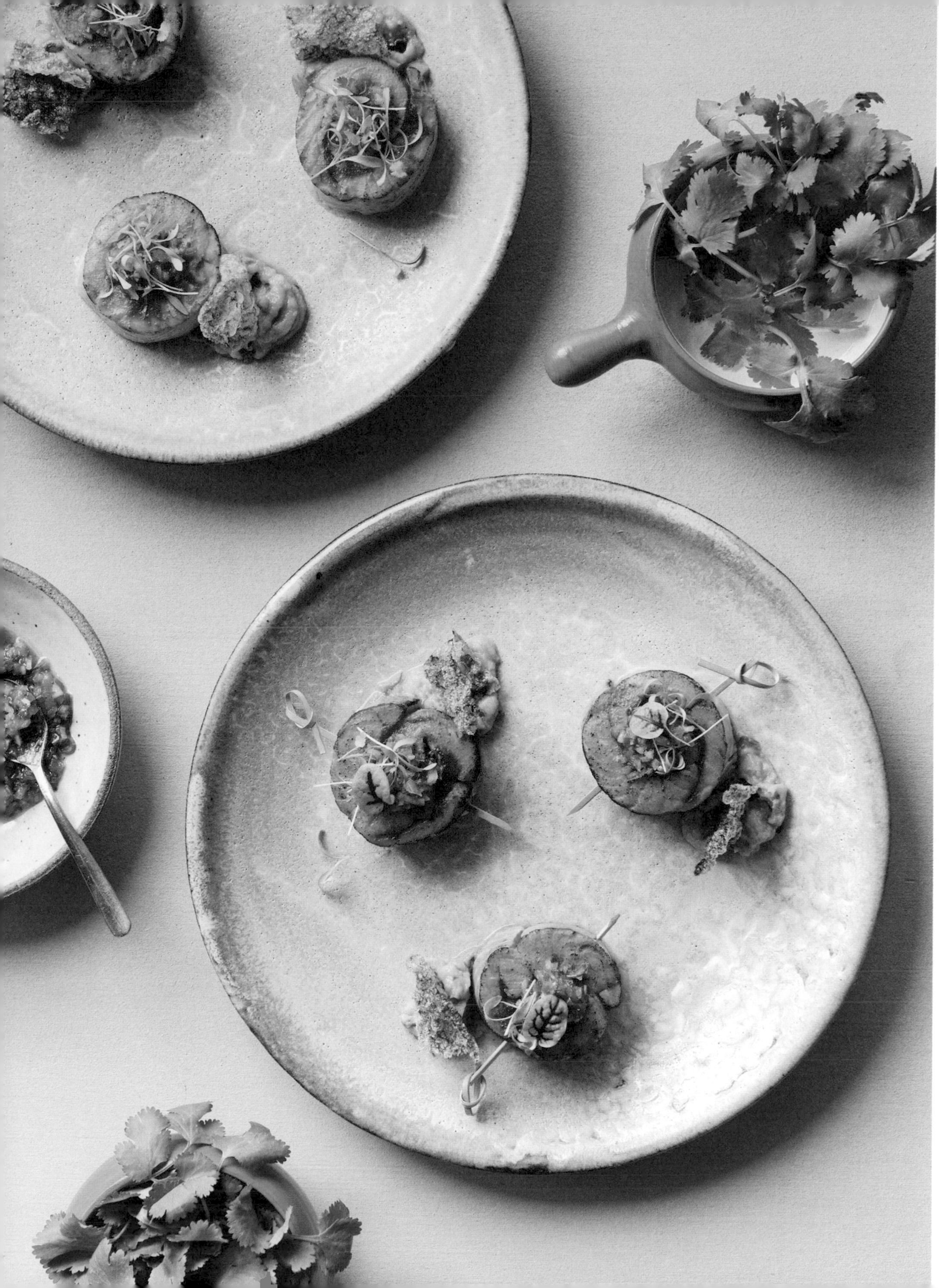

ANTICUCHO SAUCE

¾ cup Peruvian *aji panca* paste
(see Note) or ancho chili purée

⅓ cup red wine vinegar

6 Tbsp canola oil

3 cloves garlic

1 Tbsp dried oregano

1 tsp ground cumin

STEELHEAD TROUT

1 (1-lb) steelhead trout, filleted
and skin removed and reserved

2 cups canola oil, or as needed,
for deep-frying

Salt and freshly ground black
pepper, to taste

Fresh cilantro leaves, for garnish
(optional)

AVOCADO MOUSSE

1 ripe avocado, pitted

Juice of 1 lime

Salt and freshly ground black
pepper, to taste

Steelhead Trout Anticucho

SERVES 2

Traditionally, anticucho is a street food dish of marinated chunks of meat (beef heart was especially popular) grilled on skewers. It originated in the Andes and migrated to different parts of South America. Here, the dish is updated with a very West Coast ingredient: steelhead trout. Chef Valverde adds a twist by searing it first, and then serving it with an avocado mousse, pico de gallo and crispy trout skin chicharrón.

ANTICUCHO SAUCE Put all ingredients in a blender or food processor and mix for 1 minute, until smooth. Set aside. (The sauce can be stored in an airtight container in the fridge for 6 months—use it with chicken, seafood or meat.)

STEELHEAD TROUT Preheat oven to 350°F.

Slice fish lengthwise though the middle, then cut the remaining fillet into 3 or 4 pieces. (Or trim them into rounds as they do at Ancora.) Reserve belly for a sushi appetizer or a trout ceviche marinated in *leche de tigre* (page 22). Cover with plastic wrap and set aside in the fridge until needed.

To make the trout skin chicharrón, place trout skins between 2 baking sheets and bake for 30 minutes, until dried.

Pour oil into a deep saucepan or deep-fryer and heat to a temperature of 400°F. Using a slotted spoon, carefully lower dried skin into pan, taking care not to splash hot oil. Deep-fry for 5 seconds, until puffed and crispy. Drain on paper towels and season with salt and pepper.

AVOCADO MOUSSE Scoop avocado into a small bowl and using a fork, mash it into a thick paste. Add lime juice and salt and pepper and mix well. Cover tightly with plastic wrap (to prevent browning) and refrigerate until needed.

PICO DE GALLO

1 Roma tomato, peeled, seeded and finely diced

1 shallot, finely chopped

1 Tbsp sliced green onions

1 Tbsp chopped fresh cilantro

Juice of 2 limes

Salt and freshly ground black pepper, to taste

NOTE:

Aji panca paste is a versatile smoky-sweet condiment made from Peruvian peppers and available in South American markets. Use it to season everything from eggs to steak.

PICO DE GALLO Combine tomatoes, shallots, green onions and cilantro in a bowl and mix well. Season with lime juice, salt and pepper. Cover and refrigerate until needed. This can be prepared the night before and stored in the fridge for up to 3 days.

ASSEMBLY Brush anticucho sauce over trout. Place trout on a fire-resistant surface, then, using a kitchen torch, sear it lightly. (Alternatively, sear each piece in a very hot pan with a splash of olive oil for about 10 seconds on each side.)

Spread avocado mousse on a serving plate. Place trout on top of the mousse, then top with pico de gallo. Garnish with chicharrón and cilantro leaves (if using). If you like, to pay homage to the origins of the dish, you can stick small skewers into the pieces of trout.

LECHE DE TIGRE

Juice of 6 to 8 limes

1 Tbsp finely grated celery
(preferably with a Microplane)

1 Tbsp chopped fresh cilantro

1 red jalapeño pepper, seeded
and finely chopped

1 clove garlic, finely grated

¼ tsp finely grated ginger

CEVICHE

1 yam, peeled and cut crosswise
into ½-inch-thick rounds

1 red onion, thinly sliced

1 (1-lb) skinless halibut fillet, cut
into ½-inch cubes

Salt and freshly ground black
pepper, to taste

1 Tbsp chopped fresh cilantro,
plus extra leaves for garnish

Corn nuts, to serve

Peruvian-Style Halibut Ceviche

SERVES 4

Ceviche is the traditional Peruvian dish of raw seafood that is lightly cured in a citrus-based marinade known as leche de tigre, *or tiger's milk. Prepare the marinade and yam ahead of time, then mix all the ingredients together at the last minute for a bright and fresh appetizer.*

LECHE DE TIGRE In a non-reactive bowl, combine all the ingredients and mix well. Cover and refrigerate until needed. (This can be made the night before.)

CEVICHE Preheat oven to 400°F.

Place yam in a greased baking dish and roast for 10 minutes. Set aside to cool. (This can be prepared the day before since it is served cold.)

Put onion in a colander and rinse under cold running water to crisp it up and reduce its bitterness, then drain. Set aside to dry for 10 minutes.

Transfer halibut to a clean bowl and season generously with salt and pepper. Add leche de tigre, cilantro and reserved onion and mix well.

Serve immediately with corn nuts and roasted yams, and garnish with cilantro leaves. Do not drain the liquid—it's the best part of the dish.

MICHAEL ROBBINS

AnnaLena

IT'S ALL ABOUT FAMILY at AnnaLena. The Kitsilano restaurant not only is named for the grandmothers who helped raise Chef Michael Robbins, but also honours his unofficial family in the multicultural East Van neighbourhood of his childhood. "I had a lot of Filipino influences growing up, but also Chinese, Japanese and South Asian," he says. "We had a melting pot of cultures growing up on my block."

AnnaLena is modern Canadian cooking, heavily influenced by the Pacific Northwest. Robbins insists, "I don't want to be blatantly fusion. I want to use one country's technique with another country's flavour profile." For instance, he mixes the bright acidity typical of Japanese pickles with traditionally rich French fare, sprinkling pickled mustard seeds on a classic duck liver terrine. "Playing with vinegars and sugar and citrus is as important as salt, butter or cream," he says.

It's the kind of balance he saw at play with his two grandmothers, too. In fact, he based his restaurant on their personalities. "Anna liked bringing the whole family together, so she gets the bar; Lena, she's the home cook, so she gets the restaurant."

Whatever the rationale, it's proven to be a winning formula for the former executive chef of the Oakwood Canadian Bistro. Shortly after the restaurant opened early in 2015, the accolades started pouring in, including a top ten finish on *enRoute* magazine's list of Canada's best new restaurants. "We built a destination restaurant for the neighbourhood." His grandmothers would be proud.

3 L canola oil, or as needed, for deep-frying

1 lb fresh chicken skins

1 Tbsp coarsely ground Himalayan black salt (see Note)

11 oz milk chocolate, chopped

½ cup cocoa butter

NOTE:
Himalayan black salt (also known as *kala namak* or *bire noon*) is a type of pungent rock salt used in South Asian cooking. It is also considered a digestive aid and a cooling spice in Ayurveda.

AnnaLena Chicken Skins

SERVES 4 TO 6

Chicken skin? Dipped in chocolate? It might sound weird, but it turns out to be a match made in culinary heaven. In fact, this sweet-but-savoury, crispy-but-unctuous snack has become a favourite at AnnaLena.

Line 2 baking sheets with wire racks.

Pour oil into a large stockpot, filling it three-quarters full. Add chicken skins and turn heat to medium-high. Using a long slotted spoon, gently stir skins as oil heats up slowly.

Continue cooking until skins turn golden, about 1 to 1½ hours in total, lowering heat slightly if oil comes to a boil. (The skins will crisp up once you remove them from the oil.) It is important to keep scraping the bottom of the pot so the skins don't stick. Using a spider skimmer or slotted spoon, remove skins and carefully shake off any excess oil into the pot. Transfer skins to the prepared baking sheets.

Break skins into bite-sized pieces, then set aside to cool. Place them in the freezer for at least 2 hours, until frozen.

To prepare a dipping station, line 2 baking sheets with parchment paper, pour Himalayan black salt into a bowl and have a pair of kitchen tweezers ready.

Fill a small saucepan 2 inches deep with water and bring to a boil. Place chocolate and cocoa butter in a heatproof bowl that fits snugly on top of the pan without the bottom of the bowl touching the water. Melt mixture, stirring frequently until it reaches 113°F to 122°F. Try to maintain this temperature—dipping works best if chocolate stays this hot and skins remain frozen.

Using tweezers, pick up a frozen chicken skin and quickly dip into chocolate to coat. Place skin on a tray and sprinkle with salt before chocolate sets. Repeat with remaining skins.

Put tray of dipped skins in the freezer for 1 hour, until frozen. Transfer them into an airtight container. Serve frozen. (They will keep in the freezer for up to 2 months.)

DUCK LIVER PÂTÉ

2 Tbsp unsalted butter
1 cup chopped onions
½ cup chopped shallots
¼ cup finely chopped garlic
1 Tbsp kosher salt
1 tsp freshly ground black pepper
4 star anise, freshly grated or
    ground in a mortar or pestle
¼ cup brandy

¼ cup port
¼ cup vermouth
2 Tbsp honey
1 lb raw duck or chicken livers
4 large eggs
¾ cup clarified unsalted butter
Sourdough loaf, sliced
1 to 2 pears, sliced
Salad greens, for garnish (optional)

PICKLED MUSTARD SEEDS

½ cup mustard seeds
1 cup water
½ cup apple cider vinegar
¼ cup granulated sugar

Duck Liver Pâté, Sourdough, Pear and Pickled Mustard Seeds

MAKES 1 TERRINE

DUCK LIVER PÂTÉ Preheat oven to 375°F.

Melt butter in a large frying pan over medium heat. Add onions, shallots and garlic and sauté for 5 minutes, until soft and translucent. (Do not allow them to brown; reduce heat if necessary.) Add salt and pepper and star anise.

Increase heat to high. Pull the pan off the heat and add brandy (you don't want it to ignite). Return to heat and cook for another 10 to 15 minutes, until reduced by half. Add port and vermouth and cook for another 15 to 20 minutes, until reduced to one-quarter of original amount. Stir in honey.

Scrape mixture into a high-speed blender (such as a Vitamix) and process, starting at low speed and finishing on high, until fully blended.

With the motor running on medium speed, add duck (or chicken) livers one by one until well incorporated. With the motor still running, add eggs one by one until well mixed. Slowly pour butter in a steady stream until emulsified. (Make sure to maintain a vortex the entire time you are adding the ingredients.) Gradually increase speed to high and blend until smooth.

Strain mixture through a fine-mesh sieve into a terrine mould or ceramic baking dish. Place mould into a roasting pan, then pour hot water into the pan so it comes halfway up the outside of the terrine mould. Cover mould with foil and bake for 30 minutes, until it reaches an internal temperature between 150°F and 160°F. (Test it in a few different spots to be sure—if it's not cooked through, bake it a little longer.)

Remove from the oven and the roasting pan and set aside to rest at room temperature for 1 hour. Place it in the fridge for at least 8 hours.

PICKLED MUSTARD SEEDS In a small saucepan, combine mustard seeds and water and bring to a boil. Cook for 10 minutes, until water is reduced by half. Drain water. Add vinegar and sugar to the pan and cook for another 10 minutes, until liquid has reduced by half. Remove from heat and set aside to cool. (Store in the fridge for 2 to 3 months.)

ASSEMBLY Toast sourdough, then spread pâté onto each slice. Arrange pear slices on top of the pâté, then spoon pickled mustard seeds overtop. Garnish with salad greens (if using).

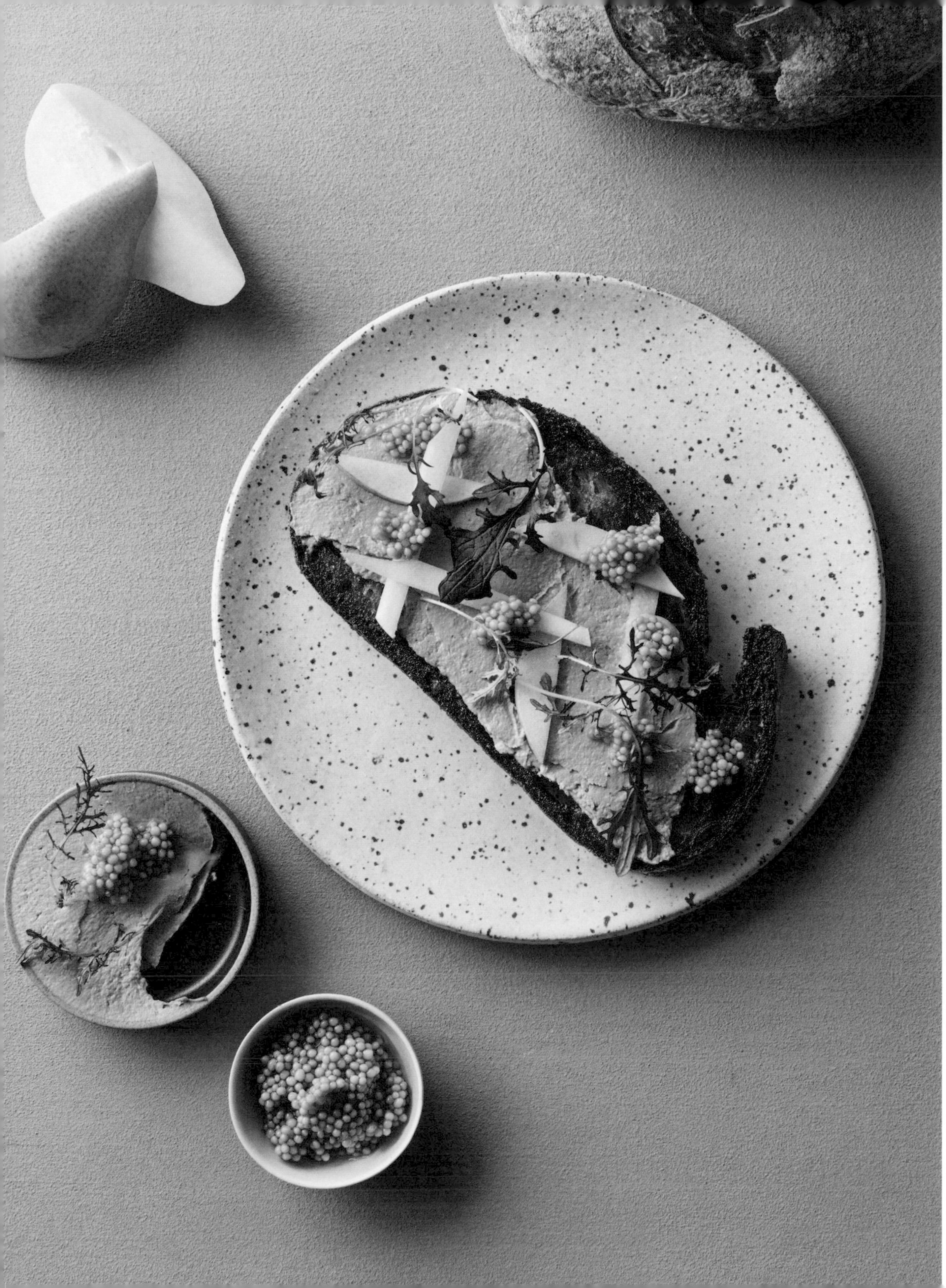

Araxi

QUANG DANG DIDN'T set out to become a chef. He was going to be an engineer like his dad. But first, he was going to play field hockey. The national team was based in Vancouver, so that's where he moved from Edmonton, working in restaurants to pay the bills while he studied structures and chased balls around muddy fields. Then one day, he says, "I met a chef and he told me, 'You can't do it all well—you have to pick one.'"

Food won. How lucky for the rest of us.

After a few years' cooking at some of Vancouver's most popular restaurants, in 2011 Dang became executive chef at Toptable Group's highly lauded West Restaurant + Bar, the youngest chef in an illustrious group of culinary talents. Then, after six years of creating delicate expressions of local seafood, foraged wild mushrooms and handcrafted pasta, he learned that James Walt, the long-time executive chef at Whistler's Araxi Restaurant, was taking on a new project. Araxi would need a new executive chef. Dang was it.

Araxi, which opened in 1981, is an oasis of cool, calm sophistication in what can sometimes be a party-hardy ski town. Mind you, when Araxi does throw a party, it's a pretty swell affair, whether it's the annual Big Guns dinner—featuring swoony vintages from award-winning wine director Samantha Rahn's spectacular cellar—or the boisterous Longtable dinners out in the fragrant fields of North Arm Farm in Pemberton. Most importantly, though, under Walt's direction, it became a passionate supporter of local producers, and that just happens to be Dang's thing, too.

"Araxi is an established restaurant, and iconic restaurants have soul. It's not like it needed a change," Dang says. For him, "It's more or less learning what James has been doing and adding my own personal touch. Essentially, to pick up where he left off." For his part, Walt, who will be around to lend a hand at Araxi even as he leads the team at Il Caminetto (page 142), says, "Bringing Quang up is a really good fit. He's got a really similar philosophy."

BEETS

3 lbs assorted beets, tops removed
2 Tbsp extra-virgin olive oil
1 bunch fresh thyme
Salt, to taste
Shaved beets, fresh herbs and/or edible flowers, for garnish (optional)

BLACK PEPPER CHEVRE

2 cups Farm House or other creamy fresh goat cheese
2 Tbsp whipping (33%) cream
2 Tbsp freshly ground black pepper

HERB VINAIGRETTE

1 shallot, sliced
1 bunch fresh tarragon
1 bunch fresh dill
1 bunch fresh thyme, leaves only
1 bunch fresh Italian parsley, leaves only
1 bunch fresh chervil (optional)

2 tsp freshly ground black pepper
1 tsp granulated sugar
1 tsp kosher salt
2 Tbsp white wine vinegar
1 Tbsp Dijon mustard
3 Tbsp extra-virgin olive oil

Beet Salad with Black Pepper Chevre and Herb Vinaigrette

SERVES 6

Araxi's chef Quang Dang has long been impressed by the produce that comes from Pemberton near Whistler, especially the German butter potatoes and sweet, tender beets. Here the earthy sweetness of roast beets is topped with a fragrant herb dressing and peppery-tart goat cheese—be sure to use beets of many colours for a bright rainbow of a salad that is both easy to make and sure to impress.

BEETS Preheat oven to 350°F.

Organize beets by colour. Place each colour on a separate piece of foil and drizzle with oil. Top with 1 to 2 sprigs of thyme and sprinkle with salt, then wrap foil to create a packet.

Place foil packages on a baking sheet and bake for 45 minutes, until beets are cooked through. To test for doneness, poke the beet with a small paring knife. The knife should slide through with ease.

Remove beets from foil and set aside to cool to room temperature. Peel off skin, then cut flesh into rounds or wedges. Keep beets in separate containers to prevent the colours from bleeding into each other.

BLACK PEPPER CHEVRE In a mixing bowl, whisk all ingredients together. Store in the fridge in an airtight container until needed.

HERB VINAIGRETTE Combine all ingredients except oil in a blender or food processor and blend until smooth. With the motor still running, gradually add oil and blend until emulsified.

ASSEMBLY Arrange beets attractively on a platter and drizzle with vinaigrette. Top with small spoonfuls of chevre. Garnish with shaved beets, fresh herbs and/or edible flowers, if using.

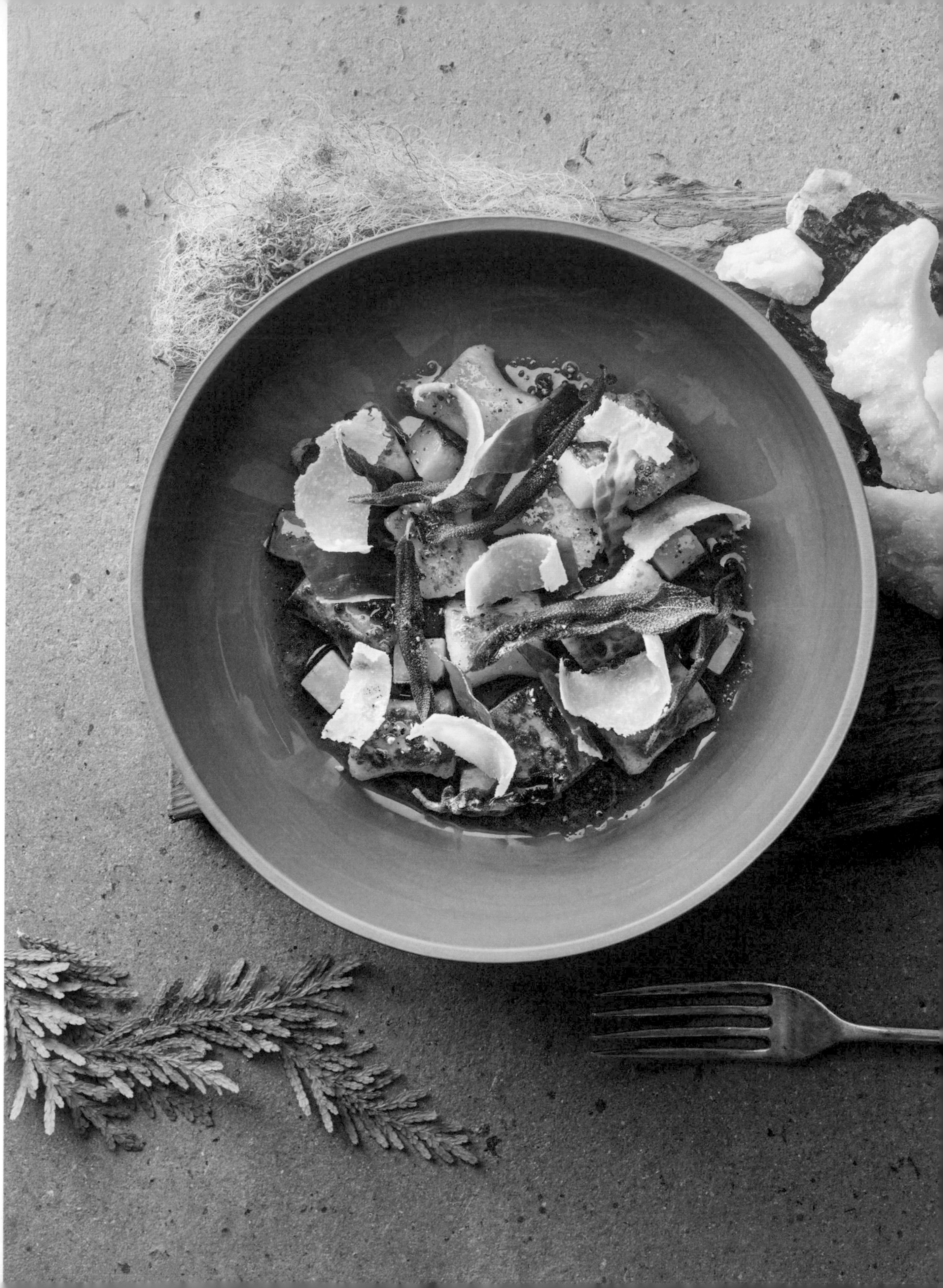

1¼ lbs russet potatoes, unpeeled

4 large egg yolks, beaten

1 cup all-purpose flour,
    plus extra for dusting

½ cup finely grated Parmesan,
    plus extra shavings for garnish

½ tsp ground nutmeg

Salt and freshly ground black
    pepper, to taste

Extra-virgin olive oil, as needed

2 tsp vegetable oil

3 Tbsp unsalted butter

1 cup chopped butternut squash
    (¼-inch cubes)

½ cup sliced prosciutto

1 sprig fresh sage

½ lemon

Gnocchi with Butternut Squash, Prosciutto and Sage Brown Butter

SERVES 6

Pemberton is famous for its potatoes, and there are few more delicious ways of preparing them than in a toothsome gnocchi tossed with simple sage brown butter. This dish presents all the flavours of fall on a plate.

Preheat oven to 450°F. Lightly oil a baking sheet.

Bake potatoes for 45 minutes, until completely tender throughout. (If you like, you can set them on a wire rack or a bed of salt on a baking sheet.) For the fluffiest gnocchi, peel and rice the potatoes while they're still hot. To avoid burning yourself, cut them in half and hold them with a pair of tongs while scooping out the flesh. Spread the riced flesh in a thin ½-inch-thick layer to cool.

Pour eggs over potatoes. Sprinkle with flour, Parmesan, nutmeg, salt and pepper. Gently mix into a pliable dough, being careful not to overwork.

Lightly flour a baking sheet. Dredge dough in flour. On a clean work surface, roll out dough by hand into a rope with a ¾-inch diameter. Cut rope into 1-inch pieces and place onto prepared baking sheet. Refrigerate until needed.

Bring a large saucepan of salted water to a boil. Drop gnocchi into the water and cook for 30 seconds, until they float to the surface. Using a slotted spoon, transfer gnocchi to a bowl of ice water to cool. Drain. Transfer to a lightly oiled baking sheet and toss with olive oil to prevent them from sticking to each other. Set aside to cool.

To caramelize gnocchi, heat vegetable oil in a large non-stick frying pan over medium heat. Add gnocchi and gently sauté until they begin to caramelize. Add butter, squash and prosciutto. Let the butter froth and foam to continue the caramelization. Cook for about 5 minutes, until gnocchi and squash become golden brown.

Add sage and a squeeze of lemon juice. Serve with a small amount of pan butter and garnish with Parmesan.

Bearfoot Bistro

AN EVENING AT Bearfoot Bistro is more than just another dinner. "It's an experience," says executive chef Melissa Craig. "It's not just about the food and wine. You visit the vodka ice room, and then you go downstairs in the wine cellar and sabre champagne. It's a bit of a crazy place."

In Whistler, Bearfoot Bistro is known for its epic events—they still talk about the night of Four Decades of Dom Pérignon and the fancy dinners aboard the PEAK 2 PEAK Gondola—which are generally instigated by host, founder and renowned bon vivant André Saint-Jacques. Credit him, too, for the twenty-thousand-plus-bottle cellar, where a sabre and a bucket of iced bubbly await the brave, as well as the minus-thirty-two-degrees-Celsius Ketel One Ice Room, where guests don Canada Goose parkas to knock back shots of icy spirit.

But all that dazzle doesn't dim the brightest light in the place: the soft-spoken Craig seemingly came out of nowhere in 2007 to beat some of the top chefs in the country and win the Canadian Culinary Championships. Although she enjoys playing with the tricks and techniques of modernist cooking and she changes her tasting menu every single day, she insists she's all about simplicity. That and the great local ingredients like Walla Walla sweet onions from Pemberton just up the road. She describes the restaurant's cuisine as "international flavours with West Coast ingredients," which doesn't even begin to describe the joyful creativity on the plate. Think black cod with sea urchin sabayon and caviar, or pastry chef Dominic Fortin's signature nitro ice cream à la minute.

Craig could be a star anywhere in the world, but she's perfectly happy right here. "In Whistler, you're feeding people who are on holiday, so people are relaxed and happy," she says. "Plus we have a close-knit community of chefs up here, and we all have each other's backs." Just watch out for flying champagne corks.

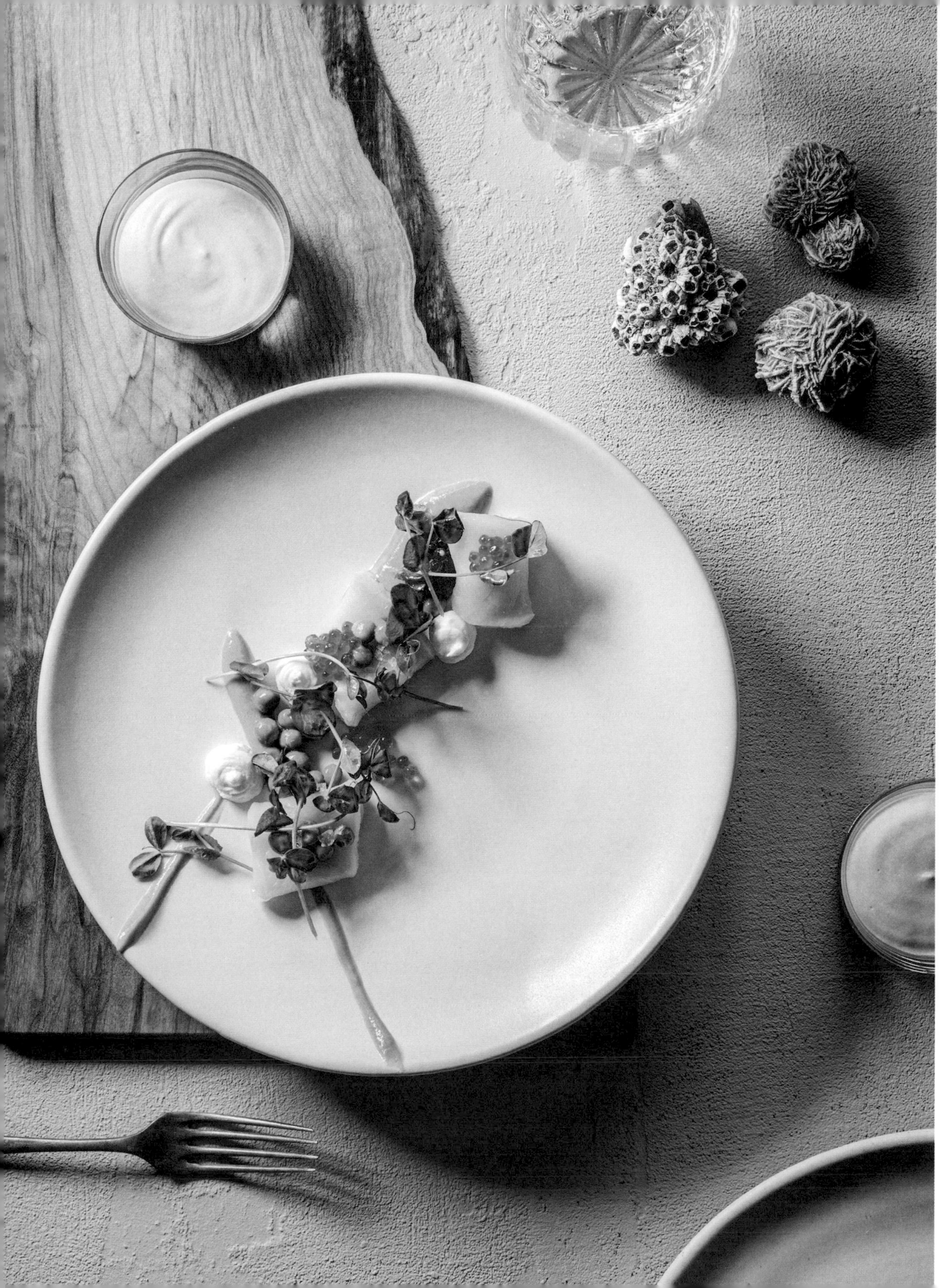

SMOKED STURGEON
½ cup kosher salt
½ cup granulated sugar
Grated zest of 1 lemon
Grated zest of ½ lime
1 lb sturgeon fillet, trimmed
    and skin removed
Ice cubes
Smoking chips (preferably a light
    wood like apple or alder)
1 oz trout roe

PEA PURÉE
1 cup vegetable stock
2 cups fresh peas
 Kosher salt, to taste

PEA MOUSSE
1½ sheets gelatin
¼ cup heavy (36%) cream
1 cup Pea Purée (see here)

Smoked Sturgeon with Textures of Green Peas, Minted Yogurt and Rye Gremolata

SERVES 8

What a showstopper of a dish this is, the sweet spring peas balancing beautifully with delicately smoked sturgeon and a crispy rye gremolata to add earthy flavour and nice texture. You'll need eight (two-ounce) shot glasses for this recipe.

SMOKED STURGEON In a small bowl, combine salt, sugar and citrus zests and mix well. Pack sturgeon top and bottom with the cure and refrigerate for 18 to 24 hours, until fish feels firm. Rinse fish under cold running water and pat dry.

To make a cold smoker, place a layer of ice in the bottom of a roasting pan. Put a piece of foil over the ice and smoking chips on top of foil. Place a rack over the foil and cured sturgeon on top. Light wood chips with a barbecue lighter or a long fireplace match. Once they start to smoke, cover pan with a lid or foil. Smoke for 30 minutes, until flesh is firm to the touch. Wrap and refrigerate for up to 1 week.

PEA PURÉE Bring stock to a boil in a medium saucepan. Add peas and cook for 3 minutes, until softened.

Place peas and stock into a high-speed blender (such as a Vitamix) and blend until smooth. Season with salt. Strain through a fine-mesh sieve into a bowl set in a larger bowl of ice water. Keep chilled until ready to use in the pea mousse.

PEA MOUSSE Place gelatin sheets into a bowl of cold water and set aside for 15 minutes, until softened.

Pour cream into a bowl and whisk until soft peaks form. Set aside. Gently warm 1 cup pea purée, setting the rest aside in the fridge to garnish the plate.

Remove bloomed gelatin from cold water, squeezing out any excess water. Add it to pea purée and mix to dissolve. Set mixture over a bowl of ice water until slightly cooled, but not set. Gently fold in whipped cream and immediately place mousse into a piping bag. Fill each shot glass with mousse, then refrigerate for 24 hours.

TEXTURES OF GREEN PEAS
¾ cup fresh peas
20 snap peas, trimmed (optional)
2 cups pea shoots

SHERRY VINAIGRETTE
1 Tbsp finely chopped shallots
1 tsp Dijon mustard
1 tsp honey
¼ cup sherry vinegar
½ cup grapeseed oil
2 Tbsp extra-virgin olive oil
Kosher salt and freshly ground
    black pepper, to taste

RYE GREMOLATA
2 cups crustless rye bread,
    cut into ½-inch cubes
2 Tbsp extra-virgin olive oil
1 small clove garlic, finely chopped
Grated zest of 1½ lemons
2 Tbsp finely chopped fresh
    Italian parsley
Kosher salt, to taste
Freshly ground black pepper,
    to taste

MINTED YOGURT
½ cup plain Greek yogurt
1 tsp honey
Grated zest of ½ lemon
1 Tbsp finely sliced fresh mint
Kosher salt, to taste

TEXTURES OF GREEN PEAS Bring a saucepan of lightly salted water to a boil, add peas and blanch for 1 to 2 minutes, until softened. Drain, then transfer to a bowl of ice water. Repeat for snap peas (if using). Split snap peas in half along their seam.

SHERRY VINAIGRETTE In a bowl, combine shallots, mustard, honey and vinegar. Whisk in oils until emulsified and season to taste with salt and pepper.

RYE GREMOLATA Preheat oven to 325°F.

Place bread cubes on a baking sheet and bake for 15 to 20 minutes, until dry. Set aside to cool, then put in a food processor and process until finely crumbled.

Heat oil in a large frying pan over medium heat, add garlic and sauté for 1 minute, until fragrant. Add bread crumbs and cook for 3 or 4 minutes, until golden and toasted. Remove from heat and add lemon zest, parsley, salt and pepper. Transfer to a plate lined with paper towels and set aside to cool completely.

MINTED YOGURT Combine all ingredients in a bowl and mix well. Season to taste with salt.

ASSEMBLY Dress 4 plates with a swipe of the pea purée and place a shot glass of pea mousse beside it. Thinly slice the smoked sturgeon and arrange around mousse.

Put peas, snap peas and pea shoots into a small bowl and dress with a little vinaigrette. Add pea mixture to each plate, then finish with gremolata, trout roe and dots of minted yogurt.

VEGETABLE STOCK

4 yellow onions, coarsely chopped
2 small leeks, white and light green
   parts only, cut into 1-inch pieces
2 carrots, cut into 1-inch pieces
4 stalks celery, cut into 1-inch pieces
1 small fennel bulb, top removed,
   cut into 1-inch pieces
12 sprigs fresh thyme
10 stems fresh parsley
1 bay leaf
1 tsp black peppercorns
6 L cold water

WALLA WALLA ONION SOUP

½ cup grapeseed oil
12 Walla Walla onions, peeled
   and sliced
3 cups Vegetable Stock (see here)
1 cup heavy (36%) cream
2 Tbsp unsalted butter
Kosher salt, to taste

GRUYÈRE ONION RINGS

¼ cup extra-virgin olive oil
3 yellow onions, peeled and diced
1 cup heavy (36%) cream
3 Tbsp unsalted butter
¼ cup all-purpose flour
¾ cup grated Parmesan
¾ cup grated cave-aged Gruyère
Ground cayenne pepper, to taste
Kosher salt, to taste
8 cups vegetable oil, or as needed,
   for deep-frying

Walla Walla Sweet Onion Soup with Gruyère Onion Rings

SERVES 8

Made with Walla Walla onions from North Arm Farm in Pemberton, this soup really showcases a single ingredient and is very easily made vegan. It is served with a side of cheese-filled onion rings, a play on French onion soup.

VEGETABLE STOCK Combine all ingredients into a large stockpot and bring to a boil over high heat. Reduce heat to low and simmer for 45 minutes to 1 hour.

Strain through a fine-mesh sieve into another pan, then set in a bowl of ice water to cool. The stock can be frozen in small batches for later use.

WALLA WALLA ONION SOUP Heat oil in a large heavy-bottomed saucepan over medium heat and add onions. Sauté for 30 to 40 minutes, until softened and slightly caramelized. Pour in stock and simmer for another 45 minutes.

Remove from heat and purée in a high-speed blender (such as a Vitamix), until smooth. If necessary, strain through a fine-mesh sieve.

Return soup to saucepan over low heat and whisk in cream and butter. Season to taste with salt. (To keep this soup vegan, omit cream and butter. This soup can be frozen for future use.)

GRUYÈRE ONION RINGS Heat oil in a large frying pan over low heat. Add onions and sauté for 30 to 40 minutes, stirring frequently, until caramelized and evenly browned. (They should not be bitter.) Transfer to a food processor and purée. Set aside.

Heat cream in a small saucepan over medium-low heat.

BREADING
¾ cup all-purpose flour
7 large eggs
½ cup whole milk
6 cups fine bread crumbs

Melt butter in a medium saucepan over medium heat, add flour and stir to form a roux. Cook for 3 to 4 minutes, until it turns slightly golden. Slowly add heated cream, stirring constantly, and cook for 5 to 10 minutes, until smooth and thickened. Reduce heat to very low and add Parmesan and Gruyère and 1 cup onion purée. Season with cayenne and salt. Set aside to cool slightly, then transfer mixture into a piping bag.

Line a baking sheet with parchment paper. Pipe cheese mixture onto the prepared baking sheet, creating onion rings that are 2 inches in diameter. Freeze for 2 hours, until solid.

BREADING Put flour in a shallow bowl. In a separate bowl, combine eggs and milk and whisk. Fill another bowl with bread crumbs.

Dredge each ring with flour, dip in egg mix and dredge in bread crumbs. Place back in freezer until ready to serve. (It can be stored in the freezer for up to 1 month.)

TO FINISH Pour oil into a deep-fryer or deep saucepan and heat to a temperature of 350°F. Carefully lower onion rings into oil, taking care not to splash hot oil. Deep-fry for 2 to 3 minutes, until golden brown. Using a slotted spoon, transfer rings to a plate lined with paper towel. Serve immediately with soup.

Beaucoup Bakery

A PROPER CROISSANT should shatter when you bite into it, exploding in flaky, buttery crumbs. The inside, though, should be pillowy and soft, a perfect vehicle for preserves. Sadly, a proper croissant is a rare treat indeed. Which is why a Beaucoup Bakery croissant is such a revelation. Oh! you realize. This is what all the fuss has been about.

Credit Betty Hung. Now the head baker and co-owner with her brother Jacky, she started at the bakery as an intern shortly after it opened in 2012 and quickly graduated to full-fledged baker. "I started on the night shift, which is all about the butter croissants," she says. Before that, she'd been a graphic designer and a passionate, self-taught home baker. But Jackie Kai Ellis, the bakery's original owner, believed that if someone had the passion, she could teach them the skills. A designer herself, she'd been inspired to open the bakery by the patisseries she fell in love with in Paris, and later sent Hung on a scholarship to study pastry in the City of Light.

Quickly the petite space with its French-vintage-inspired design became a popular destination for locals meeting friends or working on their laptops over coffee and peanut butter sandwich cookies. And it became a must for those hosting dinner parties to swing by and pick up a brioche loaf or a box of lemon tarts.

In 2017, Ellis sold the bakery to the Hungs, who continue with her vision of pretty, Parisian-inspired patisserie. "Jackie opened the bakery with the intention of providing a space to make people happier and a cookie to make themselves feel better," Hung says. "She decided to bring a bit of France to Vancouver, but also bring our own tradition to these traditions."

1⅓ cups (2⅔ sticks) unsalted butter

1¼ cups icing sugar

1 vanilla bean, split lengthwise

½ cup *kinako*, plus extra for dusting

1¾ cups all-purpose flour

1 tsp fine sea salt

2 tsp flaky sea salt

¼ cup chopped white chocolate
   (such as Valrhona Ivoire 35%)

1 Tbsp Japanese toasted brown rice,
   puffed rice or crispy rice (optional)

Kinako Brown Butter Shortbread

MAKES 20 TO 24

Kinako is a Japanese roasted soy flour that's available in Asian markets—its wonderfully nutty flavour is accentuated by the nuttiness of the brown butter in this satisfyingly indulgent treat.

Put butter in a large saucepan and stir constantly over medium heat, until light brown. (The butter will foam and boil up in the process; keep an eye on it so it doesn't boil over and burn.) Pour into a heatproof container and set aside to cool.

Preheat oven to 300°F.

In a stand mixer fitted with a paddle attachment, combine brown butter and icing sugar, then scrape in vanilla seeds. Cream together on medium speed for 5 minutes.

Add *kinako*, flour and fine sea salt. Mix on low speed, scraping bowl as necessary, until dough forms.

Line a baking sheet with parchment paper. Scoop 1½-inch-diameter balls, place them on the baking sheet and flatten slightly with your hand. Sprinkle cookies with flaky salt, chopped white chocolate and toasted (or puffed or crispy) rice (if using). Bake for 15 minutes, then rotate tray and bake for another 10 to 15 minutes, until lightly golden. Set aside to cool, then dust with *kinako*.

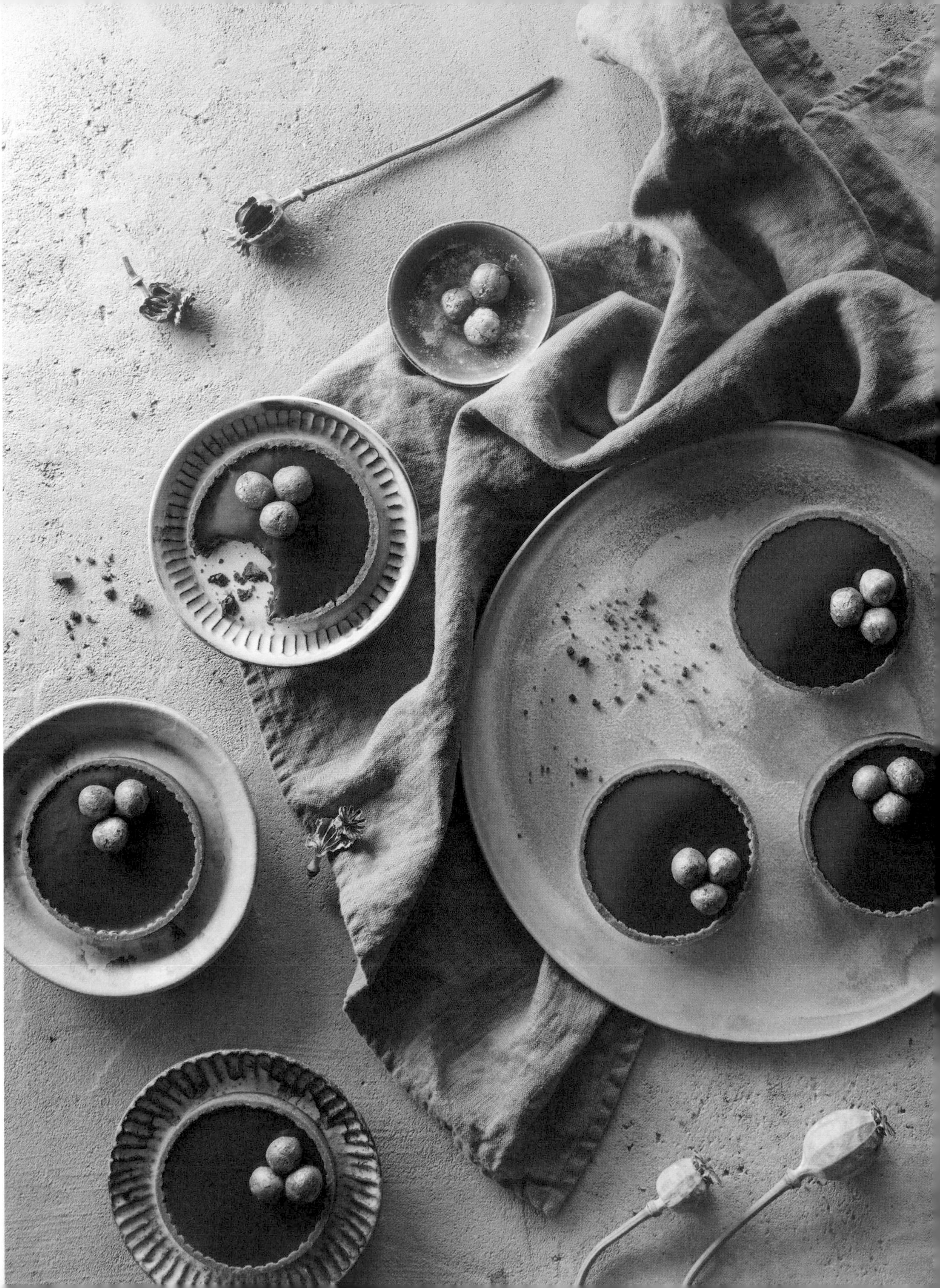

TART DOUGH

¾ cup (1½ sticks) unsalted butter, room temperature

Pinch of kosher salt

1 cup icing sugar

1½ tsp pure vanilla extract

1 large egg, slightly beaten

3¾ cups cake flour, sifted, plus extra for dusting

GANACHE FILLING

¾ cup stout beer

2 Tbsp light-coloured honey

1 vanilla bean, split lengthwise

2½ cups chopped milk chocolate (preferably Valrhona Jivara 40%)

½ cup chopped dark chocolate (preferably Valrhona Taïnori 64%)

⅓ cup (⅔ stick) unsalted butter, room temperature

Edible gold dust (optional)

Stout Chocolate Ganache Tart

MAKES 6

Stout has distinct notes of caramel and cacao. Here, it is used in place of cream to make the ganache, creating layer upon layer of rich, chocolatey flavour. Beaucoup Bakery's head chef Betty Hung advises using high-quality couverture chocolate, which contains a higher percentage of cocoa butter than regular chocolate.

TART DOUGH In a stand mixer fitted with a paddle attachment, combine butter, salt and icing sugar and beat on medium speed until well mixed and pale. Add vanilla extract, and add beaten egg, a little bit at a time, scraping down the sides of the bowl after each addition to ensure even distribution. On low speed, mix in flour until just incorporated. (Do not overmix—otherwise, tart will be tough.)

Shape dough into a disk, wrap and chill in fridge for at least 2 hours and up to overnight.

Set dough at room temperature for 10 minutes to soften. On a lightly floured surface, roll out dough to ¼-inch thickness, turning the dough after each roll to prevent sticking. Dust with flour as needed.

Cut out 6 (5-inch) rounds. Fit rounds into 6 (3½-inch) tart pans, preferably with removable bottoms. Gently press dough into bottom edges and right up to the top of the pan. Trim off excess and chill for 30 minutes.

Preheat oven to 325°F.

Using a fork, prick bottom of tart shells. Line chilled tart pans with parchment paper and fill with beans or rice. Bake for 20 minutes until set. Remove paper and weights and bake for another 5 to 10 minutes, until golden. Set aside and cool until needed.

GANACHE FILLING Combine stout and honey in a small saucepan, then scrape in vanilla seeds. Heat over low heat, just until mixture begins to simmer. (Do not boil.)

Place chocolates in a medium bowl. Pour hot stout over chocolate and set aside for 2 to 3 minutes. Using a rubber spatula, start stirring from the centre to incorporate the chocolate and liquid. Let ganache cool until it is lukewarm, then stir in butter.

Pour or spoon ganache into the baked tart shells, then chill in the fridge for at least 2 hours, until set.

Meanwhile, leftover ganache can be used to create truffle balls. Let it set, then spoon and shape into small balls. Roll them in edible gold dust (if using). To serve, top the tarts with truffles.

FRANK PABST

Blue Water Cafe + Raw Bar

VANCOUVER FOODIES KNOW to mark February on their calendars: it's when Blue Water Cafe + Raw Bar holds its annual "Unsung Heroes" festival, a celebration of little-known and underappreciated seafood. That could mean whelk paella, sea urchin trifle or a luscious pâté made from sturgeon liver. "Promoting unfamiliar seafood is something that is very close to my heart," says executive chef Frank Pabst, who notes that those rare species often get shipped to Asia, where they are considered a delicacy. He's been hosting the dinners since 2005, opening minds and palates to a wide underwater world of exotic flavours.

In many ways, Blue Water encapsulates so much of what the Vancouver food scene is all about: seafood, of course, including a vast raw bar and creative sushi (mmm, lobster and mango roll); sustainability and innovation; as well as award-winning wine and terrific cocktails. "It's not a casual restaurant; it's professional, but it's relaxed, it's approachable," Pabst says. It's stylish, too, in that not-trying-too-hard West Coast way, with exposed brick, warm wood and subtle reminders of the building's industrial past. It's one of those places where you take guests from out of town, when you want to impress them and show off something that's quintessentially Vancouver.

Mostly, though, it's about Pabst's food. Originally from Germany and trained on the French Riviera, he brings finely honed European technique and a modern sensibility to largely West Coast ingredients: sablefish with a miso-sake glaze, sturgeon with a pumpernickel crust or Dungeness crab straight from the live tanks. And every once in a while, an unsung hero or two makes an appearance, and Vancouver diners rejoice.

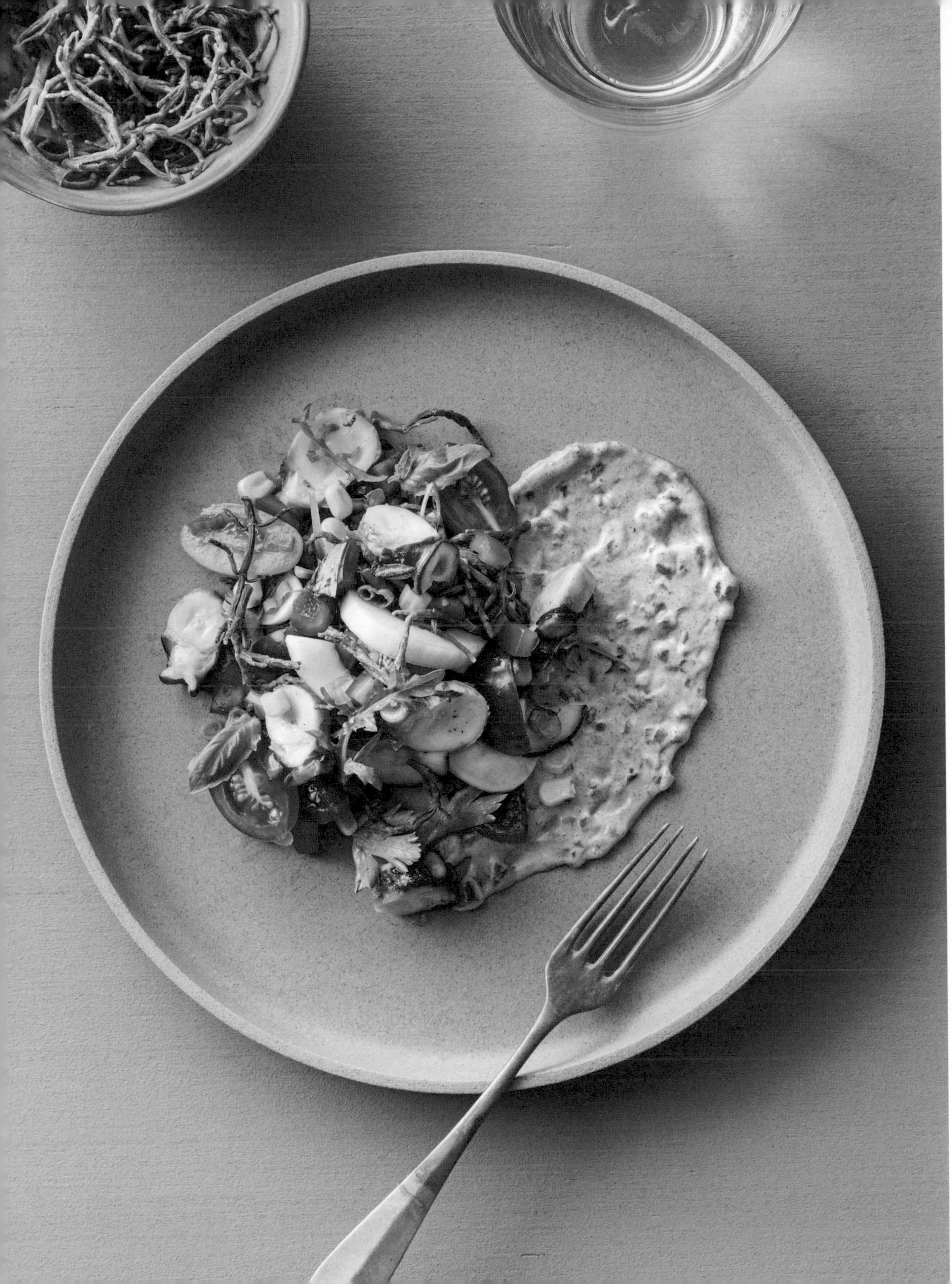

OCTOPUS

2 lbs thawed frozen octopus
or 2 prepared octopus arms
(see Note)
1 onion, cut into quarters
1 head garlic, cut in half
1 stalk celery
1 carrot, coarsely chopped
2 sprigs fresh thyme
2 bay leaves
5 L water
¼ cup extra-virgin olive oil, plus
extra as needed
Salt and freshly ground black
pepper, to taste

ROASTED JALAPEÑO– GREEN ALGAE AIOLI

1 jalapeño pepper
1 large egg
3 cloves garlic, finely grated
Juice of ¼ lime
Pinch of kosher salt
1 Tbsp spirulina, green algae powder
or ground seaweed (optional)
½ cup extra-virgin olive oil
½ cup expeller-pressed canola oil

VINAIGRETTE

½ cup extra-virgin olive oil
1 tsp honey
1 tsp Dijon mustard
2 Tbsp fresh lemon juice
Salt and freshly ground black
pepper, to taste

Grilled Pacific Octopus with Roasted Jalapeño–Green Algae Aioli

SERVES 4

Local octopus has slowly become a favourite on menus across the city. Here, it is grilled and served with a garlic mayonnaise brightened with spirulina, the sea algae that's become a rock-star ingredient among the wellness set. It's available in health food stores.

OCTOPUS If you are using thawed frozen octopus, combine all ingredients except oil, salt and pepper in a stockpot and bring to a boil. Reduce heat to medium-low and simmer for 1½ hours, until octopus arms separate easily from the body. Set aside to cool, then remove the octopus from the broth.

If you are using prepared octopus arms, skip the steps above.

Cut octopus into 3-inch pieces, with skin and suckers still attached. Put it in a bowl, toss with just enough olive oil to coat lightly (about 1 tablespoon) and season with salt and pepper.

Preheat a grill over high heat. Place octopus on the grill and grill for 4 to 5 minutes on each side, until nicely charred. (The skin might come off in some places.) Remove immediately (to avoid drying out the centre) and cut into ¼-inch slices. Toss in olive oil.

ROASTED JALAPEÑO–GREEN ALGAE AIOLI
Roast jalapeño over a gas burner or directly under a broiler until skin blisters and flesh softens. Set aside to cool. Scrape off skin, cut open, and remove the seeds.

Using a hand blender, combine jalapeño and egg. Add garlic, lime juice, salt, and spirulina, green algae powder or seaweed (if using). With the motor still running, gradually add oils and blend until emulsified.

VINAIGRETTE Whisk all ingredients together and season to taste with salt and pepper.

SUMMER VEGETABLE SALAD

1 zucchini, thinly sliced on a mandoline

1 tsp kosher salt

½ cup sea asparagus, ends trimmed and discarded (optional)

10 grape tomatoes, cut in half

2 green onions, thinly sliced

1 red bell pepper, seeded, deveined and finely chopped

¼ cucumber, peeled and cut into ¼-inch-thick half-moon shapes

3 sprigs fresh Italian parsley, leaves only, torn if large

2 sprigs fresh basil, leaves only, torn

1 cup cooked corn kernels

Handful of wild arugula

½ lemon, to serve (optional)

Sea salt, to serve

NOTE:

For this recipe, Chef Pabst recommends using frozen and thawed whole octopus rather than fresh. In any case, fresh raw octopus can be hard to find in local fish markets; you are more likely to see prepared octopus arms from Japan, usually frozen, at Asian supermarkets. These have already been poached and prepared for sushi, so you can simply defrost them, toss them in oil and put them directly on the grill. Note that the prepared arms tend to be quite chewy whereas the thawed frozen whole octopus will make a more tender dish.

SUMMER VEGETABLE SALAD In a bowl, mix zucchini and salt and set aside for 15 minutes. Rinse briefly under cold running water and gently squeeze out excess water.

Bring a small saucepan of water to a boil, add sea asparagus and blanch for 1 minute. Drain, then transfer to a bowl of ice water.

In a large bowl, combine all vegetables and vinaigrette and toss to mix.

ASSEMBLY Place 2 tablespoons of aioli on each of 4 plates and spread out using the back of a spoon or a small offset spatula. Divide salad between the plates and loosely arrange sliced octopus on top. Finish with a squeeze of fresh lemon (if using) and a sprinkle of sea salt.

TOMATO-BASIL COMPOTE
8 large Roma tomatoes
¼ cup extra-virgin olive oil
1 clove garlic, finely chopped
2 shallots, finely chopped
Grated zest of 1 lemon
8 fresh basil leaves, finely sliced
Salt, to taste
Piment d'Espelette or any fine
 ground chili powder, to taste

ARTICHOKE-CAPER SAUCE
1 large fresh artichoke or canned
 artichoke heart
1 lemon, cut in half
½ cup dry unoaked white wine
1 Tbsp white wine vinegar
½ cup (1 stick) cold unsalted butter,
 cut into cubes
2 button mushrooms, thinly sliced
2 shallots, thinly sliced
1 Tbsp capers
Salt and freshly ground black
 pepper, to taste

SPINACH
2 bunches spinach, stems trimmed
2 Tbsp unsalted butter
1 clove garlic, thinly sliced
¼ tsp kosher salt, to taste
Lemon wedge

White Sturgeon Baked with Tomato-Basil Compote

SERVES 4

Sturgeon farmed on the Sunshine Coast has become popular with Vancouver chefs for its dense flesh and clean flavour that can stand up to bold, hearty sauces like this tomato compote. If you can't find sturgeon, any other firm white fish will do as well.

TOMATO-BASIL COMPOTE Bring a saucepan of water to a boil, add tomatoes and blanch for 2 to 3 minutes. Drain, then transfer to a bowl of ice water. Peel tomatoes, remove seeds and cut into ¼-inch dice.

Heat oil in a sauté pan over medium heat, add garlic and sauté for 1 minute, until fragrant. Add shallots and cook for another 30 seconds, then add tomatoes, lemon zest and basil. Reduce heat to low and cook for 30 minutes until tomato water is evaporated and mixture has thickened. (Stir regularly to avoid burning the bottom of the tomatoes.) Season with salt and piment d'Espelette (or other chili powder). Set aside to cool and refrigerate until needed.

ARTICHOKE-CAPER SAUCE If using fresh artichoke, bring a saucepan of salted water to a boil and add artichoke and half a lemon. Reduce heat to medium-low and cook for 40 minutes. Drain and set aside to cool. Remove leaves and fuzzy centre. (Skip this step if using a canned artichoke heart.)

Finely chop artichoke heart.

Place wine and vinegar in a sauté pan over medium heat and cook until reduced to 2 tablespoons. Add butter and whisk, until emulsified. Strain through a fine-mesh sieve. Add artichokes, mushrooms, shallots and capers. Season to taste with lemon, salt and pepper.

STURGEON
4 (5-oz) skinless sturgeon fillets
Salt and freshly ground black
     pepper, to taste
½ cup panko crumbs
1 Tbsp extra-virgin olive oil

SPINACH Using paper towels, pat spinach dry. In a small saucepan, melt butter until golden brown over medium heat. Add garlic and salt and sauté for 1 minute, until fragrant. Add spinach and toss until just wilted. Squeeze a lemon wedge overtop. Set aside.

STURGEON Preheat oven to 425°F.

Season sturgeon with salt and pepper and place in a baking dish. Top with a layer of tomato compote.

In a small bowl, combine panko crumbs and oil and toss. Sprinkle mixture over sturgeon and bake for 12 to 15 minutes, until fish is just done and crust is golden.

Plate spinach in the centre of 4 plates, spoon artichoke-caper sauce around spinach and arrange sturgeon on top. Serve immediately.

Botanist

STEP THROUGH THE glass doors of Fairmont Pacific Rim with their mist of signature fragrance. Go past the conventioneers, the gleaming white marble counters and musicians by the bar and climb the steps to the mezzanine. Suddenly, you've entered another world, a garden lush with hundreds of plants—fifty different species of them—from all over the Pacific Northwest.

To your right is the cocktail bar with its bespoke cocktail lab, where creative beverage director Grant Sceney and his talented team are creating some of the most exciting cocktails in town. If you make it past the bar—it's easy to get sidetracked here—you'll likely spot wine director Jill Spoor pouring one of her terroir-driven selections near the bread station with its stacks of Provençal *fougasse*. And then there's the bright, airy, colourful dining room with the long open kitchen where Hector Laguna works his magic.

Originally from Mexico, Laguna worked his way to Vancouver via Miami, Toronto and San Francisco. He brings with him a bag of French techniques, a taste for Mexican flavours and a passion for B.C. ingredients. His charred octopus with chorizo is as pretty a plate as you're likely to see—until you try the lobster with *gnudi* or the tagliatelle with morels or any of the desserts.

In a space so clearly dedicated to the natural environment, it's not surprising that plants are at the heart of so much of the food and drink. Pollen, daisies, beets, berries, even mushrooms appear in cocktails, while Laguna uses everything from field, forest and orchard in ways both inventive and delicious. "It's very seasonal," he says. "It's very honest."

INFUSED PÈRE MAGLOIRE CALVADOS

1 Tbsp coriander seeds

1 tsp white peppercorns

1 (750-mL) bottle Père Magloire Calvados

SIMPLE SYRUP

1 cup granulated sugar

1 cup water

APPLESEED LANE COCKTAIL

1 oz Infused Père Magloire Calvados (see here)

½ oz Okanagan Spirits pear eau de vie (Poire Williams)

¾ oz fresh lemon juice

¾ oz Simple Syrup (see here)

¾ oz apple juice

1½ oz soda water

Apple slice, for garnish

Appleseed Lane Cocktail

SERVES 1

At Botanist, bartender Grant Sceney not only has all the ingredients of the Pacific Northwest to play with, he also has his own lab for concocting extraordinary cocktails like this delicately apple-scented one.

INFUSED PÈRE MAGLOIRE CALVADOS Put coriander seeds in a small frying pan and toast over medium-high heat for 1 or 2 minutes, until fragrant. Set aside to cool. Transfer to a mortar and pestle, add peppercorns and crush.

Place spices in an 8-cup jar, pour in Calvados overtop and stir. Infuse for 30 minutes, strain through a coffee filter, rebottle and label. (It'll keep indefinitely.)

SIMPLE SYRUP Mix sugar and water in a small saucepan over medium heat. Bring to a simmer, stirring, until sugar is fully dissolved. (It can be stored in the fridge for up to 2 weeks.)

APPLESEED LANE COCKTAIL Combine all ingredients except soda water and the garnish in a cocktail shaker with ice and shake. Strain into an old-fashioned glass and top with soda. Garnish with an apple slice.

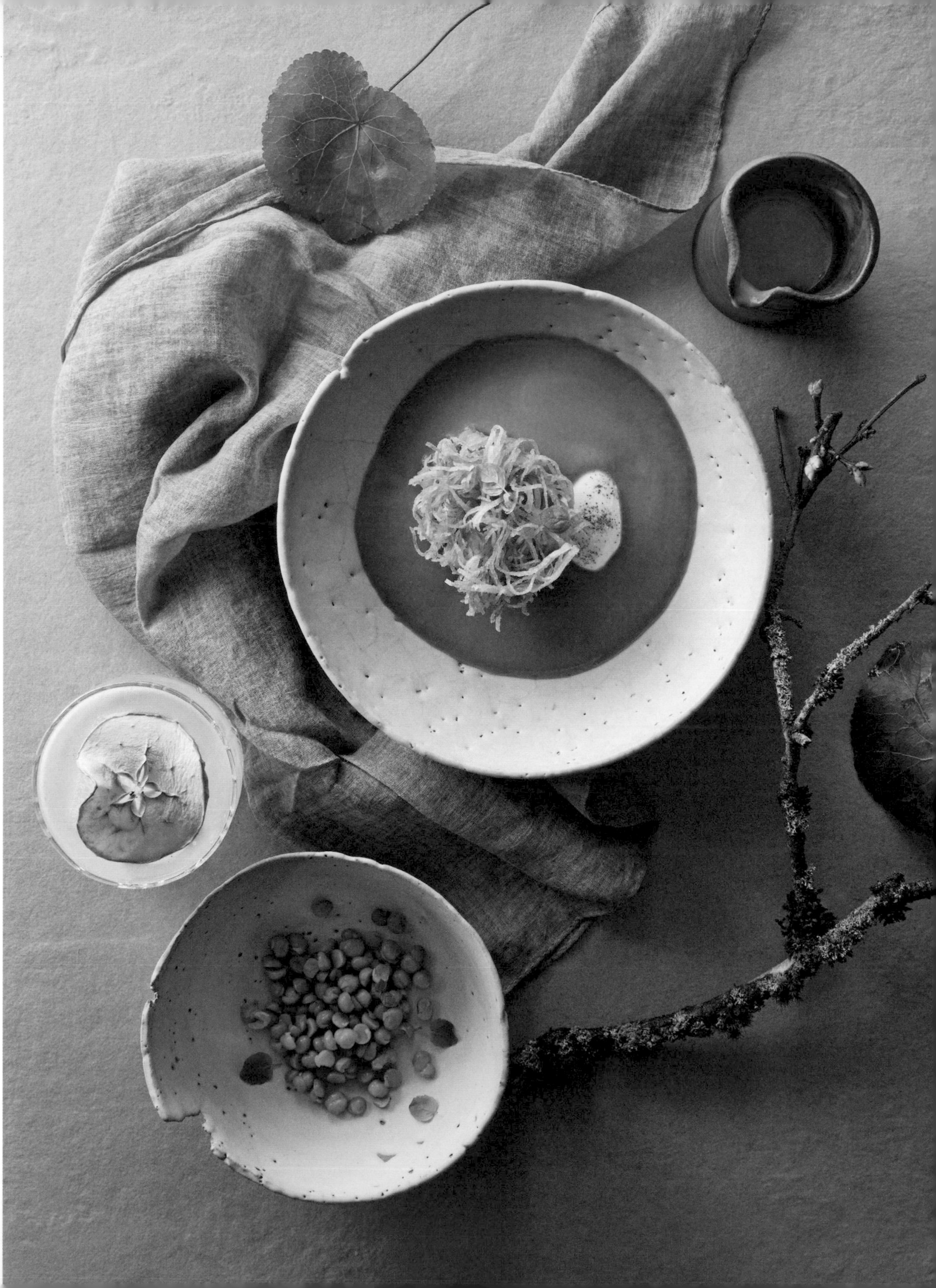

SPRING PEA SOUP

1 Tbsp unsalted butter
1 shallot, sliced
2 cloves garlic, sliced
2 cups vegetable stock
1 cup spinach leaves
2½ cups fresh peas
Salt, to taste

Fresh lemon juice, to taste
¾ cup fresh Dungeness crabmeat, picked of shells or cartilage
4 tsp crème fraîche (or 4 tsp sour cream, for garnish
Fresh mint leaves, for garnish

POTATO NESTS

1 medium potato
3 cups vegetable oil, for frying

Spring Pea Soup with Dungeness Crab

SERVES 4

Chef Hector Laguna's delicately minted pea soup with its tender crab garnish is a perfectly delectable taste of spring.

SPRING PEA SOUP Melt butter in a medium saucepan over medium-high heat. Add shallot and garlic and sauté for 5 minutes, until translucent. Pour in stock and bring to a boil, then set aside to cool to room temperature.

Bring a small saucepan of lightly salted water to a boil. Add spinach and cook for 2 minutes. Drain, then transfer to a bowl of ice water. Remove and press out excess water.

Bring a small saucepan of lightly salted water to a boil. Add peas and blanch for 3 minutes. Drain, then transfer to a bowl of ice water.

Combine stock, spinach and 2 cups of the peas in a blender. Purée for 3 minutes, until smooth. Strain through a fine-mesh sieve, then season with salt and lemon juice.

POTATO NESTS Peel the potato, then shred it using a mandoline set to the finest teeth. Soak the shredded potato in a bowl of water for 5 minutes. Drain and pat dry with paper towels.

In a small pot, heat oil over medium-high to about 350°F. Form the potato into 4 "nests" and carefully drop them in the oil. Shallow fry for 1 to 2 minutes until golden brown. Remove from the oil and drain on paper towels.

ASSEMBLY In a small bowl, combine crab and remaining ½ cup peas. Season with salt and lemon juice. Split mixture between 4 soup bowls. Ladle soup into each bowl, garnish each with a teaspoon of crème fraîche, a couple of mint leaves and a potato nest. Serve immediately.

Boulevard Kitchen
& Oyster Bar

IT'S NOT EASY running a hotel restaurant that has to be all things to all people. But that's just what Alex Chen manages to pull off at the swellegant two-hundred-seat Boulevard in the Sutton Place Hotel. He dishes up breakfast and burgers, bar snacks and group lunches—and still manages to indulge in the kind of highly creative, deeply flavourful fine dining that earned him a top ten finish at the 2013 Bocuse d'Or competition in Lyon, France.

Back then, he'd been the executive chef of the Polo Lounge at the Beverly Hills Hotel for six years, and it was time for him to come home. Chen grew up in Vancouver, dining on Cantonese-style Chinese food such as whole fish steamed and drizzled with oil. Since then he's picked up a world of culinary influences, especially from all over Asia. "It's a reflection of my travels, my childhood, classic French training and where I've worked," he says.

When Boulevard opened in 2014, people talked about the Martha Sturdy bowls, the dramatic light fixtures and the wine list heavy on natural wines. Mostly, though, they talked about Chen's crispy Vietnamese-style chicken wings drizzled in caramelized fish sauce and dotted with teeny-tiny pickled vegetables. "Only a few of our dishes are sacred," Chen says. The chicken wings are one. So is the $500 Seafood Tower Royale.

And he hadn't quite given up his competitive streak. In 2016, he won bronze and the People's Choice Award at the Canadian Culinary Championships. In 2018, he went back and won gold. Now he prides himself on mentoring a new generation of talent. People often ask him what he'd like to be known for. "I want to know that I made a difference for the young chefs who work for me," he says.

HAMACHI
1 cup kosher salt
Grated zest of ½ lime
Grated zest of ½ lemon
Grated zest of ¼ orange
1 (5-oz) sashimi-grade
  hamachi fillet

YUZU VINAIGRETTE
2 Tbsp soy sauce
2 tsp yuzu juice (available at Fujiya)
1 small shallot, finely chopped
1 Tbsp extra-virgin olive oil
Freshly ground black pepper, to taste

ASSEMBLY
Salt and freshly ground black
  pepper, to taste
½ ripe avocado, sliced
10 canned hearts of palm, thinly sliced
1 Tbsp crème fraîche (or ½ Tbsp sour cream
  mixed with ½ tsp heavy (36%) cream)
1 orange, skin and pith removed and
  segmented
4 to 6 red mustard greens
4 to 6 celery leaves, chopped
2 to 3 radishes, thinly sliced

Citrus-Cured Hamachi with Hearts of Palm, Crème Fraîche and Yuzu Vinaigrette

SERVES 2

Hamachi, *also known as Japanese amberjack or yellowtail, is a highly prized fish in Japanese cuisine. At Boulevard, Alex Chen cures it lightly with citrus flavours, making a delicate and delicious appetizer.*

HAMACHI Mix salt and citrus zests in a bowl. Cover both sides of hamachi with mixture and set aside for 8 minutes. Rinse under cold running water and pat dry. Set aside.

YUZU VINAIGRETTE In a small bowl, combine soy sauce, yuzu juice, shallot and oil and whisk. Season with pepper.

ASSEMBLY Slice hamachi and arrange on 2 plates. Season with salt and pepper.

Carefully place avocado slices and hearts of palm on top of hamachi. Top with crème fraîche and orange segments. Garnish with mustard greens, celery leaves and radish slices. Spoon yuzu vinaigrette around hamachi and serve.

POACHED LOBSTER
1 (2-lb) whole lobster

BOUQUET GARNI
3 sprigs fresh parsley, stems only
2 sprigs fresh thyme
2 sprigs fresh tarragon
1 bay leaf
1 star anise
¼ tsp fennel seeds

LOBSTER STOCK
3 Tbsp canola oil
Roasted lobster shells (see here)
1 large yellow onion, sliced
1 clove garlic, thinly sliced
1 stalk celery, chopped
¼ leek, white part only, coarsely chopped
½ cup chopped fennel
1 small carrot, chopped

½ cup white wine
¼ cup brandy
1 Roma tomato, chopped
2 Tbsp tomato paste
6 cups fish stock
1 Bouquet Garni (see here)
1 tsp fresh lemon juice
Freshly ground black pepper, to taste
Pinch of ground cayenne pepper

Lobster Bisque en Croute with Cognac Crème

SERVES 4

The ultimate in luxurious dining, this dish is for a special occasion indeed. It's always best to use live lobster, but the squeamish can ask the fishmonger to do the deed while you're not looking.

POACHED LOBSTER If using a live lobster, bring a large saucepan of water to a simmer over medium heat. Drop the lobster in the pan, cover and poach for 8 minutes. Transfer the lobster to a pot of ice water to cool, then remove the gills and innards from the head. If you are not using a live lobster, remove the gills and innards before poaching.

Remove and set aside to cool at room temperature for 10 minutes. Remove lobster meat and set aside. Reserve shells.

Preheat oven to 400°F. Cut lobster shells into 4 pieces, place on a baking sheet and roast for 20 minutes. Remove from oven and cool at room temperature for 1 hour. Reserve for later use.

BOUQUET GARNI Wrap all ingredients in a cheesecloth, tie tightly and set aside.

LOBSTER STOCK Heat oil in a large saucepan over high heat, until lightly smoking. Add lobster shells and cook for 1 minute. Reduce heat to medium-high and add onion, garlic, celery, leek, fennel and carrot. Cook for 2 minutes.

Pour in wine and brandy and cook for 10 minutes, until reduced to three-quarters of the original volume. Add tomato and tomato paste and stir. Reduce heat to medium and cook for 2 minutes. Pour in stock and add bouquet garni. Bring to a boil, reduce heat and simmer for 1 hour.

Season with lemon juice, pepper and cayenne. Discard bouquet garni.

Strain through a fine-mesh sieve. Set aside.

LOBSTER BISQUE

1 Tbsp all-purpose flour
2 Tbsp unsalted butter
1 cup heavy (36%) cream
1 quantity Lobster Stock (see here)
1 Tbsp kosher salt

COGNAC CRÈME

½ cup whipping (33%) cream
1 Tbsp cognac
Pinch of salt
Freshly ground black pepper, to taste

ASSEMBLY

2 Tbsp finely chopped celery
2 Tbsp finely chopped carrot
2 Tbsp finely chopped leeks,
  white part only
¼ to ½ cup Cognac Crème (see here)
1 sheet frozen puff pastry, thawed
All-purpose flour, for dusting
1 large egg yolk
1 Tbsp whipping (33%) cream

LOBSTER BISQUE In a small bowl, combine flour and butter and mix well. (The paste is called *beurre manié*.)

In a large saucepan, combine cream, stock and salt and bring to a boil. Divide *beurre manié* into 6 parts and drop into the bisque one at a time, whisking it in. Simmer for 15 minutes.

Strain through a fine-mesh sieve, then refrigerate at least 2 hours and preferably overnight.

COGNAC CRÈME In a bowl, whip all ingredients together until soft peaks form. Cover with plastic wrap and refrigerate until needed.

ASSEMBLY Preheat oven to 425°F.

In a bowl, combine celery, carrot and leek and mix well. Divide between 4 ovenproof serving bowls, then add lobster meat. Place bowls on a rimmed baking sheet.

Fill each bowl with lobster bisque to three-quarters full. (Do not fill to the top or it will boil over when baked.) Add 1 to 2 tablespoons cognac crème to each bowl.

Roll out puff pastry to ¼ inch thick and cut into 4 circles that are ½ inch larger than the diameter of the serving bowls. Dust your hands with a small amount of flour. Cover the top of each bowl with puff pastry, pressing the puff pastry tightly against the rim of each bowl to seal.

In a small bowl, whisk egg yolk and cream together to make an egg wash. Brush it over puff pastry. Bake for 25 to 30 minutes, until pastry is golden brown and soup is hot.

Serve immediately.

Cacao

THE CACAO TREE is native to Central America—its dried and fermented bean the basis of that most decadent of luxury foods, chocolate. "Before cacao was chocolate, it was food," says Jefferson Alvarez. "And because it was food, it was currency." Cacao, then, is a quintessential part of Latin American culture and the perfect symbol for Alvarez's dream restaurant.

"Cacao was created to demystify Latin American cuisine in this city," says the chef who arrived here in 2009 from Venezuela. "The experience and the journey at the restaurant will take you all over Latin America: from Peru and Argentina to Brazil and Colombia."

It took him a while, though, to get that journey started. Wildly innovative, highly skilled and with a flamboyant sense of flavour, Alvarez bounced from project to project and restaurant to restaurant while foodie Vancouver breathlessly followed along. Then in November 2016, everything came together when he opened Cacao with his partner and fellow chef Marcela Ramirez, who had been a celebrity TV chef and cookbook author in Mexico.

"It's every chef's dream," he says. Diners are pretty happy, too. They get to enjoy fried fish from Venezuela, ceviche from Peru, *arepas* (stuffed corn pastries) from Venezuela, *pupusas* (savoury filled corn tortillas) from El Salvador and, of course, grilled meats. "The best barbecue is from Brazil or Argentina"—known there as *asado*—"so we blend both styles in one dish," Alvarez says. Everything he makes is done with modernist flair, fragrant with chilies, citrus and exotic spices and complemented by a well-edited wine list and exceptional cocktails created by talented bartender Sergio Grandolfo.

Vancouver may not know a lot about Latin American cuisine, but with Alvarez in charge we're happy to learn, one delicious bite at a time.

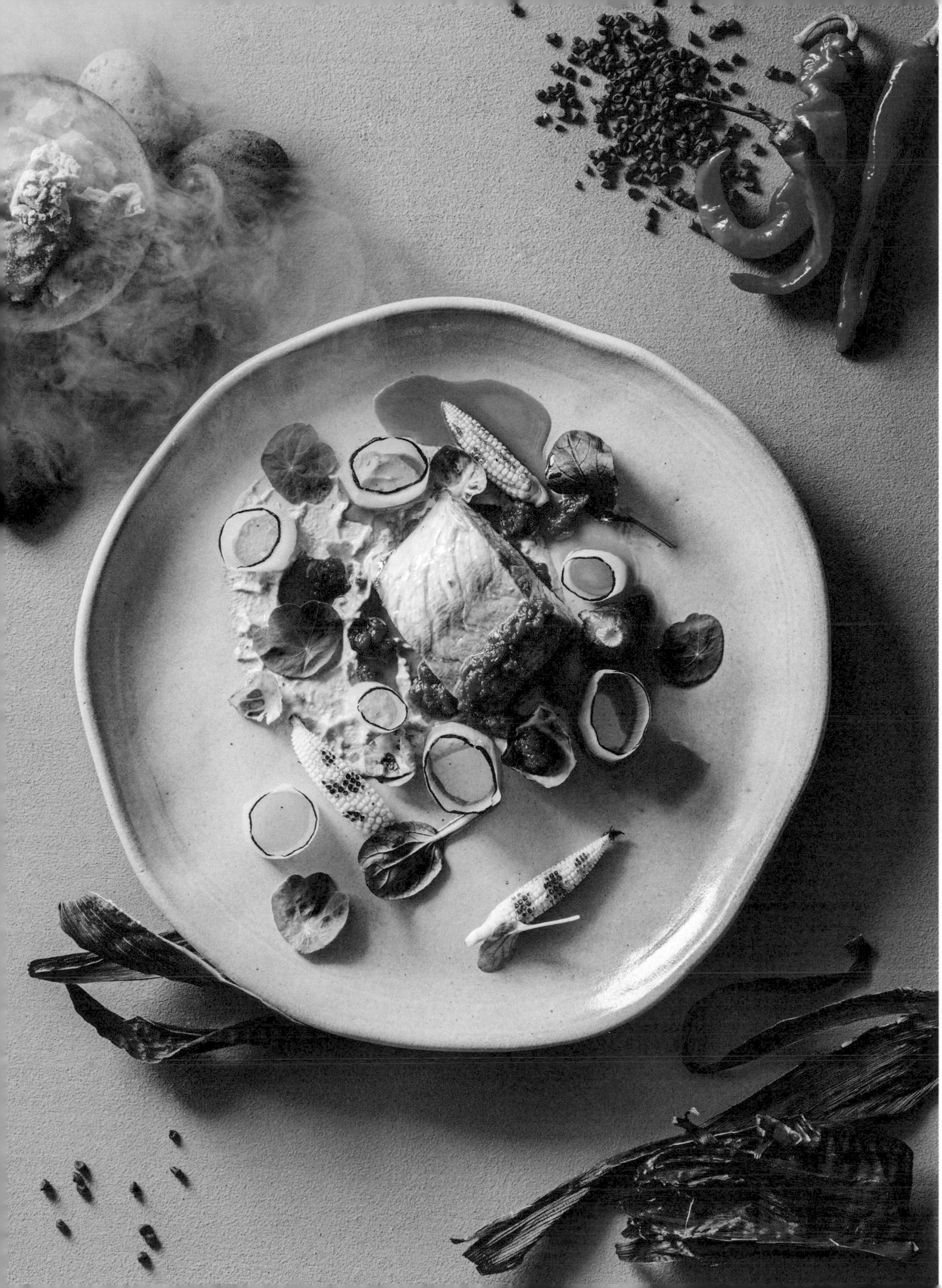

PIPIAN VERDE

¼ cup grapeseed oil

1 cup pumpkin seeds

½ onion, chopped

3 cloves garlic, finely chopped

1 jalapeño pepper, seeded, deveined and chopped

½ tsp ground cumin

½ tsp dried oregano

8 whole tomatillos, husks removed

¼ cup chopped fresh cilantro

¾ cup vegetable stock

Juice of 2 lemons

ANNATTO-CONFIT STURGEON

8 cups cold water

1 cup kosher salt

1 (1-lb) sturgeon loin or sablefish, cut into 4 portions

4 cups grapeseed oil (divided)

1 tsp annatto seeds

1 lime, cut in half

1 orange, cut in half

1 sprig fresh basil with stems, lightly crushed

3 large cloves garlic, crushed

Assorted vegetables, to serve

Annatto-Confit Sturgeon and Pipian Verde

SERVES 4

Wild sturgeon is still considered endangered, but on the Sunshine Coast, Northern Divine Aquafarms is producing a sustainable fish (and its caviar) that chefs have fallen in love with. Dense and hearty, it is ideal served with sturdy sauces like pipian verde, *a pumpkin seed pesto.*

PIPIAN VERDE Heat oil in a large frying pan over medium heat. Add pumpkin seeds, onion, garlic, jalapeño, cumin, oregano and tomatillos. Cook for 15 minutes, rotating tomatillos, until softened.

Transfer ingredients to a blender, add cilantro and pour in stock and lemon juice. Blend until smooth, then set aside.

ANNATTO-CONFIT STURGEON Combine water and salt in a large bowl and stir until salt has dissolved. Add fish and refrigerate for 20 minutes. Remove fish, rinse under cold running water and pat dry.

Heat 3 tablespoons of the oil in a small saucepan over medium heat, add annatto seeds and toast for 1 to 2 minutes until vibrant. Transfer seeds and oil to a mortar and pestle and grind to a rough paste.

In a medium saucepan, combine ground annatto, lime, orange, basil, garlic and fish. Add remaining oil, set over medium heat and maintain temperature at 200°F. Cook for 15 minutes, until fish is firm but tender.

Using a slotted spoon, remove fish from oil and place on paper towels to drain slightly. Serve with *pipian verde* and assorted vegetables.

3 cups water

1 cup good-quality dried organic
  hibiscus flowers

2 packets whipped cream stabilizer
  (such as Dr. Oetker Whip It)

¼ tsp xanthan gum

½ cup sweetened condensed milk,
  or to taste (optional)

2 Tbsp Miguelito candy chili powder,
  or to taste (see Note)

NOTE:
Miguelito is a popular spicy-sweet
condiment/confection in Latin
American cuisine. It is available in some
Latin markets or online, but if you
can't find it, replace it with a 2:1 mix
of sugar and TAJÍN Clásico Seasoning,
which is a mix of salt, chilies and lime
that's available in Latin markets. (Use
4 teaspoons sugar and 2 teaspoons
TAJÍN to make 2 tablespoons.)

Hibiscus Ice

SERVES 4

The floral prettiness of this frozen dessert gets added spice from Miguelito, a popular Latin American sweet that mixes salt, sugar and chili. You can also use it sprinkled on fruit or fried potatoes.

Bring water to a boil over high heat and add hibiscus flowers. Remove from heat and steep for 15 minutes. Strain and chill hibiscus liquid until needed.

Combine whipped cream stabilizer and xanthan gum in a medium bowl. Stir in 1 cup of cold hibiscus liquid. Set aside for 2 to 3 minutes to thicken. Using an electric mixer, beat for 4 to 6 minutes, until well mixed. Scrape mixture into a glass or metal container and freeze overnight.

Drizzle with condensed milk (if using) and sprinkle Miguelito on top. Divide between 4 bowls and serve immediately.

Café Medina

PRETTY MUCH FROM the day it opened in 2008, long lineups have snaked outside Café Medina. Understandable, since the original Beatty Street location was tiny, and Vancouver brunch spots were few at the time. But in 2014, Medina moved to bigger digs on Richards Street and, if anything, the lineups are even longer now. It seems the city is hungry for the kind of Middle Eastern–inspired breakfast fare they're dishing up. Well, that and Medina's crispy Belgian waffles with caramel sauce.

Medina was originally an offshoot of Chambar (page 74), whose owners wanted to take advantage of the space next door. Chambar was packed to the rafters each evening, so a daytime-only spot seemed like a good idea. "We wanted to create a brunch culture that was like San Francisco or New York," says owner Robbie Kane.

They pulled together a menu heavy on not just eggs but spicy merguez sausage, rich tomato sauce, couscous, olives, haloumi, the famous fricassee and really, *really* good coffee. There were plenty of vegetarian and gluten-free options, too.

In 2014, Café Medina broke away from Chambar and opened in its new location in the Library District. "It's largely a similar menu with Middle Eastern and North African influence, lots of cumin, coriander and garlic, that sort of thing," Kane says. Also adding to the mellow mood: craft cocktails like the Moroccan Maria, a variation on the Bloody Mary made with tequila and North African spices. It's food—and drink—that people are willing to wait for, even all these years later.

ANCHOVY BUTTER

7 white anchovy fillets
1 cup loosely packed fresh parsley leaves
3 Tbsp chopped fresh chives
½ tsp Worcestershire sauce
½ tsp Dijon mustard
Pinch of freshly ground black pepper
Grated zest of ½ lemon
1 cup (2 sticks) unsalted butter, softened

CHARRED BROCCOLINI

2 bunches broccolini, trimmed
2 Tbsp extra-virgin olive oil
Grated zest of 1 lemon
1 clove garlic, finely chopped
Crushed red pepper, to taste
Salt, to taste

HALIBUT WITH CHORIZO RAGÙ

2 links dry-cured chorizo, finely chopped
1 shallot, finely chopped
2 cups cherry tomatoes, or 5 to 6 Campari tomatoes cut into quarters
2 cloves garlic, sliced
2 Tbsp sherry vinegar
½ cup Castelvetrano olives, pitted and sliced
2 Tbsp extra-virgin olive oil

2 green onions, thinly sliced
2 Tbsp chopped fresh parsley
Salt and freshly ground black pepper, to taste
2 Tbsp canola oil
4 (5-oz) pieces halibut
1 Tbsp Anchovy Butter (see here)
Fresh crusty bread, to serve

Halibut with Anchovy Butter, Chorizo Ragù and Charred Broccolini

SERVES 4

This is a dish for those who prefer red wine with fish. The chorizo lends a satisfyingly spicy depth to the ragù, while the umami flavours of anchovy butter add savoury richness to the halibut. In fact, the butter recipe makes enough that you can freeze it for later. It's great on grilled meat or tucked under chicken skin for roasting.

ANCHOVY BUTTER In a food processor, combine all ingredients except butter and pulse 4 to 5 times, until coarsely chopped. Add butter and blend for 20 seconds, until ingredients come together. Scrape mixture onto a sheet of plastic wrap and roll into a log shape, tying both ends. Refrigerate until needed, or freeze for up to 6 months. Makes about 1 cup.

CHARRED BROCCOLINI Preheat broiler or barbecue to high. Combine all ingredients in a mixing bowl. If roasting in the oven, spread on a baking sheet and broil for 3 to 5 minutes. Stir and broil for another 2 minutes. If cooking on the barbecue, place on the grill or in grill basket and cook until lightly charred, turning frequently, about 5 minutes in total. Keep warm.

HALIBUT WITH CHORIZO RAGÙ Preheat oven to 400°F.

To make the ragù, heat a frying pan over high heat. Add chorizo and sauté, until caramelized and fat is released. Transfer chorizo to a plate, leaving fat in the pan.

Heat chorizo fat over medium-high heat, add shallots and sauté for 1 minute. Add tomatoes and cook for 10 minutes, until they begin to break down. Add garlic and cook for 2 minutes until softened, then pour in vinegar to deglaze pan. Add olives and return chorizo to pan. Stir in olive oil, green onions and parsley. Season with salt and pepper.

Heat canola oil in an ovenproof frying pan over medium heat. Season halibut with salt and pepper. Add halibut to pan and cook skin-side up for 2 to 3 minutes. Flip and roast in oven for 3 to 5 minutes, depending on thickness.

Remove halibut from oven and finish with a tablespoon of anchovy butter, spooning it over the halibut.

Spoon ragù onto 4 plates and arrange halibut on top. Serve with broccolini and crusty bread.

MUSHROOM DEMI

2 lbs mixed mushrooms, stems and caps separated
2 onions, chopped
5 cloves garlic, chopped
1 Tbsp extra-virgin olive oil
3 Roma tomatoes, chopped
3 bay leaves
2 sprigs fresh rosemary

1 tsp dried juniper berries
1 tsp coriander seeds
1 tsp black peppercorns
8 cups water
2 cups red wine
¼ cup red wine vinegar, plus extra to taste
¼ cup honey, plus extra to taste
¼ cup tomato paste
Salt, to taste

FRICASSEE CHAMPIGNONS

8 small potatoes
3 Tbsp extra-virgin olive oil (divided)
Reserved mushroom caps from Demi recipe
1 tsp freshly ground black pepper
1 tsp ground juniper berries
1 tsp chopped fresh rosemary
1 clove garlic, finely chopped
Salt, to taste
3 to 4 cups Mushroom Demi (see here)
¼ to ½ cup fresh goat cheese, crumbled
8 large eggs
3 cups baby arugula or kale

Fricassee Champignons

SERVES 4

Loaded with roasted mushrooms, potatoes and arugula and topped with eggs, this savoury vegetarian and gluten-free dish is one of the most popular at Café Medina. They also make a version with braised short ribs for the carnivores in the crowd. The mushroom demi is a stock that is reduced until it is thick and rich.

MUSHROOM DEMI Preheat oven to 425°F.

Spread mushroom stems, onions and garlic on a baking sheet, toss with oil and roast for 20 minutes, until golden brown. (Reserve mushroom caps for the fricassee.)

Place mixture in a large stockpot and add tomatoes, bay leaves, rosemary, juniper, coriander and peppercorns. Pour in water, wine, vinegar and honey and stir. Bring to a simmer over medium heat and simmer slowly for 1 hour. Strain and return to heat. Whisk in tomato paste and cook for another 30 minutes to 1 hour over low heat, until reduced to three-quarters of the original. Season with salt to taste. Add more vinegar or honey as desired.

FRICASSEE CHAMPIGNONS Preheat oven to 425°F.

Toss the potatoes with 1 Tbsp of the olive oil, then put potatoes in a roasting pan and roast for 20 minutes. Cool and then slice into bite-sized pieces.

Quarter reserved mushroom caps from demi recipe. In a large bowl, combine mushrooms, pepper, juniper, rosemary, garlic, remaining olive oil and salt. Spread on a baking sheet and roast for 8 to 12 minutes, until golden and crisp.

Place mushroom mixture and potatoes in a Dutch oven, cast-iron pan or baking dish. Pour in mushroom demi, then top with goat cheese. Bake for 10 minutes, until bubbly and cheese has melted.

Meanwhile, fry or poach 2 eggs per person. Remove dish from oven and top with arugula (or kale). Plate and serve with eggs.

Cartems Donuterie

IT CAME TO Jordan Cash in a dream. In the dream, he owned a doughnut shop. It made wholesome, high-quality doughnuts sustainably and in intriguing flavours. It even had a name: Cartems Donuterie. But it was just a dream.

Then in 2007, while shooting hoops, he met a guy named Rags (well, officially his name is Rajesh Narine, but no one ever calls him that), and they became friends. Fast forward to 2011, and Rags was the pastry chef at Calabash Bistro while Jordan was completing his MBA at UBC's Sauder School of Business, where he'd explored his doughnut shop dream further. One day he started to pitch the idea to Rags. "Stop!" said Rags. "You had me at doughnuts."

They opened Cartems Donuterie in February 2012, and their third partner, Krista Bailie, joined the team in 2015. As much as possible, their doughnuts are organic, sustainable and local, with no artificial colours, flavours, preservatives or stabilizers. "People can get behind that," Narine says. They offer options for vegans and the gluten sensitive. And they offer interesting flavours, like white chocolate peach or smoked maple walnut. "The Earl Grey doughnut—topped with rose petals—is hands down our most popular. People love tea, and they find this so unique and interesting."

They now have three locations, and every couple of months they hold ticketed four-course doughnut dinners that feature savoury doughnut dishes like doughnut burgers, doughnut duck confit, doughnut French toast or doughnuts in consommé. And yes, gourmet doughnuts are a trend right now, but it's not one that Narine sees dying anytime soon. "Doughnuts have been around since the early twentieth century, and people are willing to spend money on something real," he says. Besides, he adds, "I think people love the fact that we offer a friendly, approachable doughnut."

TOMATO MARMALADE

1 lb Roma tomatoes, peeled, seeded and chopped

Peel and juice of 1 navel orange, pith removed and peel cut into thin strips

2 tsp fresh lemon juice

1 cup cane sugar

⅛ tsp kosher salt

SOPAPILLA DOUGH

4 cups all-purpose flour

2 tsp baking powder

1 tsp kosher salt

1 tsp ground cumin

1 tsp ground cinnamon

1½ cups water

¼ cup coconut oil, melted

1 tsp fresh lemon juice

PAN-ROASTED HOMINY

1 Tbsp extra-virgin olive oil

1½ cups canned hominy or corn, drained and rinsed, or frozen corn kernels, thawed

1 tsp ground cumin

1 tsp ground cinnamon

1 tsp smoked paprika

1 tsp freshly ground black pepper

1 tsp kosher salt

1 green onion, finely chopped

Hominy-Stuffed Sopapillas with Tomato-Orange Marmalade

SERVES 4

Sopapilla is a traditional sweet doughnut served in Central America, topped with cinnamon, sugar and honey. This savoury version is made with hominy, a processed corn that can be found canned or dried in markets that sell Mexican foods. (If you can't find it, you could always use regular corn.)

TOMATO MARMALADE Chill a small plate in the fridge for 20 minutes.

Combine all ingredients in a saucepan and cook over medium heat, stirring constantly, until sugar is dissolved. Reduce heat to medium-low and cook for another 40 minutes, stirring occasionally.

Put a teaspoon of marmalade on the chilled plate. If marmalade stays firm on the plate, it is done. If it's still runny, cook a few minutes longer. Transfer to a small bowl.

SOPAPILLA DOUGH In a large bowl, sift together flour, baking powder, salt, cumin and cinnamon.

In a separate bowl, whisk together water, oil and lemon juice. Add to dry ingredients and mix well until smooth. Cover with a cloth and let the dough rest for 20 minutes.

PAN-ROASTED HOMINY Heat oil in a frying pan over medium heat. Add hominy (or corn), spices and salt and cook for 7 minutes, stirring frequently. Add green onions and stir for 1 minute. Remove from heat and set aside to cool.

ASSEMBLY Preheat oven to 350°F. Line a baking sheet with parchment paper. Roll out dough ¼ inch thick and cut into 4-inch squares. Cut each square in half into triangles. Place them on prepared baking sheet and bake for 20 minutes, until golden. Set aside to cool.

Slice an opening into the large side of the triangle (for stuffing like a pita). Spoon hominy into *sopapillas*. Serve with tomato marmalade.

LEMON SPRINKLES

½ cup icing sugar

1½ tsp cornstarch

½ tsp ground turmeric

½ tsp lemon extract

1 Tbsp vodka

DOUGHNUTS

2 cups all-purpose flour, plus extra for dusting

1 cup fine cane sugar

1 tsp kosher salt

2 tsp baking powder

1 tsp baking soda

1⅔ cups water

½ cup sunflower oil, plus extra for greasing

1 Tbsp apple cider vinegar

1 tsp pure vanilla extract

1 quantity Lemon Sprinkles (see here), to decorate

GANACHE

1 cup dark semi-sweet chocolate chips (55% cacao)

1 cup full-fat coconut milk

Vegan Doughnuts with Chocolate Ganache and Lemon Sprinkles

SERVES 6

This delicious vegan-friendly recipe appeals to everyone. You'll need a special doughnut pan, which is available in kitchen supply stores, but you can also use this batter to make cupcakes instead. Make the sprinkles a day in advance—or, if you prefer, just use store-bought sprinkles.

LEMON SPRINKLES In a bowl, sift together icing sugar, cornstarch and turmeric, ensuring that there are no lumps in the mixture. Slowly pour in lemon extract and vodka and stir constantly until a smooth paste forms.

Transfer paste into a piping bag with a very fine tip and pipe onto parchment paper in strips.

Set aside to dry for 24 hours, then break into small pieces with your hands.

DOUGHNUTS Preheat oven to 350°F. Grease and flour doughnut pans.

In a large mixing bowl, sift together flour, sugar, salt, baking powder and baking soda.

In a separate bowl, combine water, oil, vinegar and vanilla and mix well. Add dry ingredients to liquid ingredients and mix well.

Pour batter into prepared doughnut pans and fill each mould three-quarters full. Bake for 14 to 18 minutes, until risen, lightly golden and firm to the touch. Cool for 5 minutes in the pan, then remove to a rack and cool to room temperature.

GANACHE Put chocolate chips into a heatproof mixing bowl. Warm coconut milk in a small saucepan over medium heat. Pour coconut milk over chocolate chips and using a spatula, slowly stir until chocolate is melted and smooth. Set aside to cool slightly.

Pour ganache over cooled doughnuts (or, if you prefer, dip doughnuts into ganache) and add lemon sprinkles on top.

The Cascade Room

IT TAKES FOUR men to carry the roast pig inside, where it joins giant platters of steaks, turkey wings, sausages, ribs and all the fixin's. It's the inaugural "barbarian's feast" at the Cascade Room, and when the crowd isn't knocking back bourbon cocktails, this gang of carnivores is busy skewering massive hunks of meat with giant forks. There's even a guy in full-on Viking regalia.

Even so, the Main Street restaurant is a nod to the classic British pub. "You don't need the Guinness and Irish whiskey signs to say it's a pub. It's more about the community," says general manager Justin Taylor.

Opened in 2007, it was the first in a series of casual restaurants and bars that feature bold flavours and fun times. The restaurant group now includes El Camino's, with its Latin American street food, and the Union, with its Southeast Asian focus.

But it all started with the Cascade Room. Located right in the heart of Main Street, it serves up craft cocktails, local beer taps and a wine list heavy on B.C. wines. But mostly, it's all about executive chef Tim Evans's fun, approachable pub classics that don't scream "English pub." For instance, there's traditional roast available on Sundays, an organic beef burger and that much-loved Anglo-Indian dish, chicken tikka masala.

It's a menu sure to satisfy everyone, even a gathering of barbarians.

TIKKA MASALA PASTE

5 cloves garlic
1 (1½-inch) piece ginger, peeled and coarsely chopped
1 bird's-eye chili, seeded and coarsely chopped
2 Tbsp ground cumin
2 Tbsp ground coriander
2 Tbsp ground turmeric
2 Tbsp paprika
2 Tbsp garam masala
½ tsp ground cardamom
1 to 2 Tbsp canola oil

CHICKEN TIKKA MASALA

2 Tbsp canola oil
1 Tbsp unsalted butter
2 white onions, coarsely chopped
6 Tbsp Tikka Masala Paste (see here)
1 (796-mL) can fire-roasted tomatoes
2 Tbsp tomato paste
6 boneless, skinless chicken breasts, cut into 1½-inch cubes
6 Tbsp water
6 Tbsp heavy (36%) cream
5 Tbsp plain yogurt
Salt, to taste

Chopped fresh cilantro, for garnish
Steamed basmati rice, to serve
Store-bought mango chutney, to serve
Naan, to serve

Chicken Tikka Masala

SERVES 6

This classic of British pub fare combines traditions of English and Indian cuisine and is one of the most popular at the Cascade Room. More flavourful than hot, it has just the right amount of spice for a soul-soothing meal.

TIKKA MASALA PASTE Combine all ingredients in a food processor or blender and purée until smooth. Makes about 1 cup. (It can be stored in the fridge for 2 weeks or in the freezer for 3 months.)

CHICKEN TIKKA MASALA Heat oil and butter in a large saucepan or Dutch oven over medium heat. Add onions and sauté for 10 minutes, until softened and translucent. Add tikka masala paste and cook for 5 minutes, stirring occasionally. Add tomatoes and tomato paste and cook for another 5 minutes. Add chicken and water and simmer on low heat for 20 minutes. Stir frequently.

Stir in cream and yogurt and increase heat to medium-high. Cook, stirring frequently, until bubbling. Season with salt.

Remove from heat and divide into 6 serving bowls. Garnish with cilantro and serve with basmati rice, chutney and naan.

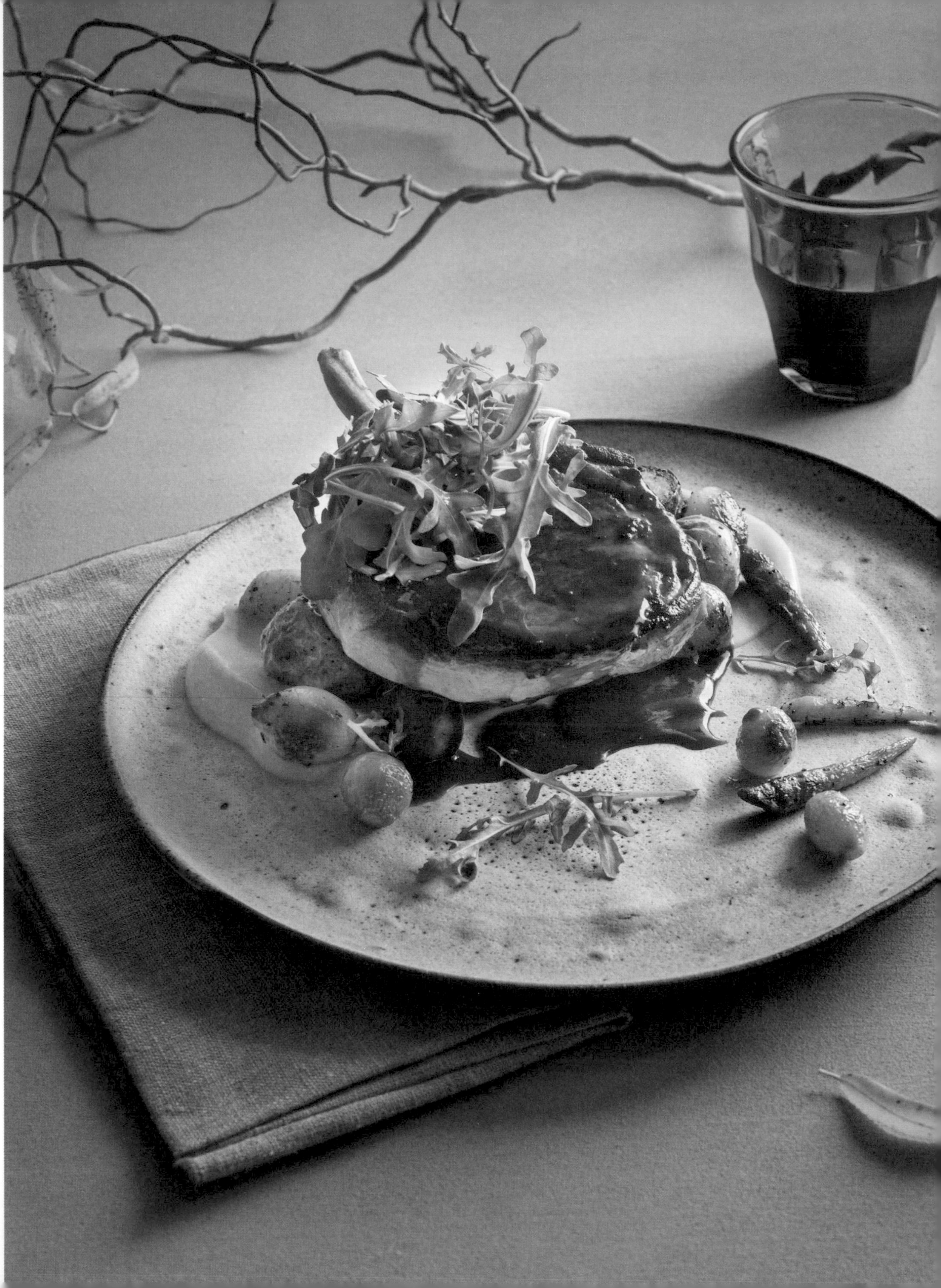

PORK CHOPS

4 cups water

⅓ cup kosher salt

1 head garlic, cloves separated and peeled (about ¼ cup)

1 Tbsp black peppercorns

5 bay leaves

Handful of fresh thyme

Handful of fresh parsley

6 Tbsp maple syrup

6 bone-in pork chops, about 1½ inches thick

1 Tbsp unsalted butter

SILKY APPLE PURÉE

6 Granny Smith apples, peeled, cored and chopped

½ cup water

¼ cup granulated sugar

¼ cup (½ stick) unsalted butter

Pinch of salt

ROASTED VEGETABLES

12 baby heirloom carrots, peeled and cut on a bias

3 lbs baby nugget potatoes

2 cups pearl onions, peeled

3 Tbsp extra-virgin olive oil

Salt and freshly ground black pepper, to taste

2 sprigs fresh rosemary, leaves chopped

Arugula, for garnish

Pork Chops with Roasted Vegetables and Silky Apple Purée

`SERVES 6`

The "wow" dish at the Cascade Room gets a hint of sweetness from the maple syrup brine, but it's the silky apple purée that puts it over the top.

PORK CHOPS Combine all ingredients except pork chops and butter in a large saucepan and bring to a boil, stirring until salt has dissolved. Remove from heat and set aside to cool completely.

Place pork chops in brine and refrigerate for 1 hour.

SILKY APPLE PURÉE Place apples in a large saucepan over low heat. Add remaining ingredients and simmer for 15 minutes, until apples soften. Transfer to a blender or food processor and blend until silky smooth. Set aside and keep warm.

ROASTED VEGETABLES Preheat oven to 400°F.

In a large bowl, combine all ingredients except rosemary and toss until well coated. Spread evenly on a baking sheet, sprinkle with the rosemary and roast for 15 to 20 minutes, until just starting to brown. Set aside and keep warm. Leave oven on.

ASSEMBLY Remove pork chops from brine and pat dry.

Melt butter in a large cast-iron pan over medium-high heat. Add pork chops and sear for 2 minutes. Flip and roast in oven for 5 minutes. Remove from oven and rest for 5 minutes.

Spread apple purée on each of 6 plates. Arrange vegetables, then add pork chop. Season with salt and pepper to taste. Once pork chops are removed from the pan, reduce the pork drippings and butter and spoon over the chops. Top with arugula.

Chambar

BACK IN 2004, when Nico and Karri Schuermans decided to open a Belgian-by-way-of-Morocco restaurant in an old warehouse space in the urban wasteland of Crosstown, there were more than a few raised eyebrows. "We were the first restaurant in the neighbourhood, and nobody really believed in it. It was Karri who said it would work," Nico says. "All I do is cook."

Chambar became the coolest spot in town, its cozy lounge area packed with people night after night. Its proximity to the arenas and Queen Elizabeth Theatre certainly helped, but so did the funky vibe, the inventive cocktails and the fragrant pots of Mussels Congolaise served with perfectly cooked frites. Over time, Chambar became a launching spot for many of Vancouver's most celebrated chefs, bartenders and restaurateurs.

A little surprisingly, given all the tagines, couscous and spices on the menu, the Belgian-born and Michelin-trained Nico has never actually been to Morocco, although he's cooked all over the world. These days, he's just as heavily influenced by the great produce he finds here on the West Coast and the easy mix of culinary styles that seems to appeal to Vancouver palates. "I want to come up with ideas that surprise people. The classics at Chambar are so popular that I can't take them off the menu, but for the rest of the menu, we go with the seasons. Once you use seasonal ingredients, everything falls into place."

A decade after it first opened, Chambar moved two doors up the street to a bigger space, with a patio, private event space and a huge lounge. It still has the vintage charm of the original, though now brightened with natural light and eye-catching modern art—and if anything, it's busier than ever. Turns out Karri, of course, was right.

NICO SCHUERMANS

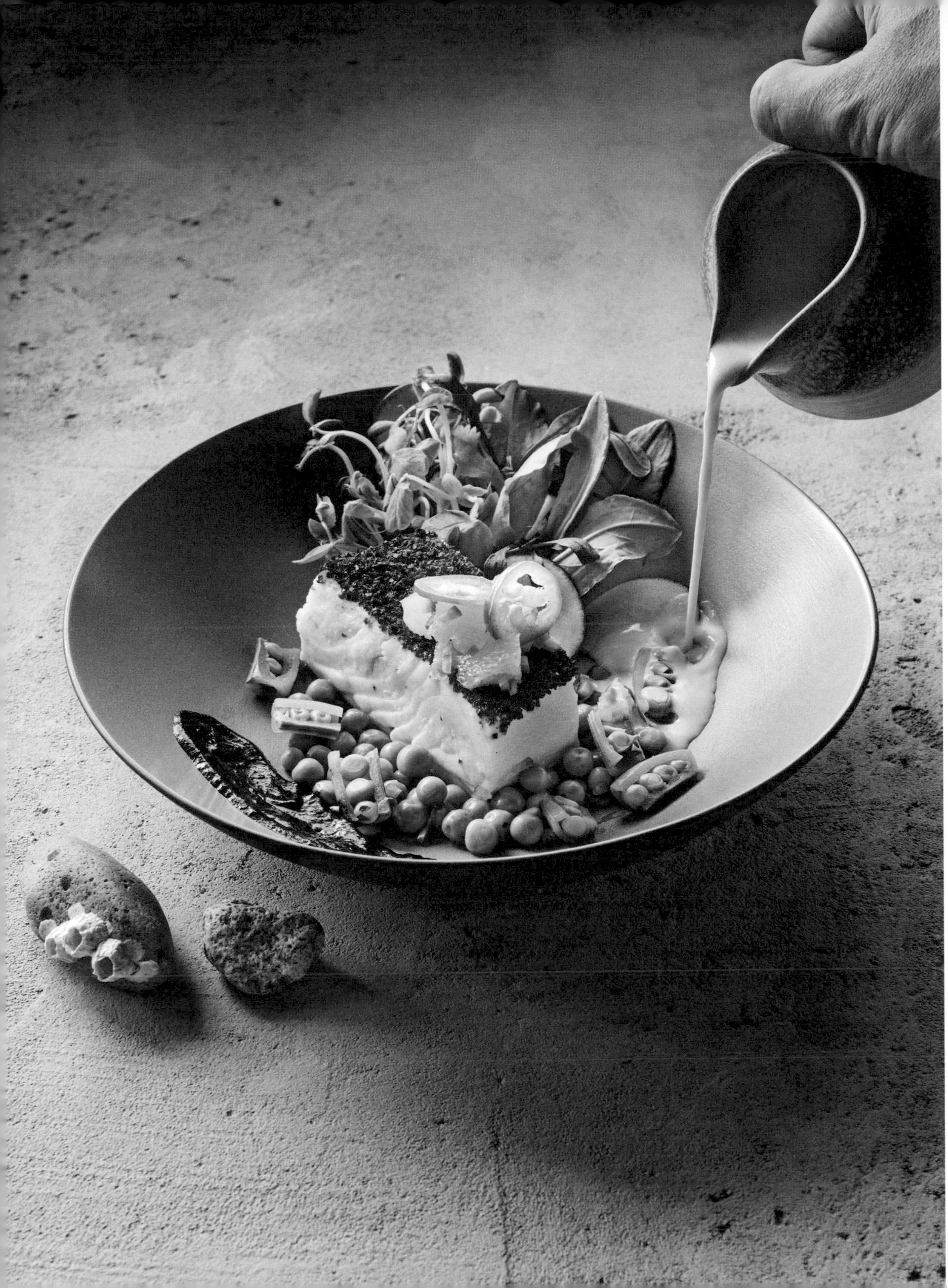

ORANGE-JALAPEÑO BROTH

8 cups water

1 lb white fish bones

½ white onion, cut in half

3 cloves garlic

3 stalks celery, cut in half widthwise

1 carrot, cut in half widthwise

1 Tbsp coriander seeds

6 star anise

3 Tbsp kosher salt

4 oranges, peeled and quartered

2 jalapeño peppers, seeded, deveined and chopped

Pinch of saffron

2 cups heavy (36%) cream

Juice of 3 lemons

BLACK GARLIC-NORI EMULSION

¼ cup peeled black garlic (available at South China Seas)

1½ tsp nori paste

ORANGE-JALAPEÑO SALSA

1 orange, skin and pith removed and segmented

1 small jalapeño pepper, seeded, deveined and diced

2 radishes, sliced into fine matchsticks

1 Tbsp chopped fresh cilantro

1 tsp fresh lemon juice, or to taste

1 tsp extra-virgin olive oil, or to taste

Salt, to taste

Nage de Flétan (Halibut in Orange-Jalapeño Broth)

SERVES 4

Halibut caught off the B.C. coast is a true delicacy with a firm, clean flesh that's highlighted by this bright and flavourful sauce.

ORANGE-JALAPEÑO BROTH In a large saucepan, combine water, bones, onion, garlic, celery and carrot and bring to a boil. Skim surface and discard foam. Add coriander seeds, star anise and salt. Reduce heat to medium-low and s immer for 1 hour. Strain liquid into a clean pan. Discard solids.

Add oranges, jalapeño and saffron. Pour in cream and bring to a boil. Reduce heat to medium-low and simmer for 30 minutes. Remove from heat and stir in lemon juice. Transfer mixture to a food processor and process until smooth. Strain through a fine-mesh sieve, then season to taste. Set aside.

BLACK GARLIC-NORI EMULSION Put black garlic in a small saucepan, add just enough water to cover and bring to boil. Remove from heat and set aside for 5 minutes. Transfer mixture to a food processor, add nori paste and pulse. Set aside.

ORANGE-JALAPEÑO SALSA Slice orange segments into 1-inch pieces. Combine with jalapeños, radishes and cilantro. Season with lemon juice, oil and salt.

HALIBUT

1 cup snap peas, trimmed and cut into 1-inch pieces

1 cup fresh peas

1 cup white wine, or as needed

4 (5-oz) skinless halibut fillets

Pinch of tagine spice (available in gourmet markets)

1 Tbsp extra-virgin olive oil

1 cup pea shoots, cut in half

1 cup sorrel, small leaves only

1 cup mustard greens, small leaves only

1 cup watercress leaves

HALIBUT Bring a small saucepan of water to a boil. Add snap peas and fresh peas and cook for 1 minute. Drain, then transfer to a bowl of ice water. Drain and set aside.

Turn the broiler to high.

Heat a frying pan over medium-high heat and add ½ inch of wine.

Season halibut with tagine spice and place in pan. Bring liquid to a boil, then reduce heat to medium-low and simmer for 3 to 5 minutes, until almost cooked. Place under the broiler for 1 minute, until fish is flaky but not dry.

In a separate frying pan, heat oil over medium-high heat, add snap peas and fresh peas and sauté for 1 minute. Toss in pea shoots. Remove from heat.

ASSEMBLY Prepare 4 shallow bowls. On one side of each bowl, place pea mixture. On the other side, form a row of sorrel, mustard greens and watercress. Place fish on pea mixture and finish with 1 tablespoon of black garlic-nori emulsion. Spoon orange-jalapeño salsa overtop. Pour 1 cup of broth around the finished dish. Serve immediately.

VICHYSSOISE BASE
¼ cup extra-virgin olive oil
2 cups chopped leeks, white and light green parts only
½ cup chopped shallots
1 tsp chopped garlic
1 tsp kosher salt
½ tsp coriander seeds
½ tsp black peppercorns
½ tsp fennel seeds
½ cup beef stock

VICHYSSOISE VEGETABLES
2 cups chopped black (lacinato) kale
⅔ cup chopped watercress
½ cup chopped fresh chervil
½ tsp ground white pepper
½ clove garlic
Salt, to taste
1 quantity Vichyssoise Base (see here)

SUN-DRIED TOMATO DRESSING
1 cup sun-dried tomatoes packed in oil, drained and oil reserved
1 Tbsp truffle oil
2 Tbsp soy sauce
1 Tbsp sherry vinegar
2 Tbsp reserved sun-dried-tomato oil

Le Bison (Bison Tartare with "Vichyssoise")

SERVES 4

Bison is leaner and more deeply flavourful than beef; here it is accompanied by Chef Nico Schuermans's take on classic vichyssoise—in this case, a bright green and fragrant sauce that adds vibrancy.

VICHYSSOISE BASE Heat oil in a large frying pan over medium-high heat. Add all ingredients except stock. Cook for 5 minutes until vegetables are soft.

Add stock and cook for another 2 minutes. Remove from heat and set aside to cool for 5 minutes. Transfer mixture to a blender or food processor and blend until smooth. Strain through a fine-mesh sieve and discard pulp. Set aside.

VICHYSSOISE VEGETABLES Bring a medium saucepan of salted water to a boil over high heat. Add kale, watercress and chervil and blanch for 1½ minutes. Drain, then transfer to a bowl of ice water. Drain again.

In a food processor, combine watercress mixture, pepper, garlic and salt and blend until very smooth. If necessary, strain through a fine-mesh sieve.

In a mixing bowl, combine vichyssoise base and puréed greens and mix well. Refrigerate until ready to serve.

SUN-DRIED TOMATO DRESSING In a food processor, combine all ingredients except sun-dried tomato oil and process until smooth. With the motor still running, gradually add sun-dried tomato oil and blend until emulsified. Set aside.

CROSTINI

4 thin slices sourdough bread
1 tsp melted unsalted butter
Pinch of paprika
Salt, to taste

TARTARE

4 quail eggs
2½ cup bison tenderloin,
    cut into ¼-inch cubes
¼ cup finely chopped shallots
¼ cup finely chopped gherkins
¼ cup finely chopped capers
¼ cup chopped fresh chervil
Sun-Dried Tomato Dressing (see here),
    to taste plus ¼ cup for frisée
Salt, to taste
Piment d'Espelette or any fine-ground
    chili powder, to taste (optional)
1 head frisée lettuce, leaves separated

CROSTINI Preheat oven to 325°F.

Brush sourdough with melted butter and sprinkle with paprika. Place on a baking sheet and bake for 10 minutes, until golden brown and crispy. Season with salt.

TARTARE Bring a small saucepan to a boil, add quail eggs and cook for 2 minutes and 45 seconds. Drain, then transfer to a bowl of ice water. Peel and set aside.

In a mixing bowl, combine bison, shallots, gherkins, capers and chervil. Season with sun-dried tomato dressing to taste.

Spoon a row of bison tartare on 4 plates or shallow bowls. Spoon vichyssoise around bison. Slice quail eggs in half and season each egg with salt and piment d'Espelette (or other chili powder) (if using). Place egg at bottom of plate beside bison.

Combine frisée with ¼ cup sun-dried tomato dressing and toss. Arrange around bison. Garnish with crostini.

JOSH GONNEAU

SABRINE DHALIWAL

Cibo Trattoria /
UVA Wine & Cocktail Bar

BACK IN THE day, the Dufferin was one of the swankiest hotels in town. Built in 1908, it went through decades of ups and downs and changing fashions until, a century after opening its doors, it was reborn as the chic boutique Moda Hotel, home to both UVA and Cibo. It's coolly modern now, but still embraces vintage details like mosaic-tiled floors, delicate wall mouldings and dramatic gilded cornices.

You could say the same about the food and drink. When Cibo opened in 2009, its modern Italian fare propelled it to the top of *enRoute*'s best new restaurant list. Executive chef Josh Gonneau continues with a contemporary approach, but with a friendly nod to the classics. "We're keeping in mind that Italian philosophy of fresh, seasonal and local and allowing the ingredients to speak for themselves," he says. "It's simple, but big in flavours."

It's the kind of menu that appeals to both the hip urban professionals who stay at the hotel and the culture vultures who swing by for a quick bite before heading over to the Orpheum Theatre. That is, unless they drop by UVA first.

Originally a wine bar, the focus shifted to cocktails as the city's top bartenders took turns behind the wood here. Now it's the talented Sabrine Dhaliwal who runs the show, serving up some of Vancouver's most innovative, well-crafted cocktails. "I try to play outside the box," she says, "and to do intriguing things that you wouldn't necessarily do at home."

That could mean low-proof cocktails, seasonal drinks or bar classics like the Chartreuse Milkshake or Pink Skies, Dhaliwal's award-winning update on the martini. They just happen to pair nicely with Gonneau's grazing menu of Italian snacks. Moda, it seems, is back in style, and this time to stay.

HONEY SYRUP
1 cup honey
1 cup hot water

CROSSING BORDERS
1½ oz Belvedere vodka
½ oz fino sherry
½ oz Amontillado sherry
¼ oz Luxardo Bitter Bianco
¼ oz Honey Syrup (see here)
2 dashes Bittered Sling Suius
   Cherry bitters
Lemon twist, for garnish

Crossing Borders Cocktail

SERVES 1

Sabrine Dhaliwal won Belvedere Vodka's worldwide martini competition with her Pink Skies cocktail made with Lillet Rose. Here, she uses another favourite ingredient, sherry, for a subtle and delicate drink made with Vancouver's own Bittered Sling bitters.

HONEY SYRUP Mix honey and water in a bowl and stir until fully dissolved. It can be stored in a clean glass jar in the fridge for 2 weeks.

CROSSING BORDERS Combine all ingredients except garnish into a mixing glass with ice. Stir for 10 to 15 seconds, until well diluted. Strain into a chilled coupe glass and garnish with lemon twist.

PASTA DOUGH
6 large eggs
5 cups Italian "00" flour, plus extra for dusting
¼ cup water
1 Tbsp extra-virgin olive oil

MUSHROOM FILLING
1½ lbs portobello mushrooms
1 Tbsp chopped fresh rosemary
1 clove garlic
Juice of ½ lemon
Salt and freshly ground black pepper, to taste

TOMATO CONSERVA
2 cups cherry tomatoes (preferably organic heirloom)
½ cup extra-virgin olive oil
2 Tbsp red wine vinegar
½ cinnamon stick

ASSEMBLY
3 to 4 oz Gorgonzola
1 Tbsp unsalted butter
Salt and freshly ground black pepper, to taste
¼ cup baby arugula
Extra-virgin olive oil, for drizzling

Mushroom Ravioli with Gorgonzola, Tomato Conserva and Baby Arugula

SERVES 2 TO 4

Layer upon layer of savoury flavours are tucked in and around toothsome pillows of pasta. Earthy mushrooms, tangy blue cheese, sweet tomatoes and peppery arugula make this a winner for dinner. If you can't find the Italian "00" flour, all-purpose will work almost as well.

PASTA DOUGH Lightly beat eggs in a large mixing bowl. Add remaining ingredients and knead for 5 to 7 minutes. Cover with plastic wrap and refrigerate for at least 30 minutes.

MUSHROOM FILLING Combine mushrooms, rosemary and garlic in a food processor and process until finely chopped. Transfer the mushroom mixture into a large frying pan and cook over low heat for 30 to 40 minutes, stirring constantly, until almost all the liquid has evaporated. Add lemon juice and season with salt and pepper. Set aside and cool.

TOMATO CONSERVA Preheat oven to 300°F. Place all ingredients in an ovenproof pan, toss to combine and roast for 30 minutes, until tomato skins begin to crack. Remove from heat and set aside. Discard the cinnamon stick before plating.

ASSEMBLY Dust a baking sheet with flour.

Using a pasta roller or rolling pin, roll pasta dough into 2 even-sized sheets, ⅛ inch thick.

Using a piping bag or spoon, place small balls of mushroom filling on top of the first sheet of dough, evenly spacing them 2 inches apart. Using a water spray bottle, lightly spritz the pasta sheet around the filling.

Carefully place the second sheet overtop, using your fingers to press out air and avoid creating any air pockets. Using a circle cutter, cut ravioli and remove the remaining unfilled pasta.

Place ravioli on the prepared baking sheet and refrigerate until needed.

Bring a large saucepan of salted water to a boil. Gently lower ravioli into pan and cook for 3 minutes.

Using a slotted spoon, transfer ravioli to a frying pan. Add ½ cup of salted pasta water and stir in Gorgonzola until melted and smooth. Stir in butter. Season with salt and pepper.

Transfer Gorgonzola and ravioli to a serving dish. Top with tomato conserva and baby arugula. Drizzle with olive oil and finish with pepper.

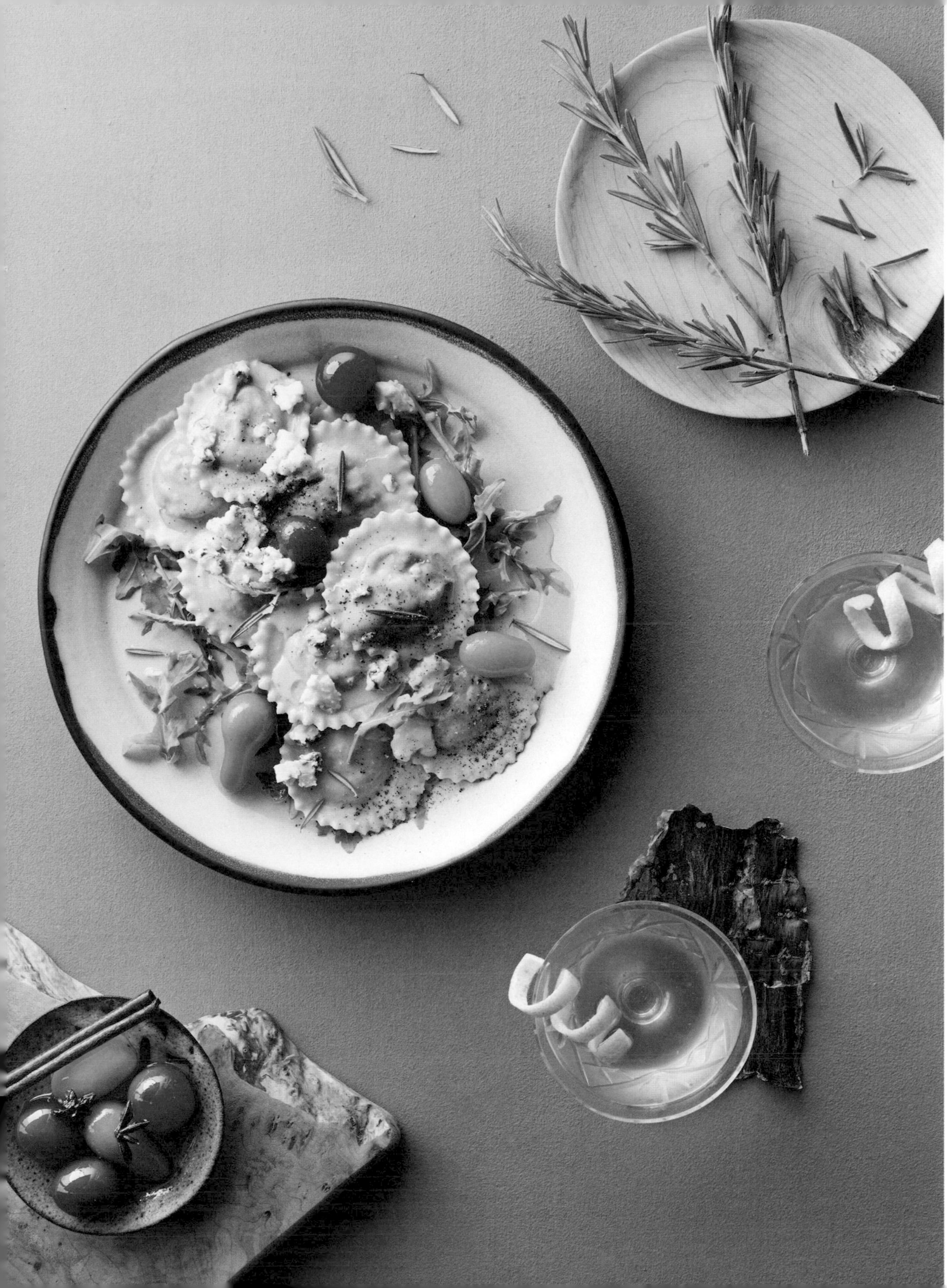

CinCin Ristorante

ANDREW RICHARDSON IS all fired up these days. That's thanks to his Grillworks Infierno, a massive wood-burning grill and rotisserie that's the source of those deliciously smoky aromas that waft over Robson Street. "The grill is the heart and soul of the kitchen and the whole restaurant," Richardson says.

That love of live fire brought Francis Mallmann, the famous Argentinian barbecue chef, for a visit in 2014. He and Richardson took over half a block of parking spots on Robson for a giant *asado*, slow-roasting whole prime ribs and chickens over glowing coals. Vancouver had never seen, or tasted, anything like it.

Nor had the city experienced anything like CinCin when it first opened back in 1990. It brought a sexy little slice of Tuscany to Vancouver and, like a fine Brunello, it has only improved with time. Venture up the winding stone stairs, and the doors open onto a warm and opulent space. Here, guests dine on truffles and pasta and whole *branzino* (European sea bass) from the grill and sip from a cellar curated by one of the city's most refined palates, Shane Taylor, 2017's B.C. Sommelier of the Year.

"We're loosely an Italian-style restaurant, but we do stretch the boundaries a little bit," says Richardson. Originally from Newcastle, he worked in Michelin-starred restaurants in the U.K. before moving to Vancouver and falling in love with local produce. "Italian cuisine is really driven by seasonality," he says. "Here in B.C., and the west coast of Canada, the range of produce is incredible. It makes it stimulating to be a chef."

That, and a bit of fire.

TARTARE

1½ lbs beef tenderloin
2 Tbsp finely chopped shallots
2 Tbsp small capers, called *nonpareil*
2 Tbsp finely chopped gherkins
¼ cup finely chopped fresh parsley
2 Tbsp Dijon mustard
2 tsp extra-virgin olive oil
8 extremely fresh large egg yolks, lightly beaten
Sea salt and freshly ground black pepper, to taste

SMOKED MAYONNAISE

2 large egg yolks
1 tsp Dijon mustard
Sea salt and freshly ground black pepper, to taste
1 cup + 1 Tbsp grapeseed or vegetable oil
2 tsp white wine vinegar
1 tsp fresh lemon juice
2 Tbsp water
Apple or cherry wood chips, for smoking

SHALLOT RINGS

2 small shallots
2 cups canola oil, or as needed, for deep-frying
3 Tbsp rice flour
Salt, to taste

ASSEMBLY

4 slices sourdough (preferably made with Red Fife wheat)
Pinch of salt
Extra-virgin olive oil, for drizzling
1 bunch watercress, leaves only
16 nasturtium leaves

Beef Tartare with Smoked Mayonnaise and Shallot Rings

SERVES 4

Mayonnaise is always delicious, but adding smoke to it, as Andrew Richardson does here, makes it divine. And it can be surprisingly easy, if you follow the instructions below. It takes an old-school classic and makes it exciting and modern.

TARTARE Using a mincer fitted with the smallest gauge, grind the beef into a bowl. Fold in remaining ingredients and adjust seasoning to taste. Keep refrigerated until ready to serve.

SMOKED MAYONNAISE In a food processor, combine egg yolks, mustard, salt and pepper. With the motor still running, gradually add oil and blend until emulsified. Season with vinegar and lemon juice. Stir in water to thin out. Adjust seasoning to taste.

To smoke the mayonnaise, place a smoker box filled with fruitwood chips at one end of a 6-inch-deep metal roasting pan or at one end of your barbecue. Pour mayonnaise into a shallow bowl and place at the other end of the pan or the barbecue. Light wood chips with a barbecue lighter or a long fireplace match. Once they start to smoke, cover pan with foil, or close the lid on the barbecue, and set aside for 7 minutes. Remove foil and stir mayonnaise well. Set aside.

SHALLOT RINGS Using a mandoline, slice shallots into very thin rings. Transfer to a plate lined with paper towels and set aside to dry for 2 to 3 minutes.

Heat 2 inches of oil in a deep saucepan or deep-fryer until it reaches a temperature of 350°F.

Dust the shallots with rice flour, then shake them in a sieve to sift off excess. Gently lower shallots into oil and deep-fry for 1 to 2 minutes, until golden brown. Using a slotted spoon, transfer shallots to a plate lined with paper towel to drain. Season with salt.

ASSEMBLY Toast or grill sourdough and season with salt.

Spoon the beef tartare onto one side of the plate—use a ring mould, if you like, to make it more attractive. On the other side, place a spoonful of smoked mayonnaise and drizzle oil in a line down the plate. Scatter watercress, nasturtium leaves and shallot rings on top. Cut the grilled bread into 3 pieces and arrange on one side of each plate.

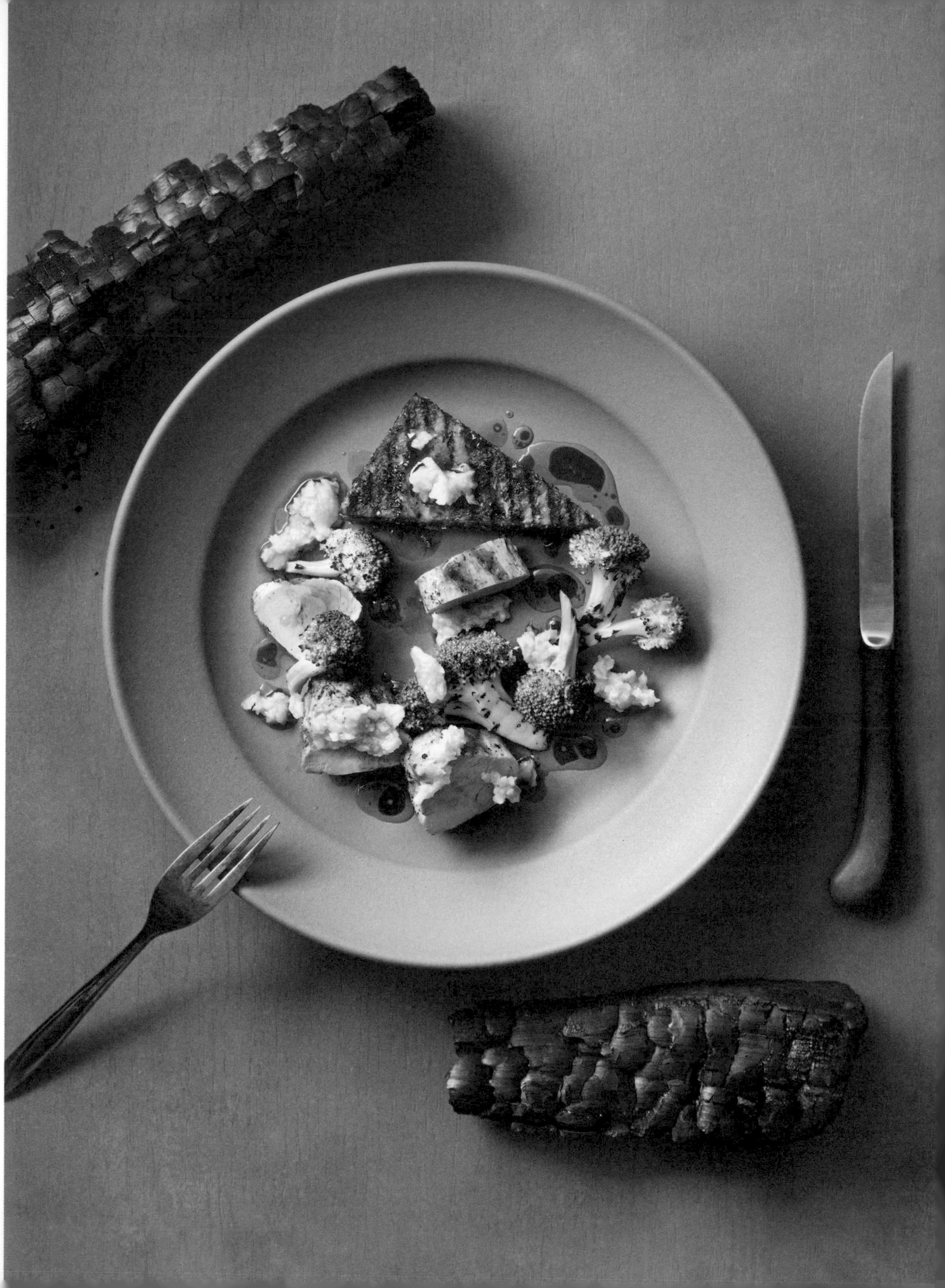

BUCKWHEAT POLENTA

2½ cups water

½ cup coarse-ground polenta (cornmeal), preferably Bob's Red Mill or Anson Mills, plus extra for dredging

2 Tbsp buckwheat flour

2 Tbsp unsalted butter

½ cup grated Parmesan

Salt and freshly ground black pepper, to taste

KUMQUAT, HONEY AND SAKE MOSTARDA

1½ lbs kumquats, washed, cut into quarters and seeds removed

⅔ cup honey

⅓ cup sake

BALSAMIC VINAIGRETTE

6 Tbsp balsamic vinegar (preferably Venturi-Schulze)

6 Tbsp extra-virgin olive oil

Sea salt and freshly ground black pepper

PORK TENDERLOIN

10 oz broccolini or broccoli, trimmed

4 (6-oz) pork tenderloins

2 to 3 Tbsp canola oil (divided)

Sea salt and freshly ground black pepper, to taste

Pork Tenderloin with Kumquat Mostarda, Buckwheat Polenta and Broccolini

SERVES 4

All the components for this dish can be prepared ahead of time and then finished on the grill, making it perfect for an elegant backyard barbecue dinner party.

BUCKWHEAT POLENTA Line a small baking pan with parchment paper.

Bring a small saucepan of water to a boil. Combine cornmeal and buckwheat flour together, then gradually add into water and stir constantly. Reduce heat to medium-low and simmer for 40 minutes, stirring frequently. Stir in butter and Parmesan. Season with salt and pepper. Transfer to the prepared baking pan and refrigerate for 1 hour, until set. Cut into 2-inch squares.

Preheat a grill over high heat. Dredge polenta in polenta flour, tapping off any excess and place on grill. Cook, turning occasionally, for 10 minutes, until tender and grill marks have been achieved.

KUMQUAT, HONEY AND SAKE MOSTARDA Combine all ingredients in a saucepan and bring to a boil over medium-high heat. Reduce heat to medium-low, cover and cook for 5 minutes. Remove lid and cook for another 20 to 25 minutes. Cool to room temperature.

BALSAMIC VINAIGRETTE Stir vinegar and oil together in a bowl. Season with the salt and pepper.

PORK TENDERLOIN Bring a medium saucepan of water to a boil and generously season with enough salt so that the water tastes like sea water. Put broccolini (or broccoli) into water and cook for 2 minutes. Transfer broccolini to a bowl of ice water. Drain, then pat dry.

Preheat a barbecue to medium-high or cast-iron grill plate over medium-high heat. Rub 1 to 2 tablespoons of oil over 4 tenderloins and season with salt and pepper. Place on barbecue or grill and cook for 20 minutes, turning every 2 minutes. Remove from heat and allow to rest.

Toss broccolini in 1 tablespoon of oil and season with salt and pepper. Place on grill and cook for 2 minutes, until nicely charred.

Slice each tenderloin into 3 and place on one side of the plate. Add grilled polenta and broccolini. Drizzle vinaigrette over polenta and spoon *mostarda* over tenderloin. Serve immediately.

Cioppino's Mediterranean Grill

ONE OF THE "three amigos" is what Anthony Bourdain called him when he visited Vancouver a few years ago. Giuseppe Posteraro, known to all as "Pino," helped introduce the bad boy of celebrity chefdom to Vancouver's food scene. And what better guide could you ask for?

"Vancouver is most like where I grew up in southern Italy," Posteraro says, "unpretentious and laid back." He was born in Calabria, but he has not only made his home here, he has changed the way the city dines. His multiple-award-winning restaurant may represent high-end, Old World cuisine, but it has been revolutionary in this city.

When Cioppino's opened in 1999, Yaletown wasn't yet the restaurant mecca it is now. Neither was Vancouver. It's one reason Posteraro insists his is not an Italian restaurant. Despite all that pasta and risotto on the menu, it's not exactly an old-school meatballs-and-red-sauce kind of joint. "Cioppino's is a restaurant that has the soul intrinsically tied to Italian culture but sets the stage in beautiful British Columbia," Posteraro says. "When people think about Italian food, they think spaghetti and pizza. I call it Mediterranean to have more freedom."

He was one of the first chefs to bring sous vide cuisine to North America and has mentored some of the most exciting young chefs in the city. He introduced countless diners to the addictive pleasures of burrata, veal cheeks and Iberian ham. He helped lead the way in using local and seasonal ingredients. Even now, when he could easily rest on his laurels, he's just undertaken a major renovation and is constantly reinventing his cuisine.

"My distinctive dishes are never the same. I never sit still. The same dish—I always try to make it fresher, lighter, more evolved," he says. "I'm always the first to arrive and the last to leave. To me, it's not work—it's what I love."

2 Tbsp red wine vinegar

2 slices white bread

6 heirloom tomatoes, peeled, seeded and coarsely chopped

1 Persian cucumber, chopped

1 stalk young celery, chopped

1 red bell pepper, seeded, deveined and chopped

½ jalapeño pepper, seeded, deveined and chopped

1 tsp chopped red onion

1 clove garlic, finely chopped

6 Tbsp tomato juice

1 tsp coarse salt

Extra-virgin olive oil, for drizzling

1 ball buffalo mozzarella, chopped

Fresh basil leaves, torn, for garnish

Chilled Heirloom Tomato and Garden Vegetable Soup

SERVES 4

Cool and refreshing, this soup makes the most of your summer garden and is an ideal starter for a hot day. Heirloom tomatoes have a more intense tomato flavour than modern ones, which have been bred for good appearances and shelf life rather than for taste. If you can't find heirloom tomatoes, you can use ripe plum tomatoes instead.

Chill 4 soup bowls in the fridge.

Drizzle vinegar over bread and leave to soften for a few minutes. Tear it into pieces and place in a food processor. Add vegetables, garlic, tomato juice and salt and process until smooth. If you like it chunky, leave as is; if you prefer a smooth soup, pass it through a coarse strainer. Chill until ready to serve.

Stir in oil, then divide between the chilled soup bowls. Arrange mozzarella and basil leaves overtop. Serve.

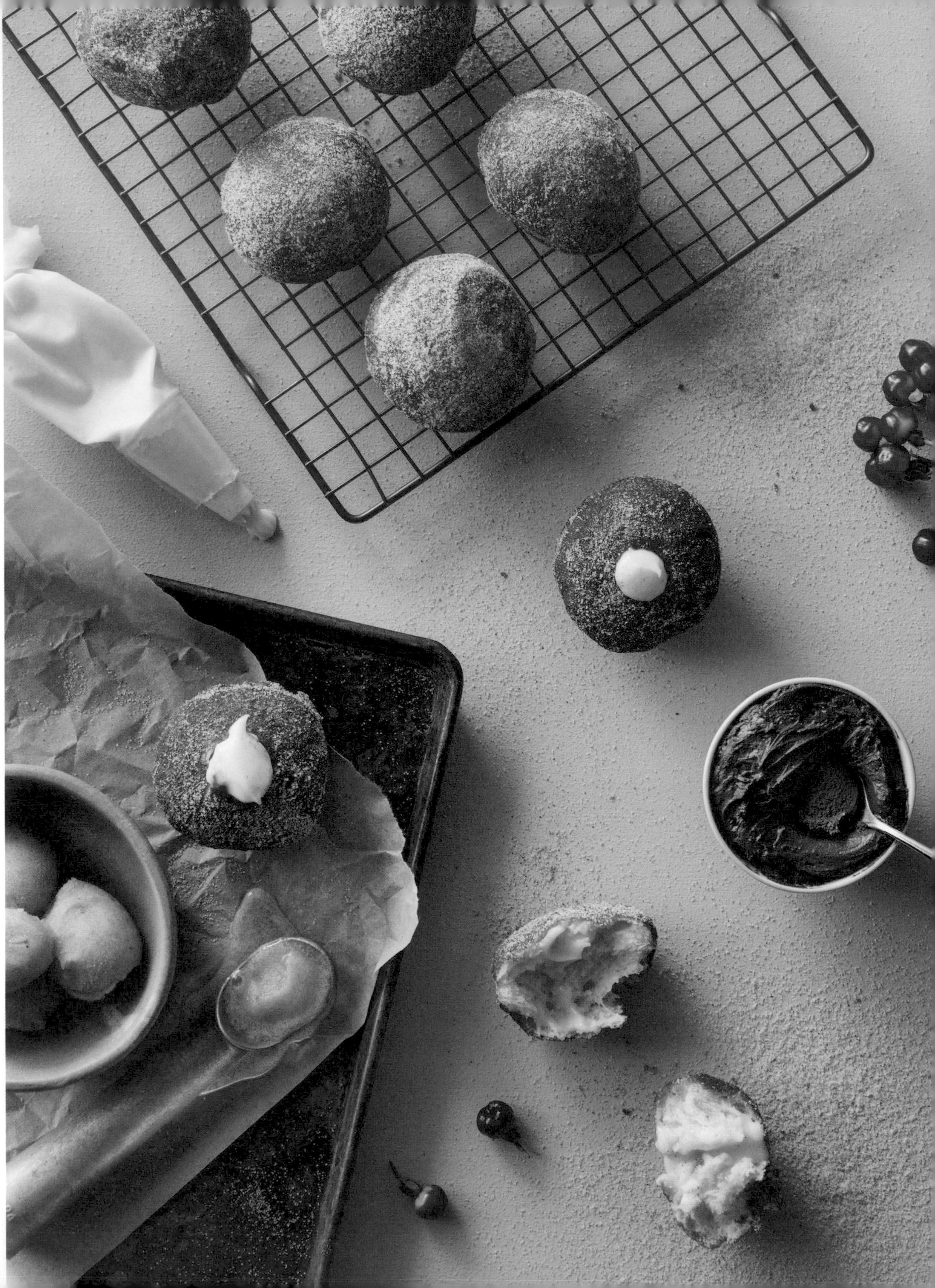

¾ cup lukewarm whole milk
   (about 110°F)
1 Tbsp active dry yeast
¼ cup granulated sugar,
   plus extra for sprinkling
⅓ cup vegetable oil, plus 3 cups
   or as needed for deep-frying
2 large eggs

1 tsp pure vanilla extract
Grated zest of ½ orange
4½ cups unbleached
   all-purpose flour
Pinch of salt
Granulated sugar, for coating
Jam, lemon curd or chocolate
   ganache, for filling (optional)

Bomboloni (Italian Doughnuts)

MAKES ABOUT 24

*Light, crispy and fun to say, these sweet treats are an
excellent way to end a meal—or to enjoy anytime.
Fill them with jam, pastry cream or chocolate ganache,
or simply enjoy as is.*

Place milk in a stand mixer fitted with a dough
hook. Stir in yeast and sugar and leave it to
dissolve. Add ⅓ cup oil, eggs, vanilla extract and
orange zest and mix well. Stir in flour and salt.
Leave dough in a warm place to proof for 1 hour,
until doubled in size.

   Roll dough out, about 1½ inches thick. Using a
cookie cutter, cut out 1¼-inch disks. Cover them
with a cloth and proof them again for another
2 hours, until doubled in size.

Heat remaining 3 cups oil in a deep saucepan
or deep-fryer (the oil should be at least 3 inches
deep; add more oil, if necessary) until it reaches
a temperature of 375°F. Gently lower bomboloni,
in small batches, into oil and deep-fry for 2 to
3 minutes, until golden. Using a slotted spoon,
transfer to a plate lined with paper towels and
drain. Roll in sugar. If you like, use a piping bag
fitted with a small tip to fill the bomboloni with
jam, lemon curd or chocolate ganache.

DAVID ROBERTSON

The Dirty Apron Cooking School

IT'S SAFE TO say that many a Vancouverite wouldn't even know how to chop an onion if it weren't for the Dirty Apron Cooking School.

"I've always enjoyed passing on knowledge of cooking," says Chef David Robertson, who owns the school with his wife, Sara. "It's fun to share passion, educate the public about food and demystify the process behind the scenes at restaurants."

While he was still chef de cuisine at Chambar (page 74), he realized what he liked best about cooking was teaching others how to do it. He figured that in an "amazing food city" like Vancouver, plenty of people would want to learn. And he was right.

The school opened in 2009, and the staff has grown from six to forty. It's added a deli that serves three hundred people every day ("Best sandwiches in town," Robertson insists) as well as a busy catering arm. But the school is still the heart of the business. It now offers forty different styles of classes, including both demonstration and hands-on cooking lessons that cover everything from knife skills to seafood, vegetarian, Italian, French, Spanish and Thai cuisine. And more than ten thousand students a year sign up for the classes.

In part, it's because they're just so much fun. After you've tried your hand at making, say, pasta from scratch, you get to sit down to enjoy it over a glass of wine with your classmates. But mainly it's because Robertson is just so dedicated to the kind of whole, hearty food that we want to eat. In other words, don't expect any classes in molecular gastronomy.

"It's just not me," he says with a laugh. "I'm more about flavour. I want to take a simple approach to it and let the food do the talking."

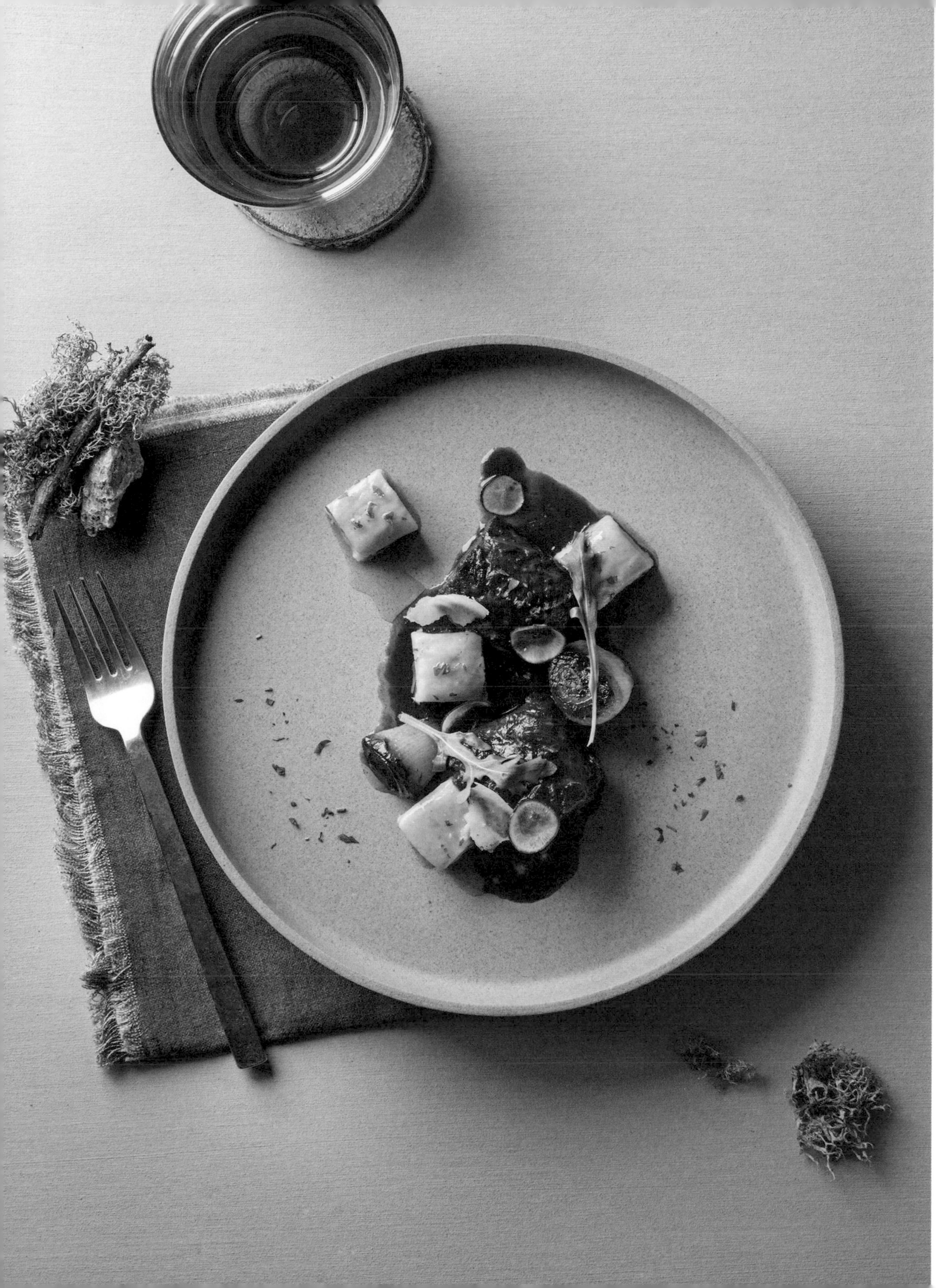

2 Tbsp vegetable oil, or as needed

1½ lbs boneless lamb shoulder, cut into
   3 equal pieces

Salt and freshly ground black pepper,
   to taste

1 large onion, chopped

1 carrot, chopped

1 stalk celery, chopped

4 cloves garlic, finely chopped (divided)

1½ cups dry red wine

1 cup canned crushed tomatoes

½ cup beef stock, or as needed

½ cup chicken stock, or as needed

¼ cup maple syrup

2 Tbsp sherry vinegar

2 sprigs fresh thyme

1 sprig fresh rosemary

1 bay leaf

1 Tbsp extra-virgin olive oil

Shaved Parmesan, for garnish

Handful of arugula, for garnish

**BUTTERNUT SQUASH–RICOTTA
GNOCCHI**

1 medium butternut squash, cut in half
   lengthwise and seeds removed

Vegetable oil, for brushing

1 cup drained ricotta

1 large egg, lightly beaten

¾ cup grated Parmesan

1 tsp freshly grated nutmeg

1 tsp kosher salt

Freshly ground black pepper, to taste

1⅓ cups all-purpose flour, plus extra for
   dusting and dredging

Braised Lamb Shoulder with Butternut Squash–Ricotta Gnocchi

SERVES 4

Every part of this perfect dinner-party dish can be made ahead of time. The lamb can be reheated, the gnocchi boiled and everything assembled at the last minute. Impress your friends, and yourself.

BRAISED LAMB SHOULDER Preheat oven to 300°F.

Heat a large frying pan over high heat and add enough vegetable oil to coat. Season lamb on all sides with salt and pepper. Carefully add lamb to pan and sear until brown on all sides. Place in a Dutch oven or braising pan and set aside.

Add onion, carrot, celery and half of garlic to the frying pan and cook for 5 minutes, until tender. Pour in wine and bring to a boil, scraping any bits of meat from the bottom of the pan. Cook for 10 minutes, until liquid is reduced by half.

Stir in canned tomatoes, stocks, maple syrup and vinegar and bring to a boil. Pour mixture over lamb. The liquid should almost cover the lamb—if it doesn't, add more stock or water. Add thyme, rosemary and bay leaf. Cover with a lid or foil and braise in the oven for 3 hours, until meat is fork tender. Set aside to cool to room temperature, then refrigerate for at least 4 hours or preferably overnight to let the flavours settle and develop.

Remove fat, which will have solidified. Gently reheat over low heat. Once the braising liquid has come to liquid form, remove the lamb. Strain the liquid into a bowl and discard the solids.

Cut lamb into bite-sized cubes.

BUTTERNUT SQUASH–RICOTTA GNOCCHI

Preheat oven to 400°F. Lightly flour a baking sheet.

Lightly brush cut side of butternut squash with oil. Place squash cut-side down on a baking sheet and roast for 1 hour, until tender. Set aside to cool slightly, then scoop out flesh. Discard skin. Measure 2 cups squash and chill in the fridge for at least 1 hour. (You can freeze any remaining squash to use another time.)

In a large bowl, combine 2 cups squash, ricotta, egg, Parmesan and nutmeg. Season with salt and pepper and mix well. Gradually fold in flour, taking care not to overwork the dough.

Dredge dough in flour. On a clean work surface, roll out dough by hand into a rope with a ¾-inch diameter. Cut rope into 1-inch pieces and place onto prepared baking sheet. Refrigerate until needed.

Bring a large saucepan of salted water to a boil. Drop gnocchi into the water and cook for 1 minute, until they float to the surface. Using a slotted spoon, transfer gnocchi onto a lightly oiled baking sheet and toss lightly to prevent them from sticking to each other. Set aside to cool.

ASSEMBLY Heat olive oil in a large frying pan over medium heat. Add remaining garlic and sauté for 1 minute, until fragrant. Add lamb and quickly sauté. Pour in 2 cups of braising liquid and simmer until reduced to your desired consistency.

Add gnocchi and gently toss together. Season with salt and pepper to taste. Garnish with shaved Parmesan and arugula and serve.

SABLEFISH
3 cups whole milk
4 sprigs fresh thyme
2 bay leaves
4 cloves garlic
4 (3-oz) smoked sablefish pieces

BUTTERED CRAB
3 Tbsp unsalted butter
1 leek, white and light green parts only, sliced
⅓ cup dry vermouth
Juice of 1 lemon
1 cup heavy (36%) cream
4 oz fresh crabmeat, picked of shells or cartilage

4 sprigs fresh Italian parsley, leaves only, chopped
4 sprigs fresh tarragon, leaves only, chopped
Salt and freshly ground black pepper, to taste

Poached Sablefish with Buttered Crab

SERVES 4

Sablefish is one of the great little-known seafood stars of the West Coast. Also known as black cod, it has a buttery taste and velvety texture that is ideal for smoking. Plus, it is highly sustainable, making it as guilt-free as it is delicious.

SABLEFISH In a saucepan, combine milk, thyme, bay leaves and garlic and bring to a simmer over medium heat. Reduce heat to low, place sablefish into pan and cook for 6 minutes, until softened and tender. Set aside.

BUTTERED CRAB Heat butter in a small saucepan over medium-high heat, add leeks and sauté for 2 minutes. Pour in vermouth and lemon juice and cook for another minute. Stir in cream and cook for 10 minutes, until reduced by half. Add crabmeat, fresh herbs, salt and pepper.

ASSEMBLY Divide buttered crab between 4 plates, mounding it in the centre, and stack sablefish on top. Serve.

Fable Kitchen

IT WAS DURING the "Restaurant Wars" episode of *Top Chef Canada* season two that Trevor Bird came up with the name for his dream restaurant: Fable, a mash-up of "farm" and "table." When he placed second in the final, he took his winnings and made the plunge. "I was wrapping up my time on *Top Chef*, and I always wanted to open a restaurant. The timing was perfect," he says.

Fable is a down-home kind of place, with chalkboard walls, light fixtures made from mason jars or pitchforks, and specials written on a hanging roll of butcher paper. Dishes sound simple and straightforward, but don't be fooled—there's serious technique behind them. "Canned tuna," for instance, is a subtly sophisticated confit; the meatball of "spaghetti and meatball" is duck filled with a hidden pool of Madeira and finished with Parmesan foam.

And as much as possible is sourced locally and ethically. "I wanted to make a difference in how we source our food and get to know our farmers," he says. "Straightforward. Seasonally driven. Technically inspired." It's that access to exceptional local produce that he says is the very best thing about being a chef in Vancouver.

In 2016, he opened the even more casual Fable Diner and has now turned his attention to mentoring the young cooks coming up through his restaurants. "Leadership is huge," he says. "It's about learning how to educate and empower people while sharing your vision."

PANNA COTTA

5 oz high-quality milk chocolate, chopped
8 sheets gelatin or 3 Tbsp gelatin powder
4 cups whipping (33%) cream
1¼ cups whole milk
¼ cup granulated sugar
½ tsp kosher salt
8 (8-oz) wide-mouth mason jars
Raspberries, for garnish

OREO COOKIE CRUMB

1 cup (2 sticks) unsalted butter, room temperature
¾ cup granulated sugar
1 cup all-purpose flour
1 cup black cocoa powder
½ tsp baking powder
½ tsp kosher salt

Milk Chocolate Panna Cotta with Oreo Crumb and Raspberries

SERVES 8

"Panna cotta" means cooked cream, and this is reminiscent of a chocolate pudding—only so much better. For the crumbs, you can purchase Oreo cookies or make your own. Just note that you will need black cocoa to get that distinct dark Oreo colour—it's an ultra-Dutch-processed cocoa powder available at bakery supply stores or online.

PANNA COTTA Place the chopped chocolate in a large bowl.

Soak gelatin leaves in ice water for 5 minutes, then squeeze out the excess water. (If using gelatin powder, sprinkle it over ¾ cup cold water and allow it to sit for 5 to 10 minutes, until it has bloomed and turned the texture of applesauce.)

Combine cream, milk, sugar and salt in a saucepan and heat over medium-high heat, until it just comes to a boil. Remove from heat. Add prepared gelatin to mixture, stirring to dissolve.

Pour hot liquid over chocolate and whisk, scraping down the sides of the bowl, until chocolate is melted and well mixed in. Pour into jars, cover tightly and refrigerate overnight to set.

OREO COOKIE CRUMB In a stand mixer fitted with a paddle attachment, cream butter and sugar together until light and fluffy.

In a separate bowl, mix together remaining ingredients, then add them to the butter mixture. Mix until it becomes a very soft dough. Refrigerate for 1 hour.

Preheat oven to 325°F and line a baking sheet with parchment paper.

Roll out dough ¼ inch thick, then cut into pieces and place on the prepared baking sheet, evenly spaced about 2 inches apart. (No need to be fancy: the cookies will just be turned into crumbs later.) Bake for 12 to 15 minutes, until the cookie crumbles easily. Cool to room temperature.

Store any leftover cookies in an airtight container in the freezer. It can be crumbled on top of ice cream, yogurt, puddings or other desserts.

ASSEMBLY When you're ready to serve the panna cotta, remove the jars from the fridge. Crumble the cookies on top, then garnish with raspberries.

GARLIC CRACKERS

¼ cup all-purpose flour

2 Tbsp granulated sugar

1 tsp kosher salt

1 large egg white

¼ cup (½ stick) unsalted butter, room temperature

1 Tbsp finely grated Parmesan

1 Tbsp finely grated garlic

SHALLOT VINAIGRETTE

¼ cup finely chopped shallots

¼ cup honey

¼ cup white wine vinegar

¾ cup Canadian organic cold-pressed canola oil or extra-virgin olive oil

½ tsp kosher salt

1½ tsp chopped fresh thyme leaves

SALAD

2 lbs assorted heirloom tomatoes, room temperature

1 large ball burrata

4 to 6 fresh basil leaves, torn

Leaves of frisée, curly kale or other greens, for garnish (optional)

Heirloom Tomato Salad with Burrata, Shallot Vinaigrette and Garlic Crackers

SERVES 4 TO 6

Trevor Bird serves this signature salad at his restaurants every summer when tomatoes are ripe. It's topped with the luscious cream-filled fresh cheese known as burrata—the more, the better, he advises. "It's simple and so, so good," he says.

GARLIC CRACKERS Preheat oven to 350°F. Line a baking sheet with parchment paper.

Combine all ingredients in a medium bowl and mix to form a thick paste. Using a spatula, spread paste thinly over prepared baking sheet. Bake for 6 minutes, until golden brown. If it's still too pale, bake for another 2 minutes and check again—adding more time, if needed. (Don't bake more than 15 minutes—if the cracker gets too dark, the garlic will burn and make it very bitter.) Set aside to cool and break into large pieces.

SHALLOT VINAIGRETTE Combine all ingredients in a mason jar and shake well. It can be stored in an airtight container in the fridge for 1 week.

SALAD Cut tomatoes into wedges and rounds and arrange them on a serving platter or divide them between 4 to 6 plates. Top with burrata, drizzle shallot vinaigrette overtop and finish with torn basil. If you like, garnish with frisée, curly kale or other greens. Serve with garlic crackers.

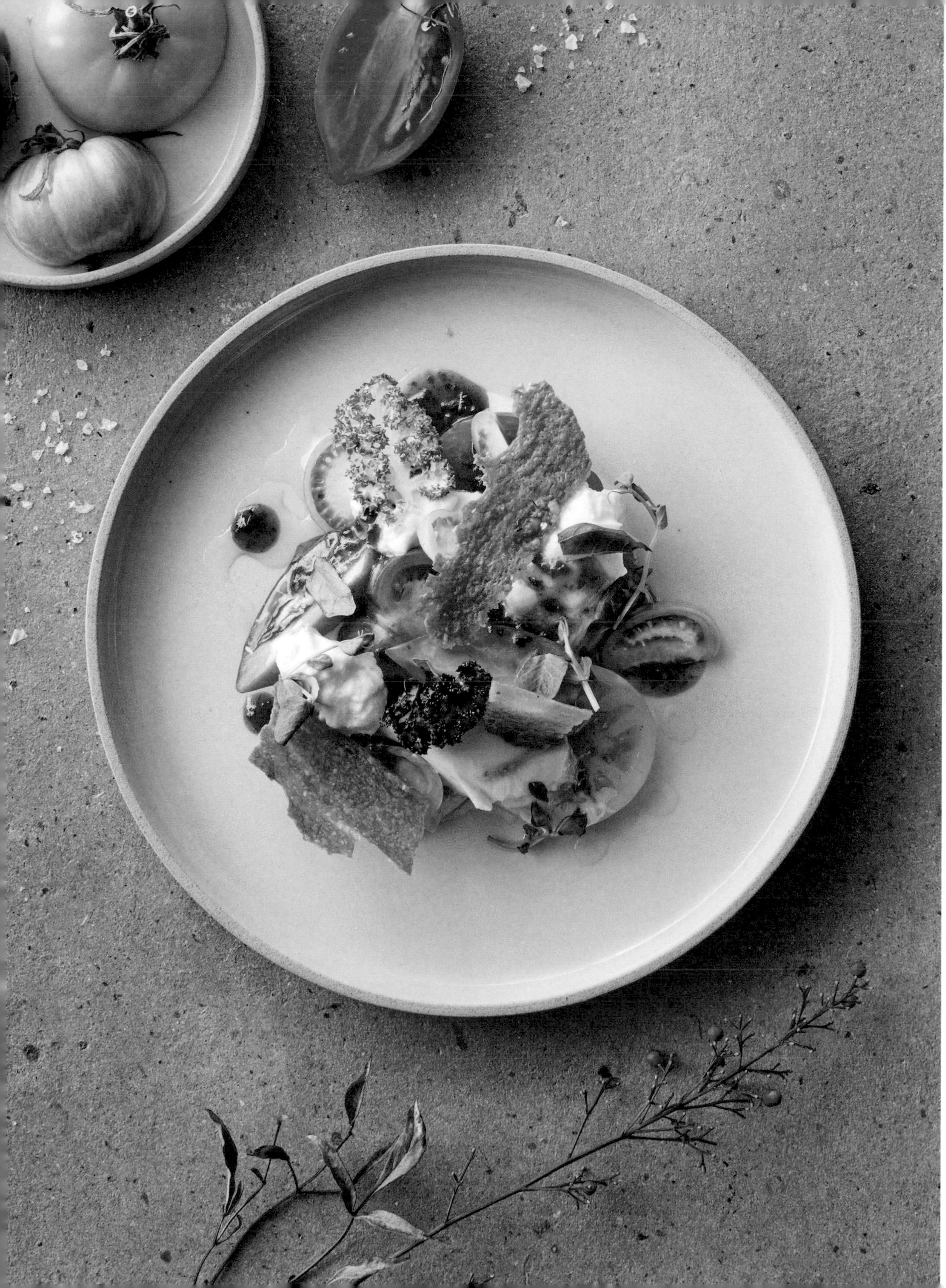

DAVID GUNAWAN

Farmer's Apprentice

VANCOUVERITES—EVEN THE ONES who follow restaurant openings like others follow the travails of the Canucks—were taken aback when a tiny, vegetable-forward restaurant took the 2014 Vancouver Magazine Awards for Best New Restaurant, Best Casual Restaurant and Restaurant of the Year. It also nabbed the number-two spot on *enRoute* magazine's annual list of Canada's best new restaurants. But those who knew David Gunawan weren't surprised at all.

Long a champion of sustainable locavorism, he'd honed his skills at top restaurants in Chicago, Seattle, Belgium and Vancouver, where he was executive chef at West and then Wildebeest before opening Farmer's Apprentice in 2013.

"For us, it's about fostering people and their creative freedom. It's not a traditional restaurant. We're trying to cultivate knowledge and education," he says. "The food is very minimal, very seasonal, very resourceful and very local. Our whole idea is to let nature express herself."

That means when he does cook animal protein, he breaks down the whole animal, letting nothing go to waste. He puts the smoker to good use, smoking everything from hay to bacon to the bones for broth. He ferments things and pickles them, dishes up whole grains, sources heirloom vegetables and uses all sorts of weird botanical things that show up at his door. The menu changes all the time, so every visit is a whole new experience.

Most importantly, he sees his role as an opportunity to promote sustainability and to change our perceptions of food. "Our generation of chefs is being heard," he says. "Chefs are more proactive and have the power to change policy and the way people eat." Deliciously, sustainably, creatively, at least when Gunawan is in the kitchen.

PICTURED ON P.104

1 small white onion
¼ cup extra-virgin olive oil, plus extra
  for drizzling
Salt and freshly ground black pepper,
  to taste
4 ice cubes
2 cups sorrel leaves, chilled
¼ cup apple juice, chilled

1 (3-inch) piece cucumber, peeled
  and chilled
½ cup fresh mint leaves, chilled
Fresh lemon juice, to taste
1 cup fresh berries, to taste
White wine vinegar, to taste
Wild herbs, such as elderflower
  or dandelion leaves, for garnish

Sorrel Gazpacho with Berries and Wild Herbs

SERVES 4

At Farmer's Apprentice, this chilled soup will change depending on what wild herbs and berries are in season—try it with huckleberries, salmonberries or even blueberries, and if you can't find foraged herbs, you can always use whatever is fresh in your garden, such as parsley or mint. Just remember that all ingredients must be cold, and stay cold, in order for the sorrel to retain its bright-green colour.

Preheat oven to 350°F.

Cut top off onion, but leave most of the skin on. Put onion in a small baking dish, drizzle oil overtop and sprinkle with salt and pepper. Cover with foil and roast for 25 minutes, until softened and tender. Set aside to cool and chill in fridge.

Peel onion, then put into a blender or food processor. Add ice cubes, sorrel, apple juice, cucumber, mint and ¼ cup oil and blend until smooth. Add lemon juice and salt to taste.

Divide gazpacho equally into 4 serving bowls. Dress berries with a drizzle of oil and vinegar and arrange in bowls as garnish. Top with wild herbs and serve.

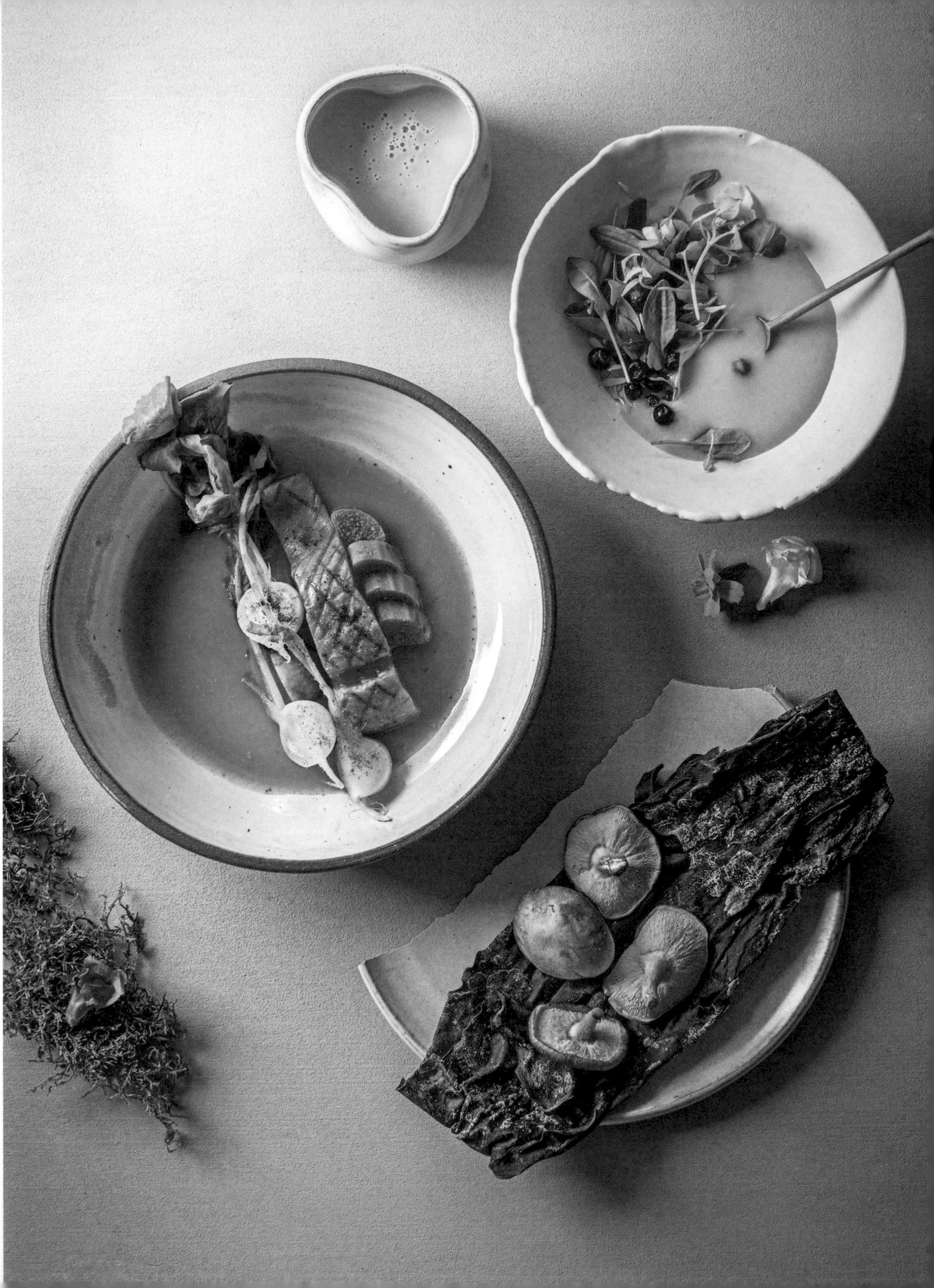

BRINED RHUBARB

2 cups water

1 Tbsp kosher salt

2 stalks rhubarb, cut into
    4-inch segments

SALMON AND SMOKED BONE BROTH

Alder wood chips, soaked, for smoking

1 (5-lb) whole salmon, filleted and bone
    reserved (ask your fishmonger)

4 cups water

3 dried shiitake mushrooms

1 (3-inch) piece kombu (dried seaweed),
    wiped clean with a damp cloth

4 (5 g) packets bonito flakes (optional)

1½ Tbsp granulated sugar

1½ Tbsp kosher salt

4 small turnips, cut into quarters and leaves
    reserved, for garnish

Spring Salmon with Brined Rhubarb, Turnips and Smoked Bone Broth

SERVES 4

Chef David Gunawan loves adding the sweet, savoury flavour of smoke to his dishes, and this one is no exception. In this case, he smokes a whole salmon bone before adding it to the broth that surrounds his grilled salmon. If you don't have access to a smoker, you can use bonito flakes instead.

BRINED RHUBARB Combine water and salt in a large sealable jar and stir mixture until the salt dissolves. Add rhubarb pieces, making sure they're submerged, then seal.

Leave at room temperature for 4 days, until rhubarb has fermented.

SALMON AND SMOKED BONE BROTH Light a smoker and add soaked alder chips to the coals. Add salmon bone and smoke for 30 minutes.

In a large saucepan, bring the water to a simmer over medium-low heat. Add smoked bone, shiitakes and kombu and simmer for 10 minutes. Remove from heat and set aside to steep for 20 minutes. (Alternatively, if you are not using the smoked salmon bone, simmer mushrooms and kombu together for 10 minutes, then add bonito flakes during the steeping process.)

In a small bowl, mix together sugar and salt. Place the salmon fillets in a deep dish. Pat the salt mixture over salmon, covering it thoroughly and leave it to cure in the fridge for 45 minutes. Rinse salmon under cold running water and pat dry before grilling.

Heat a grill to medium-high heat. Grill the salmon fillets for 20 to 30 seconds on each side.

ASSEMBLY Depending on the weather and your preference, this dish can be consumed warm or cold. Slice salmon fillet into 4 pieces. Place salmon pieces in the middle of 4 serving bowls. Slice rhubarb to desired thickness and garnish salmon with rhubarb and turnips. For each dish, pour ½ cup broth around salmon. Garnish with a turnip leaf.

The Flying Pig

WHEN JOHN CROOK was a kid back in Ontario, money was tight for his big family. Even so, his mom, Margaret, managed to cook up healthy, hearty meals straight from the garden for the mob of kids and all their friends. "I used to say to my mom, 'One day I'll open my own restaurant, and you'll never have to clean or cook again.' And she'd say, 'I'll believe that when pigs fly.'"

After nearly twenty years of cooking around the world, including gigs in New York and at Vancouver's Four Seasons hotel, Crook and his business partner Erik Heck opened the first Flying Pig in Yaletown in 2011. "We met while working at Joe Fortes and immediately hit it off," Heck says. "We soon found we shared the same dream of creating a friendly spot for hanging out with friends over good food in Vancouver."

Two more branches quickly followed in Gastown and Olympic Village. "The formula for us has always been just hard work and patience and luck," Crook says.

The Flying Pigs are casual and lighthearted, a place for friends to gather over shareable plates of charcuterie, crispy Brussels sprouts or pulled-pork poutine. "We try to think about what it was like sitting down to dinner with my family. And we try to focus on good value," Crook says. Keeping his mother and her garden-fresh veggies in mind, he also makes a point of sourcing fresh, local ingredients when he can. "It's what being a chef is all about in Vancouver, and I love the availability of absolutely amazing products from the farms to the ocean."

But whether he's serving potatoes from Pemberton, halibut from Haida Gwaii or chicken from Mount Lehman Farm, what matters most is the spirit of the Flying Pig. "Someone said a long time ago, it feels like it's just people serving people," Crook says. "There's a humbleness about the Pig. It's like butcher meets farmer. We're talking true hospitality."

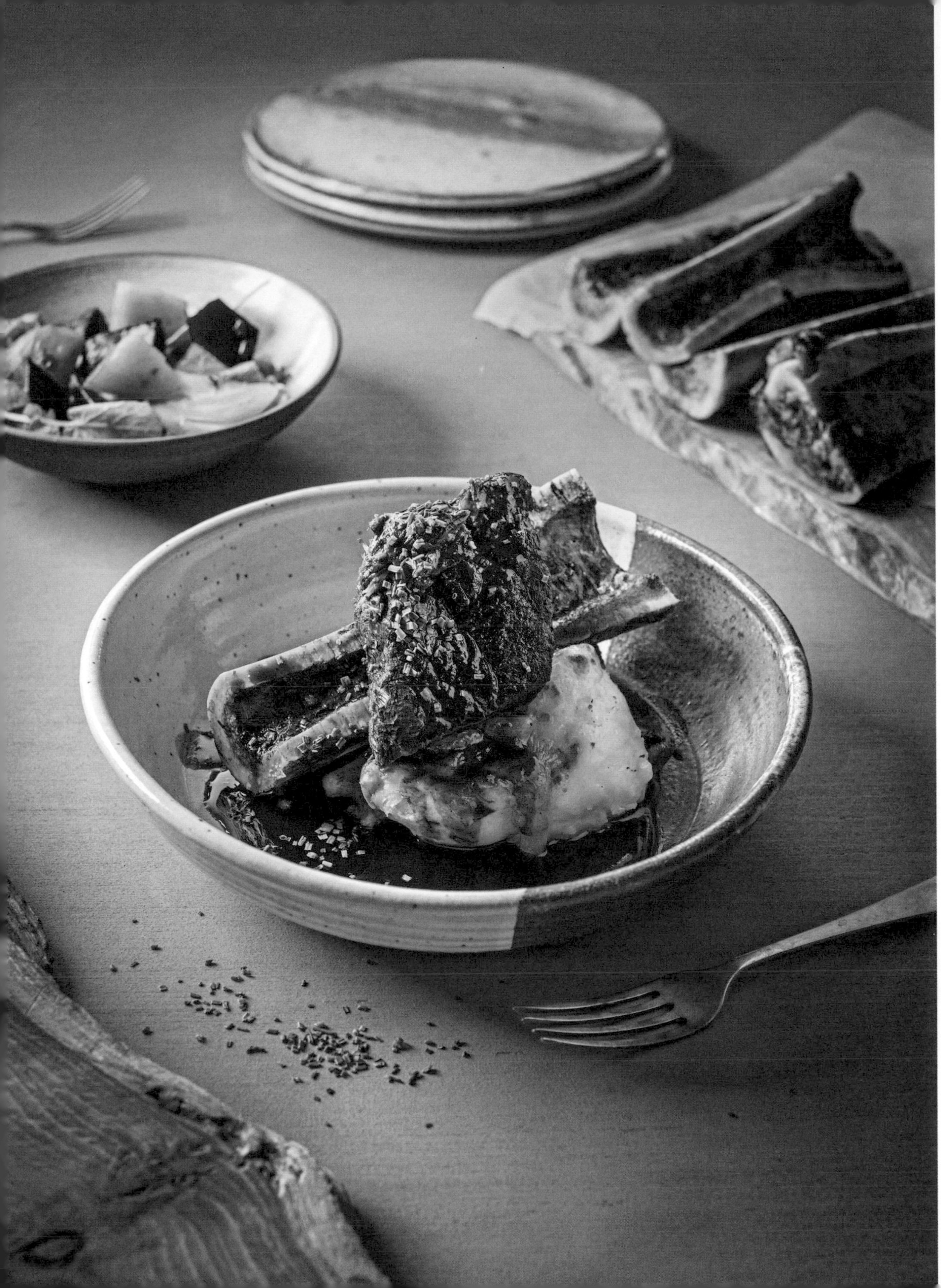

BRAISED SHORT RIBS

5 lbs boneless short ribs or
chuck flat, cleaned and trimmed
of excess fat and silver skin
Salt and freshly ground black
pepper, to taste
3 Tbsp vegetable oil
1 (750-mL) bottle red wine
(preferably Cabernet Sauvignon)
3 onions, chopped

3 carrots, chopped
1 stalk celery, chopped
1 Tbsp tomato paste
8 sprigs fresh thyme
2 sprigs fresh rosemary
2 bay leaves
4 cups veal stock
2 Tbsp chopped fresh chives,
for garnish

MASHED POTATO

4 lbs Yukon Gold potatoes (about 8),
peeled and cut into quarters
1 Tbsp kosher salt
6 Tbsp (¾ stick) unsalted butter
2 cups whole milk
Salt and freshly ground black
pepper, to taste

Red Wine–Braised Short Ribs with Bone Marrow

SERVES 6

Chef John Crook considers this one of his personal signature dishes. Instead of bone-in short ribs, Crook makes the dish a step easier by using "chuck flat," a cut that's also known as boneless short rib. It is among the tastiest and most affordable cuts of beef. And when you're finished scraping the marrow out of the bone, pour a shot of bourbon down the channel for a "bone luge."

BRAISED SHORT RIBS Preheat oven to 275°F.

Divide short ribs (or chuck flat) into 8-ounce portions and season with salt and pepper. Heat oil in a large Dutch oven over medium-high heat. Working in 2 batches, brown short ribs on all sides, about 8 minutes per batch. Transfer short ribs to a plate.

Pour out all but 3 tablespoons of drippings from pan and add red wine, stirring up any browned bits and cooking until reduced by a third. Add onions, carrots, celery and tomato paste, stirring constantly until combined. Add short ribs and any accumulated juices, thyme, rosemary and bay leaves. Pour in stock, ensuring ribs are completely covered with liquid. Bring to a boil, then cover Dutch oven with lid and transfer to oven. Cook for 8 hours.

Transfer short ribs to a platter. Strain sauce through a sieve to remove solids and discard. Pour sauce into a heavy-bottomed saucepan. Spoon fat from surface of sauce and discard. Reduce sauce until slightly thickened, then season with salt and pepper.

MARROW

2 Tbsp extra-virgin olive oil

6 (8-oz) beef marrow bones, split in half
   (ask your butcher)

Salt and freshly ground black pepper

1½ cups grated aged white cheddar

MASHED POTATO Place potatoes in large saucepan and add enough water to cover and the 1 tablespoon salt. Bring to a simmer and cook for 15 to 20 minutes, until tender. Drain. Do not wash the saucepan.

In a small saucepan, heat butter and milk over low heat until butter is melted and liquid is simmering. Using a potato ricer or masher, press potatoes back into large saucepan. Stir in butter and milk, then season with salt and pepper.

MARROW Preheat oven to 325°F. Drizzle oil over cut sides of marrow bones and season with salt and pepper. Place in a roasting pan and roast cut-side up for 15 to 20 minutes.

ASSEMBLY Preheat oven to 350°F.

Spoon mashed potatoes into one side of 6 (15-oz) oval casserole dishes. Sprinkle cheddar overtop, then place cooked bone marrow in the dish, leaving room for short ribs. Bake for 10 minutes, until cheese has melted. Place a portion of short ribs in the casserole dish and spoon sauce over meat. (Alternatively, scoop the mashed potatoes onto a plate, angle one marrow bone and one piece of braised beef over the potatoes and spoon sauce on top.) Garnish with chopped chives.

PIE SHELL

1¼ cups all-purpose flour,
  plus extra for dusting
1 tsp granulated sugar
Pinch of salt
¼ cup (½ stick) cold unsalted butter,
  cut into cubes
¼ cup chilled lard or shortening
3 Tbsp ice water
Non-stick vegetable spray

FILLING

2 cups packed light brown sugar
1 cup whipping (33%) cream
½ cup (1 stick) unsalted butter
1 Tbsp whisky
2 tsp pure vanilla extract
5 large eggs, room temperature
½ cup all-purpose flour
¾ tsp kosher salt
Whipped cream, to serve

Margaret's Maple Sugar Pie

MAKES 1 (9-INCH) PIE

This sweet treat is a great classic of Quebecois cuisine and one of John Crook's mother's favourite recipes. Although it doesn't actually contain maple sugar, the combination of ingredients tastes like it does.

PIE SHELL Combine flour, sugar and salt in a food processor and pulse to combine. Add butter and pulse until the largest pieces are pea-sized. Add lard (or shortening) and pulse again until mixture resembles coarse meal. Transfer to a large bowl and slowly drizzle ice water, mixing with a fork to combine. Knead 3 to 4 times to bring dough together (only a couple of floury spots should remain). Flatten dough into ½-inch-thick disk and wrap in plastic wrap. Chill for 2 hours, until firm.

Remove dough from fridge and set aside at room temperature for 5 minutes, until softened. Roll out dough on a lightly floured surface to a 12-inch round, rotating often and dusting with more flour as needed to prevent sticking. Transfer to a 9-inch pie dish. Lift up edges and allow dough to slump down into dish. You should have about 1-inch overhang. Fold edges under and crimp. Freeze for 15 minutes.

Preheat oven to 400°F.

Lightly coat a sheet of foil with non-stick spray and place into the pie crust, coated-side down, pressing into bottom and sides. Fill with pie weights or dried beans and bake for 15 to 20 minutes, until edges of crust are pale golden. Carefully remove foil and weights, then bake crust for another 8 to 12 minutes, until bottom is golden and dry. Transfer dish to a wire rack and set aside to cool.

FILLING Preheat oven to 325°F. Line a baking sheet with foil.

Pour a couple of inches of water into a large saucepan and bring to a simmer over medium heat.

Combine brown sugar, cream and butter in a large heatproof bowl and set it over the pan of water. (Do not let bowl touch water.) Heat, stirring constantly, until butter is melted, sugar is dissolved and mixture is smooth.

Remove bowl from heat and stir in whisky and vanilla. Whisking constantly, add eggs one at a time, incorporating completely after each addition. Add flour and salt and whisk just until smooth. Scrape filling into crust and place pie plate on the prepared baking sheet. Bake pie for 45 to 55 minutes, until filling is browned all over, puffed around the edges and slightly wobbly in the centre. Transfer dish to a wire rack and set aside to cool for at least 4 hours before slicing. (The longer you can wait, the easier it'll be to slice—do not refrigerate.) Top with whipped cream and serve.

Forage

PLENTY OF CHEFS are willing to forage for morel mushrooms and wild asparagus. They might even cast a line for trout or salmon every once in a while. But Chris Whittaker goes a step further. "I'm a hunter," he says. "I'm predominantly a moose hunter, and moose hunting is a lot of hiking and sitting and watching. That's when the size of our country really hits me. And that really makes me respect our land even more."

You won't find Whittaker's moose steaks on the menu at Forage (though if you're lucky, he might invite you to a barbecue sometime), but you will find meat from Turtle Valley Bison Co. and salmon from Pacific Provider. They're just two of the relationships he's carefully cultivated with small-scale suppliers who emphasize sustainability and quality. He happily credits them for the success of what comes out of his kitchen. After all, he points out, "They spend way more time growing and taking risks on crops and animals than we do."

Cozy, welcoming and unpretentious, Forage opened in 2012 in the Listel Hotel. Right away it was clear that this was not going to be hotel dining as usual: no bland Cobb salads or clubhouse sandwiches on this menu. Chef Whittaker believes that when it comes to flavour, it's go big or go home. He roasts pork bellies and salmon collars; lavishes them with ferments and smoked preserves; adds texture with puffed rice, black pepper praline and the crispy chicharrón that garnishes his award-winning seafood chowder. And he always has a few foraged surprises up the sleeves of his chef's whites.

That could mean wild mushrooms, cattails, sea asparagus or herbs he found growing by a road. "The big thing for me is when spring nettles come out," he says. "That tells me it's spring and everything is going to be awesome again." At Forage, everything already is.

SAUCE

2 Tbsp *usukuchi* (see Note)

6 Tbsp *koikuchi* or all-purpose soy sauce (see Note)

1 Tbsp Worcestershire sauce

1½ tsp fish sauce

6 Tbsp brown sugar

1½ tsp sambal oelek

1 clove garlic, crushed

BISON

1 cup grapeseed oil

4 shallots, thinly sliced

1 lb bison tenderloin, cut into ¼-inch-thick medallions

1 small bunch fresh cilantro, coarsely chopped

¾ cup toasted hazelnuts, lightly crushed

NOTE:

Soy sauce is one of the oldest condiments in the world, a by-product of fermented soybeans and (usually) wheat mixed with brine. It was invented in China some 3,000 years ago, then travelled to Japan and elsewhere. What Western cooks think of when they think of soy sauce is what the Japanese call *shoyu*, which is sweeter, milder and thinner than traditional Chinese soy sauce. Japanese sauces are divided into dark (*koikuchi*) and light (*usukuchi*)—most supermarket brands, even if they are not labelled as such, are considered dark. Light soy sauce tastes slightly sweeter and saltier, thanks to the addition of mirin (rice wine). There is also tamari, a thicker, richer, more intensely flavoured sauce, and the delicate white soy or *shiro*, which has the lightest flavour of all and is typically used for dipping sashimi.

"Vietnamese-Style" Bison Carpaccio

SERVES 4

Bison is lean, healthy and sustainable, with a deep but not gamy flavour. It's no wonder it's growing so fast in popularity. At Forage, Chris Whittaker sources his bison from Turtle Valley, but if you have a hard time finding it, you can always use venison or beef tenderloin in this recipe. Just be sure to use the best quality you can find.

SAUCE Combine all ingredients in a medium saucepan and bring to boil over medium-high heat. Immediately, set aside to cool completely. Refrigerate until needed.

BISON Heat oil in a medium saucepan over medium-high heat, until it reaches a temperature of 300°F. Carefully lower shallots into pan and cook for 2 to 3 minutes, stirring constantly, until lightly golden. Remove from heat and using a slotted spoon, transfer shallots to a plate lined with paper towels. Set aside to drain.

Place bison tenderloin medallions, one at a time, between 2 heavy freezer bags. Using a meat mallet or heavy-bottomed pan, gently pound each medallion to about ⅛ inch thick. Divide medallions between 4 plates. Generously garnish each with the sauce, cilantro, shallots and hazelnuts. Serve immediately.

TART SHELL

1¼ cups all-purpose flour, plus extra for dusting

½ tsp kosher salt

½ cup (1 stick) cold unsalted butter, cut into cubes

¼ cup ice water

FILLING

½ cup stinging nettles (see Note)

2 Tbsp extra-virgin olive oil

1 clove garlic, finely chopped

1 shallot, finely chopped

1½ cups fresh morel mushrooms, cleaned and sliced into ½-inch rounds

4 large eggs

¼ cup whole milk

½ cup whipping (36%) cream

⅛ tsp ground nutmeg

Salt and freshly ground black pepper, to taste

8 oz brie, diced (about 1 cup), plus 8 to 12 slices for garnish

Wild watercress or other greens, for garnish (optional)

NOTE:

Stinging nettle grows wild in many parts of B.C., mainly in disturbed areas like forest clearings and roadsides, and the best time to forage for it is in early spring when it is tender. Stinging nettle is both good and good for you and has for centuries been used as a tonic. Wear gloves while picking and preparing stinging nettles; they have tiny hairs that contain an acid that can trigger an itchy skin rash. Blanching the nettles stops them from stinging.

Morel Mushroom and Stinging Nettle Tart with Brie

SERVES 4

Stinging nettles—along with fiddleheads, morels and a few patio umbrellas—are among the surest signs of spring in Vancouver. Yes, they pack a sting if you stumble upon them while hiking, but prepared carefully, peppery nettles are delicious and nutritious. If you can't find nettles or morels, you can use chopped, steamed spinach and any other wild mushroom instead.

TART SHELL In a large bowl, combine flour and salt. Using a fork, pastry cutter or your fingers, cut in butter until mixture resembles coarse crumbs. Stir in ice water, a tablespoon at a time, until mixture forms a ball. Wrap in plastic wrap and refrigerate for 4 hours or overnight.

Remove dough from fridge and set aside at room temperature for 5 minutes, until softened. Roll out dough on a lightly floured surface to a 12-inch round. Transfer to a 9-inch pie dish or tart pan with a removable bottom. Press dough evenly into bottom and sides of pie plate and trim any excess. Refrigerate until ready to fill.

FILLING Preheat oven to 400°F.

Bring a saucepan of lightly salted water to a boil. Wearing gloves, drop the stinging nettles in the pan and blanch for 2 minutes. Drain, then transfer to a bowl of ice water. Drain again and coarsely chop. Remove gloves.

Heat oil in a frying pan over medium heat. Add garlic, shallots and mushrooms and sauté until just tender. Gently fold in nettles. Remove from heat and set aside to cool to room temperature.

In a bowl, combine eggs, milk, cream, nutmeg, salt and pepper. Whisk.

Once mushroom mixture has cooled, stir in brie. Put mixture into tart shell. Pour in egg mixture evenly over the filling and place on a baking sheet. Bake for 45 to 50 minutes, until quiche is lightly puffed and browned. (A toothpick inserted into the centre should come out clean.) Set aside to cool for 1 hour before serving. Top each tart with 2 to 3 slices of brie and, if you like, garnish with wild watercress or other greens.

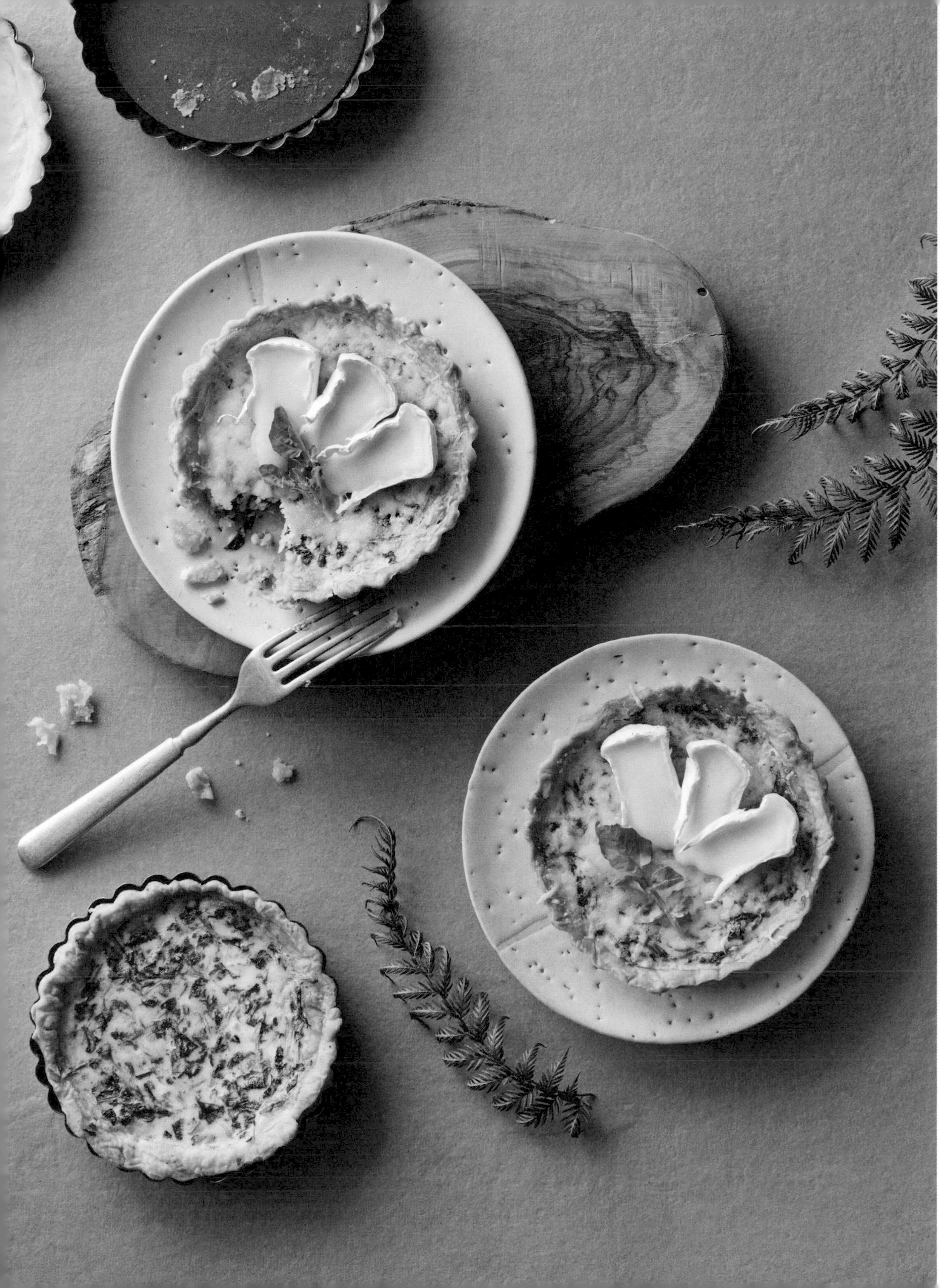

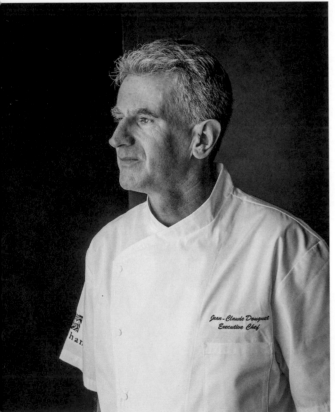

JEAN-CLAUDE DOUGUET

Gotham Steakhouse & Bar

WALK BY WHAT looks like just an unassuming small building on Seymour Street and you might not think twice. Look a bit closer, though, and you'll notice the intricate waterfall detailing of one of Vancouver's few surviving art deco buildings. Step inside, and it's like stepping through the looking glass. It's simply grand in here: two vast, darkly sexy and graciously appointed rooms with high ceilings, white tablecloths, a sweeping bar and one of Vancouver's best hidden patios. Who knew?

Well, plenty of professional athletes, for one, and most celebrities to hit town, for another. If fame's your game, the Gotham bar is one of the best places in the city to hang out. It's also one of the best places for well-made cocktails and well-marbled, perfectly seared steaks.

"It's a classic steakhouse, with big cuts of meat and elegant surroundings," says Jean-Claude Douguet, the restaurant's French-born and -trained chef. "Some of the dishes on our menu are true standards, like the porterhouse steak, or the classic Caesar salad. It's what people come to expect when they dine at a high-end steakhouse."

Think prime Alberta beef, aged at least twenty-eight days, with classic steakhouse sides combined with creative, fresh dishes. Like Hy's Steakhouse (page 138)—they're part of the same family—Gotham has gone out of its way to source Canadian beef since long before going local was a thing. Douguet, who joined the restaurant in 2005, has also made an effort to source locally. The incredible bounty of the land and sea is one of the things he loves best about Vancouver. That, and the culture. "The culinary scene has evolved a lot," he says. "People really know their food now, and that's a great thing."

TARRAGON REDUCTION

2 Tbsp chopped fresh tarragon

¼ cup chopped shallots

½ cup dry white wine

1 Tbsp white wine vinegar

1 bay leaf

½ tsp freshly ground black pepper

HOLLANDAISE SAUCE

4 large egg yolks

2 Tbsp dry white wine

1 Tbsp white wine vinegar

1¼ cups warm clarified unsalted butter

1½ tsp fresh lemon juice

1 tsp Worcestershire sauce

½ tsp Tabasco sauce

1 quantity Tarragon Reduction (see here)

Salt and freshly ground black pepper, to taste

STEAK

4 (10- to 12-oz) New York strip steaks, about 1½ inches thick

Canola oil, for brushing

Coarse salt and freshly ground black pepper, to taste

Steak with Béarnaise Sauce

SERVES 4

Nothing pushes a steak over the edge into sublime richness like a healthy dollop of Béarnaise sauce, a classic hollandaise with the licorice-y taste of tarragon.

TARRAGON REDUCTION Combine all ingredients in a small saucepan and cook for 10 minutes over medium-low heat, until 90 percent of the liquid has evaporated. Remove from heat and set aside to cool to room temperature.

HOLLANDAISE SAUCE Combine egg yolks, wine and vinegar in a heatproof bowl, then place the bowl over a pot of simmering water. Whisk vigorously for 5 minutes, until yolks change colour and ribbons have formed when you lift whisk from bowl. (Be careful not to overheat—otherwise, you will end up with scrambled eggs.) Remove from heat.

While whisking vigorously, drizzle in butter until emulsified. If mixture is too thick, add a few drops of hot water. Add lemon juice, Worcestershire and Tabasco.

Remove bay leaf from tarragon reduction, then pour reduction into hollandaise. Season with salt and pepper to taste. Keep at room temperature and serve within 1 hour.

STEAK Preheat barbecue, with one zone between 450°F to 500°F and a second zone at 350°F.

Take your steaks out of the fridge and set aside for 2 to 3 minutes before grilling. Pat dry with a towel to remove any moisture. Brush steaks lightly with oil. Season with salt and pepper.

Put steaks on high heat, in the first zone, and brown on all sides. (When doing this, you bring aroma to your steak; this is called the Maillard reaction.)

Transfer your steaks to the lower-heat zone of your grill to finish cooking, turning them once. Do not cover the barbecue. In total, it will take 8 minutes for rare, 10 minutes for medium-rare, 13 minutes for medium and 18 minutes for well done. Rest meat for 3 to 5 minutes.

Serve with Béarnaise sauce and the sides of your choice.

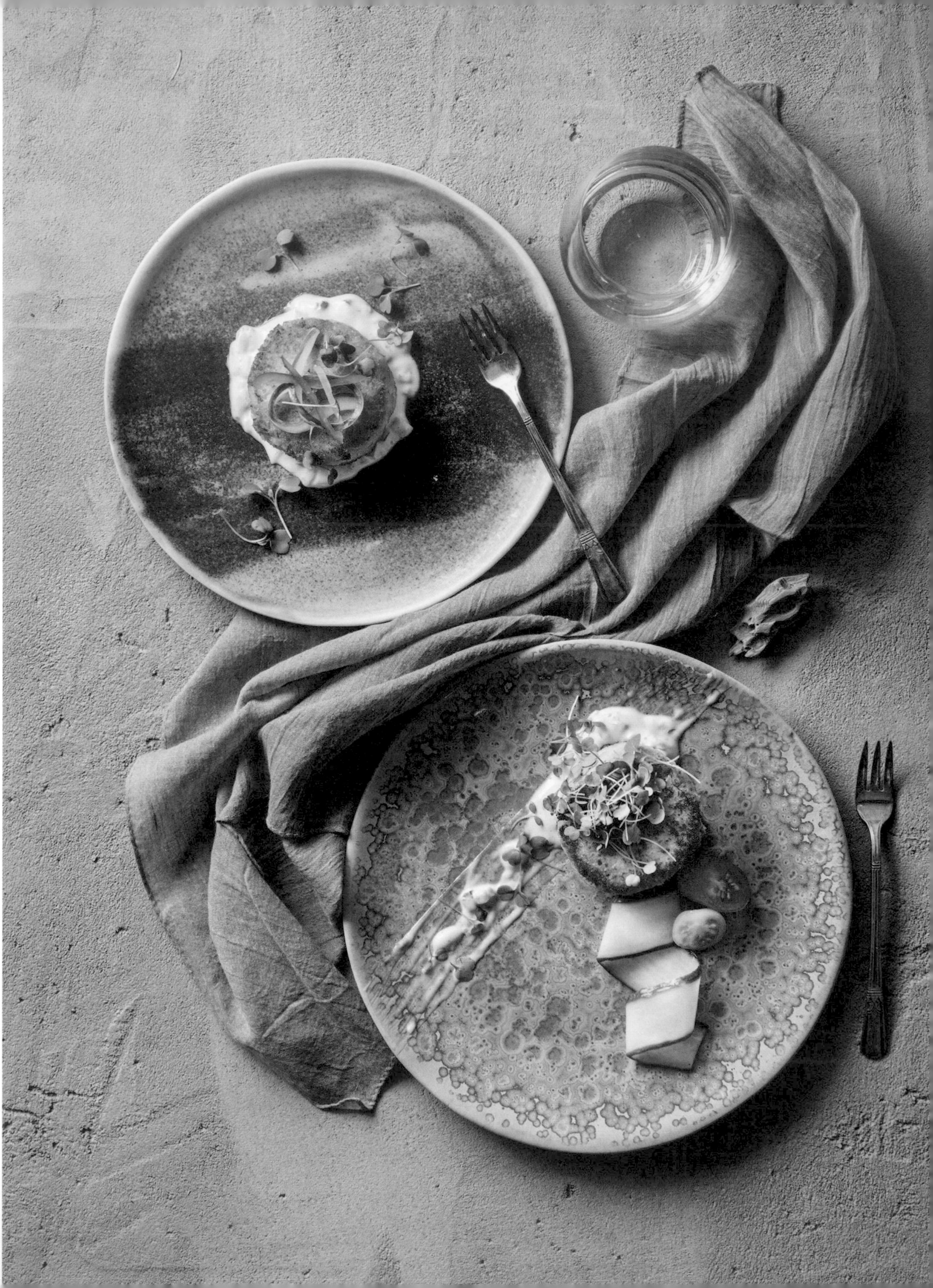

ROASTED JALAPEÑO TARTAR SAUCE
1 jalapeño pepper
1 tsp canola oil
1 cup mayonnaise
1 Tbsp green relish
Juice of ½ lemon (1 Tbsp)

PICKLED CUCUMBER
1½ cups water
1 cup granulated sugar
½ cup white vinegar
1 small English cucumber
    or 2 Persian cucumbers,
    thinly sliced

CRAB CAKES
3 Tbsp unsalted butter (divided)
½ onion, finely chopped
½ red bell pepper, seeded and finely
    chopped
12 oz fresh Dungeness crabmeat,
    picked of shells or cartilage
2 Tbsp mayonnaise
1 Tbsp Dijon mustard
1 Tbsp chopped fresh Italian parsley
1 cup panko crumbs (divided)
Microgreens, for garnish (optional)
Cherry tomatoes, halved, for garnish
    (optional)

Crab Cakes with Pickled Cucumber and Roasted Jalapeño Tartar Sauce

`SERVES 4`

These delicate crab cakes are pillowy soft and absolutely jam-packed with crabmeat, so it's best to use sweet, buttery Dungeness crab and to be very gentle when cooking them. Roasted jalapeño in the tartar adds just enough heat to balance the richness of the crab.

ROASTED JALAPEÑO TARTAR SAUCE Preheat oven to 400°F.

Lightly coat the jalapeño with oil and place on a small baking sheet. Roast for 20 minutes, then place in a small bowl. Tightly seal the bowl with plastic wrap and set aside for 1 hour, until cooled to room temperature.

Peel, devein and seed pepper. Chop, then mix it with remaining ingredients. Cover and refrigerate until needed.

PICKLED CUCUMBER Place water, sugar and vinegar in a saucepan and bring to a simmer. When sugar is dissolved, remove from heat and refrigerate for 1 hour, until chilled.

Place cucumber slices in chilled pickling solution in the fridge for at least 1 hour or overnight.

CRAB CAKES Preheat oven to 400°F.

Heat 1 tablespoon butter in a small sauté pan over medium heat, add onions and peppers and cook for 7 minutes, until onions are translucent. Set aside to cool.

In a medium bowl, combine crab, mayonnaise, mustard, parsley and onion-pepper mixture and mix gently, trying not to break up the crabmeat.

Add ½ cup panko crumbs and mix until everything binds. Form into 4 cakes and lightly coat each cake with remaining panko.

In a large ovenproof frying pan, heat remaining 2 tablespoons butter over medium heat. Add crab cakes and pan-fry for 5 minutes, turning once very carefully, until golden on both sides. Bake in oven for 8 minutes.

Divide crab cakes between 4 small plates and garnish with pickled cucumbers, a spoonful of roasted jalapeño tartar sauce, and microgreens and tomatoes (if using).

Guu

THINK OF THE izakaya as a boozy kind of Japanese gastropub-meets-tapas bar, with lots of tasty little bites to go alongside beer, wine and cocktails. They've been popular after-work spots in Japan since the eighteenth century, places where salarymen—and more recently, women—would stop by for a relaxing drink, or two or three, on the way home. They're loud, boisterous and, above all, fun.

They're just the sort of place Vancouver loves.

Although there are a number of izakayas around the city, especially in Vancouver, Guu was the original. It opened in the 1990s and now has five locations in town, plus one in Toronto. Walk in the door of any of them, and you're sure to be greeted with a chorus of cheerful shouts from the chefs. Soon a cup of sake is in front of you, the croquettes are on their way and the evening is off to a fine start.

Suspend any ideas you might have about what Japanese food is. While you're likely to find some sushi, robata and udon on the menu, for the most part this is fun, freewheeling food: marinated octopus, hanger steak with pepper sauce, barbecue lamb with honey soy and deep-fried pumpkin croquettes with a boiled egg inside.

"The basic idea is Japanese product and cooking techniques," says Guu's chef and executive vice-president Takeshi Hasegawa. He mixes those with local ingredients, such as seafood and vegetables. "It's something we couldn't do in Japan because Japan is an island and you can't get foods from other countries." He smiles. "That is kind of fun."

DASHI
1 (6-inch) piece kombu
(dried seaweed), wiped
clean with a damp cloth
5 cups water
2 cups bonito flakes

BRAISED DAIKON
1 or 2 daikon radishes,
peeled and cut into
2-inch-thick disks
1 quantity Dashi (see here)
¼ cup *shoyu* (soy sauce)

SPINACH SAUCE
1 bunch spinach
¼ cup (½ stick) unsalted butter
1 clove garlic, finely chopped
1 cup whipping (33%) cream
½ tsp kosher salt
Pinch of freshly ground black
pepper

LING COD
1 cup *shoyu* (soy sauce)
1 cup mirin
1 cup sake
1 Tbsp finely grated ginger
4 (5-oz) ling cod fillets
Potato starch, for dredging
1 to 2 Tbsp canola oil
1 tsp yuzu juice (available at
Fujiya)
2 Tbsp sliced green onions

Sautéed Shoyu Ling Cod with Braised Daikon

SERVES 4

Ling cod is one of the great sustainable fishes on the West Coast, unfamiliar outside these waters but highly prized by those in the know. It is not actually related to either the ling or cod families but kind of resembles both. In any case, it makes a terrific foil for the savoury flavours in this recipe, especially the shoyu, which is the Japanese word for soy sauce (see Note on page 113).

DASHI Soak kombu in the water for at least 3 hours and up to 1 day in the fridge.

Put the water and kombu in a medium saucepan and bring to a simmer. Remove from heat and steep for 10 minutes. Remove kombu, add bonito flakes and bring back up to a simmer. Cook for 5 minutes, then strain dashi. Set aside.

BRAISED DAIKON Place daikon, dashi and *shoyu* in a medium saucepan. Bring to a simmer and cook for 20 to 30 minutes, until tender but not falling apart. Remove from heat and set aside to cool. Refrigerate for at least 2 hours or up to 1 day.

SPINACH SAUCE Steam spinach for 5 minutes. When it is cool enough to handle, squeeze out excess water and coarsely chop.

Melt the butter in a small saucepan over medium heat, add garlic and cook for 2 to 3 minutes, until softened. Add spinach and cream and mix until heated through.

Transfer mixture to a blender and purée until smooth. Season with salt and pepper and keep warm.

LING COD Combine *shoyu*, mirin, sake and ginger in a large bowl and mix well. Add ling cod, making sure each piece is well coated in marinade, then refrigerate for 3 hours.

Remove ling cod from marinade and wipe off excess liquid. Dredge fish in potato starch. Remove daikon from the braising liquid.

Heat oil in a large frying pan over medium-high heat. Add fish and pan-fry for 5 minutes, flipping once or twice, until just crispy. Remove from pan. Add daikon to the pan and cook until lightly browned. Remove from pan. Add spinach sauce to the pan to heat through.

Divide daikon between 4 plates, then place fish on top of daikon. Pour spinach sauce over the fish. Drizzle with yuzu juice and sprinkle with green onions.

PONZU SAUCE

1 cup soy sauce

¾ cup yuzu juice (available at Fujiya)

½ cup mirin

¼ cup rice vinegar

1 (1-inch) piece kombu (dried seaweed),
 wiped clean with a damp cloth

SALMON TATAKI

8 oz sashimi-grade Atlantic salmon

1 tsp kosher salt

1 tsp freshly ground black pepper

1 tsp garlic powder

½ small onion, sliced

1 Tbsp Japanese mayonnaise

¼ cup Ponzu Sauce (see here)

2 Tbsp chopped green onions (optional)

Garlic Salmon Tataki

SERVES 4

Tataki *is the Japanese process of searing meat or fish over high heat, leaving the inside cool and uncooked. Here,* tataki-*style salmon is served with an umami-rich ponzu sauce that you will want to add to pantry staples.*

PONZU SAUCE Combine all ingredients in a bowl, cover and refrigerate for 2 days for the flavours to mingle and mature. Remove kombu. Ponzu will keep at least 2 weeks refrigerated.

SALMON TATAKI Trim the salmon into a neat block. In a small bowl, mix together salt, pepper and garlic powder and pat gently over the salmon.

Heat a frying pan over high heat and quickly sear the salmon on all sides. Remove from the pan and place salmon in the fridge for 30 minutes, until cooled down. Slice the salmon into ½-inch-thick pieces.

In another bowl, combine onion and mayonnaise and mix well. Place onion on a plate. Top with salmon slices, then drizzle ponzu sauce overtop. Garnish with green onions (if using) and serve.

DAVID HAWKSWORTH

Hawksworth Restaurant / Nightingale

WHAT AWARDS HASN'T David Hawksworth won? *Vancouver* magazine's Restaurant of the Year—twice. Chef of the Year—four times. Best Upscale Dining—six times. *enRoute* magazine's Best New Restaurants. *Maclean's* Restaurant of the Year. Canada's 100 Best Restaurants. More diamonds, stars and Golden Plates than you can shake a whisk at.

Born and raised in Vancouver, Hawksworth spent a decade honing his skills in some of Europe's top Michelin-starred kitchens, including Le Manoir aux Quat'Saisons, L'Escargot and the Square. He returned home in 2000, ready to turn up the heat in his hometown. And Vancouver, it seemed, was hungry for what he wanted to cook.

In 2011, he opened Hawksworth Restaurant in the gorgeously renovated Rosewood Hotel Georgia. Filled with light and art, its chic rooms, beautiful food and attentive service simply took the city's breath away.

He describes the cuisine as "contemporary Canadian," but that barely does justice to his exquisitely elegant food. Dishes evolve constantly, depending on what's new, what's exciting and what's in season. Wine and cocktails are treated as seriously as the food, thanks to the five sommeliers on staff and the serious talent behind the bar.

And, not content to helm the city's fine-dining go-to, in 2016 Hawksworth opened the casual Nightingale in another beautifully renovated historic building. (The name refers to the Aesop's fable that gave us the proverb "A bird in the hand is worth two in the bush.")

You might think running two busy and popular restaurants would keep Hawksworth busy enough, but he's also designing signature dishes for Air Canada business class as well as leading a number of charitable initiatives, notably the Hawksworth Young Chef Scholarship Foundation, which annually awards $10,000 to boost the career of a young professional chef.

Best of all though, he says, is cooking for a dining city as sophisticated as Vancouver. "It's a dream come true to be able to do what we do here in our hometown."

TOMATO-ANCHOVY VINAIGRETTE

¼ cup extra-virgin olive oil
¼ white onion, chopped
2 cloves garlic, finely chopped
¼ cup tomato paste
3 cups canned San Marzano
   tomatoes
¼ cup red wine vinegar
¼ cup granulated sugar

1 cup water
½ cup chopped fresh herbs
   (parsley, basil and tarragon),
   leaves only
¼ tsp crushed red pepper
3 anchovy fillets, finely chopped
Salt, to taste

HALIBUT

⅓ cup grapeseed oil
4 (4-oz) pieces halibut
Salt, to taste
2 tsp unsalted butter
2 cloves garlic, unpeeled
4 sprigs fresh thyme
½ lemon

Pan-Roasted Halibut with Tomato-Anchovy Vinaigrette

SERVES 4

Don't let halibut's mild nature fool you: its firm flesh can stand up to powerful flavours like the tomatoes, anchovies and fresh herbs of this Mediterranean sauce. It's the kind of elegant but flavourful dish that Hawksworth Restaurant is known for, made with local ingredients and international flair.

TOMATO-ANCHOVY VINAIGRETTE Heat oil in a saucepan over medium-low heat. Add onion and garlic and sauté for 5 minutes, until softened and translucent. (Do not let them brown.)

Add tomato paste and cook for 5 minutes. Stir in tomatoes, vinegar, sugar and water. Remove from heat and, using an immersion blender, pulse until blended.

Return to heat and bring to a simmer over medium-low heat. Cook for 30 minutes, until reduced to desired consistency. Strain through a fine-mesh sieve. Add chopped herbs, crushed red pepper and anchovy and season with salt. Set aside and keep warm until ready to serve.

HALIBUT Preheat oven to 400°F.

Heat oil in a cast-iron or ovenproof non-stick frying pan over high heat. Season fish with salt and place gently in pan. Cook for 2 to 3 minutes, until golden around the edge. Put in oven and roast for 6 minutes, until fish has just warmed through. Do not flip the fish.

Remove from oven and strain out oil. Add butter, garlic and thyme to the pan. Baste fish with foaming butter for 30 seconds and remove from pan. Squeeze lemon juice over fish.

Spoon ½ cup vinaigrette onto each of 4 plates, then arrange halibut on top. Serve immediately.

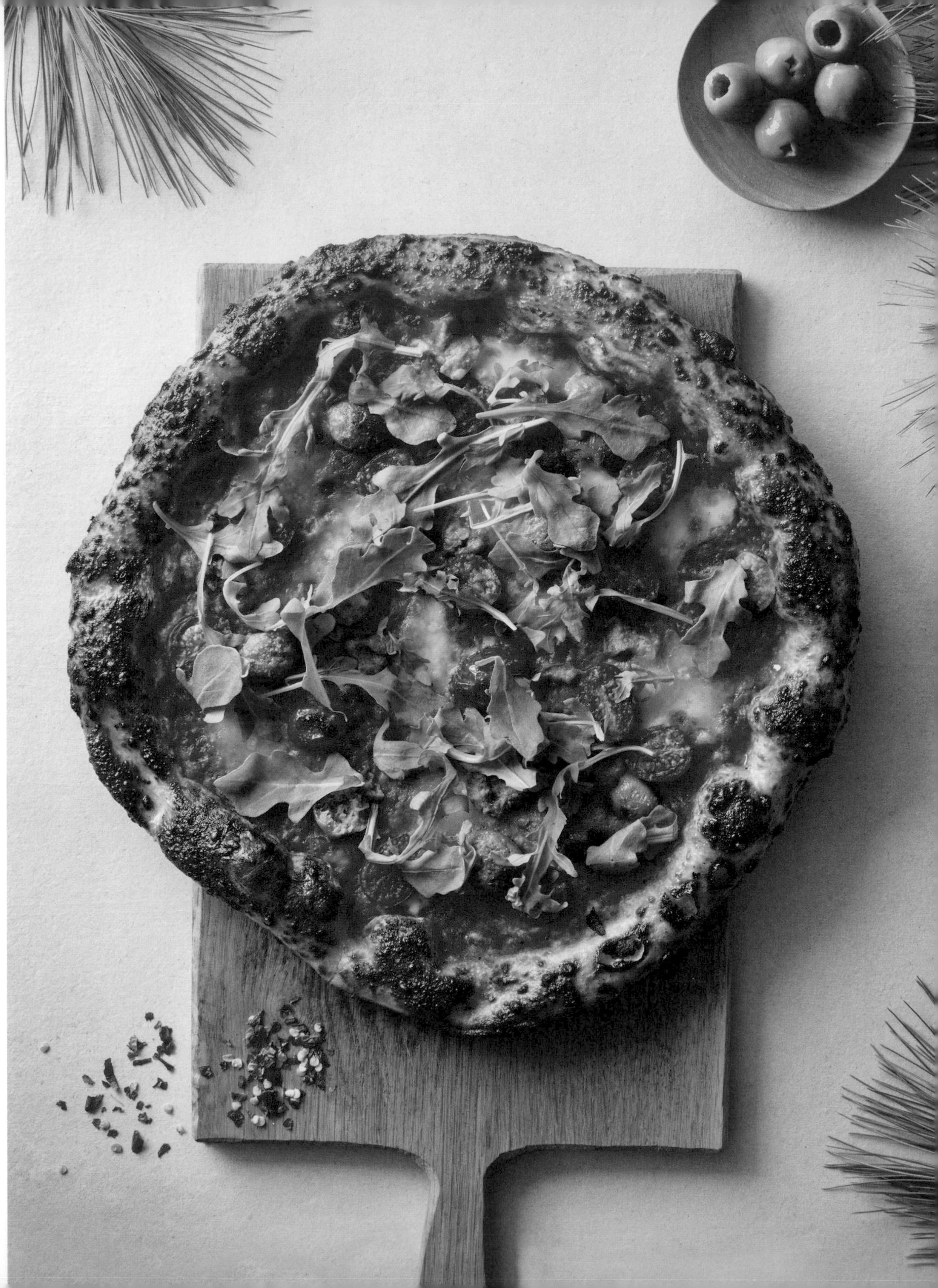

PIZZA DOUGH

1⅓ cups Italian "00" flour, plus extra for dusting

2 cups bread flour

1 tsp active dry yeast

1 Tbsp sea salt

1 tsp granulated sugar

1¼ cups warm water (100°F to 110°F)

2 Tbsp extra-virgin olive oil, plus extra for coating

TOMATO SAUCE

1 (796-mL) can San Marzano tomatoes

¼ cup extra-virgin olive oil

1 tsp granulated sugar

1 tsp kosher salt, plus extra to taste

6 fresh basil leaves, torn

PIZZA TOPPINGS (PER PIZZA)

½ cup *fior di latte*, sliced

Fresh basil leaves, torn

5 cherry tomatoes

4 green olives

Pinch of crushed red pepper

Extra-virgin olive oil, for drizzling

Handful of arugula

Pizza with Cherry Tomatoes, Olives and Arugula

SERVES 2

When David Hawksworth decided his restaurant Nightingale would serve pizza, he knew it would have to be the best pizza possible—like this simple, and simply delicious, version. The dough makes enough for three pizzas, but the toppings are for one. You can make the dough ahead and use it during the week.

PIZZA DOUGH Using a stand mixer with the dough hook attachment, combine flours, yeast, salt and sugar and mix well on low speed. With the motor still running, slowly add water and oil and mix for 8 to 10 minutes, until very smooth.

Coat the inside of a metal bowl with 1 to 2 teaspoons of olive oil, then add dough and cover loosely with plastic wrap. Rest in a warm place for 1 hour, until doubled in size. Punch the dough down and continue to let it proof for at least another 2 hours, but preferably overnight.

Divide dough into 3 portions and reserve in the fridge until required (it will keep for up to a week). Pull dough out 1 hour before you want to use it.

TOMATO SAUCE In a medium saucepan over medium-low heat, combine tomatoes, olive oil, sugar and salt and slowly simmer for 20 minutes. Add basil and cool. Check seasoning and add more salt if needed.

ASSEMBLY Place a pizza stone in the middle of the oven and heat it to the highest temperature possible (most likely 550°F).

Sprinkle a good pinch of flour on a counter or marble slab. Using your fingertips, press the air out of the dough. Gently pull dough until it is about ¼ inch thick.

With a large spoon, spread tomato sauce around on the dough, leaving a 1-inch space along the perimeter. Place cheese, basil, tomatoes and olives on top, season with crushed red pepper and drizzle olive oil overtop.

Slide pizza onto pizza stone and bake for 7 to 10 minutes, until crust is golden brown. If you do not have a pizza stone, you can use a well-oiled baking sheet or pizza pan instead. Carefully remove from oven and scatter arugula on top. Serve.

Heritage Asian Eatery

FELIX ZHOU HAS cooked at some of Vancouver's finest restaurants as well as starred ones in the U.K. So what's he doing running a casual lunch counter in the financial district? Turns out he's making the kind of food he loves, just the way he wants to: umami-rich rice bowls, overstuffed baos and crispy five-spice chicken wings.

A little ironically for a chef who was born in China, he'd never really cooked Asian food before. He was classically trained in French technique and was more likely to be making hollandaise than hoisin. "Moving into Asian-inspired dishes was a challenge for me, and it was fun," Zhou says. "Vancouver is very multicultural, and everyone loves Asian food, so it seemed like a natural fit."

Heritage Asian Eatery opened as a weekday lunch joint to serve the hungry office workers in nearby towers. But dishes like the signature duck rice bowl—with its combination of confit and roast duck—quickly became so popular that Zhou has expanded his hours to include early dinners.

"At Heritage, it's a hundred percent about the food. It's a casual environment, and the food has to be good for you to want to come back," he says. "When you start with high-quality product, you don't have to do very much to it. It's amazing."

PEKING SAUCE

1 Tbsp finely grated ginger
1 Tbsp finely chopped garlic
2 Tbsp hoisin sauce
2 Tbsp soy sauce
1 Tbsp sesame oil
1 green onion, finely chopped
½ tsp rice vinegar
½ tsp granulated sugar

DUCK

1 (5-lb) whole duck
½ cup kosher salt
½ cup granulated sugar
1 Tbsp ground white pepper
1 Tbsp five-spice powder
3 to 4 cups melted duck fat
Watercress, for garnish (optional)

YUZU COLESLAW

½ cup canola oil
3 Tbsp yuzu juice (available at Fujiya)
1 Tbsp Dijon mustard
Kosher salt and freshly ground black
    pepper, to taste
½ cabbage, thinly sliced
1 carrot, cut into matchsticks
1 fennel bulb, thinly sliced
4 radishes, thinly sliced

Heritage Duck Rice Bowl

SERVES 4

Plan to start this dish a couple of days before you intend to serve it. The steps aren't hard, but the duck does need time to cure, confit and marinate. It's worth it though for the layers upon layers of umami-rich flavour.

PEKING SAUCE Combine all ingredients in a medium bowl and whisk. Set aside half for glazing and half for duck marinade.

DUCK To prepare duck, cut into skin between thigh and breast. Pull leg down away from the body and pop it out of the joint. Cut through any attached skin to remove leg. Repeat on the other side.

To remove breasts, run knife down one side of the breast bone. Then, keeping your knife as close to the bone as possible, use stroking movements to remove meat from rib cage. Repeat for other breast. Cover duck breast in half of the Peking sauce and marinate in fridge overnight.

Combine salt, sugar, white pepper and five-spice powder in a small bowl and mix well. Rub mixture over duck legs and refrigerate overnight.

The next day, finish the duck. Preheat oven to 325°F.

Rinse duck legs under cold running water, then pat dry. Place duck legs in a small, deep baking dish and pour in fat, making sure legs are well coated. Bake for 2 hours, until tender. Remove from oven and set aside to cool.

Shred the meat and mix with remaining half of the Peking sauce. Reserve duck fat for another use.

Increase the oven temperature to 500°F. Wipe the marinated duck breasts dry with paper towel. Place in a roasting pan and roast for 16 minutes. Let rest for 15 minutes.

YUZU COLESLAW Whisk oil, yuzu juice and mustard in a small bowl. Season with salt and pepper.

In a large bowl, combine all vegetables and dressing and toss. Refrigerate for at least 30 minutes.

MARINATED EGG
4 large eggs, chilled
6 Tbsp water
2 Tbsp soy sauce
2 Tbsp mirin

RICE
1 cup short-, medium- or long-grain white rice
1½ cups water (or as rice-cooker instructions or package directions suggest)

MARINATED EGG Place eggs in a saucepan and add enough water to cover. Bring to a boil over high heat. Reduce heat to medium and boil for 8 minutes. Drain, then transfer to a bowl of ice water.

Once chilled, peel the eggs and marinate in water, soy sauce and mirin for 6 hours.

RICE Place the rice in a colander and rinse under cold running water, until water runs clear.

Add rice and water to a rice cooker and cook until tender. (Alternatively, place in a saucepan and bring to a boil, then cover and reduce heat to low. Cook for 20 to 30 minutes, depending on the type of rice.)

Let rice rest for 10 to 15 minutes, covered (to prevent rice from becoming overly sticky or mushy). Use a wooden spatula to fluff the rice.

ASSEMBLY Divide warm rice between 4 bowls, then top each with yuzu coleslaw and duck confit. Slice duck breast and add to each bowl. Halve the marinated eggs and add 2 egg halves to each bowl. Garnish with a few sprigs of watercress (if using).

PICKLED SHIMEJI MUSHROOMS
⅔ cup white wine vinegar
½ cup granulated sugar
¼ cup water
½ tsp sea salt
3 oz *shimeji* mushrooms, trimmed

DASHI
4 cups water
2 (6-inch) pieces kombu (dried seaweed), wiped clean with a damp cloth
1½ cups dried shiitake mushrooms
1½ cups bonito flakes (optional)
⅓ cup soy sauce
6 Tbsp mirin

BRAISED DAIKON
1 daikon radish, cut into ¼-inch cubes
2 cups Dashi (see here)

HIRAMASA
1 lb *hiramasa* (yellowtail amberjack) side, cleaned and filleted
Salt and freshly ground black pepper, to taste
¼ cup canola oil
2 cups Dashi (see here)
2 green onions, white parts only, sliced

Seared Hiramasa with Dashi and Vegetables

SERVES 4

Hiramasa *is also known as the yellowtail amberjack, and on sushi menus as* hamachi. *It is similar in taste and texture to tuna, and here is served with umami-rich dashi and pickled mushrooms. For best results, pre-pare pickled* shimeji *mushrooms a day in advance.*

PICKLED SHIMEJI MUSHROOMS Combine all ingredients except *shimeji* mushrooms in a medium saucepan and bring to a boil over high heat. Place *shimeji* mushrooms in an airtight container, such as a mason jar, and pour in pickling liquid. Seal container and set aside to pickle for at least 4 hours and preferably overnight.

DASHI Combine water, kombu and shiitake mushrooms in a medium saucepan and heat over medium heat. Just before it comes to a full boil, remove kombu from water and reserve for *hiramasa*.

Add bonito flakes (if using) and simmer for 1 minute.

Remove from heat and set aside to steep for 5 minutes. Strain stock into a bowl. Discard bonito flakes and shiitake mushrooms. Season stock with soy sauce and mirin. It can be stored for 1 week in the fridge or for 3 months in the freezer.

BRAISED DAIKON Combine daikon and dashi in a saucepan and simmer for 10 minutes, until tender. Set aside.

HIRAMASA Season the *hiramasa* with salt and pepper.

Heat oil in a frying pan over medium-high heat. Add fish and sear on one side for 3 minutes, then flip and cook for another 3 minutes, until opaque but still tender inside. Remove from heat.

Pour dashi in a medium saucepan and bring to a boil. Add green onions.

Thinly slice the reserved kombu seaweed, then place in the bottom of a serving bowl. Pour dashi over the kombu. Place the seared *hiramasa* on top. Garnish with braised daikon and pickled *shimeji* mushrooms. Serve immediately.

KAYLA DHALIWALL

Hook Seabar

AFTER MICHAEL GAYMAN opened his gastropub, the Blind Sparrow, near the Georgia Street entrance to Stanley Park, visitors would ask him all the time: Where can we find good, local and affordable seafood? Vancouver, he realized, had plenty of terrific high-end seafood restaurants, but when it came to casual fare, there wasn't quite as much choice, not, at least, outside of the countless sushi bars.

And so, says Chef Kayla Dhaliwall, who oversaw the menu at Blind Sparrow and now runs the kitchen at Hook Seabar, "We thought it would be great to open a fun, unpretentious year-round seafood restaurant." Gayman started looking around for the perfect location, just in time for the old Milestones on English Bay to become available. Could there be a better place for a seafood eatery? It's just steps from the beach and Stanley Park and right in the heart of all the city's biggest events from Pride to Honda Celebration of Light. Even better, Dhaliwall says, "The landlord wanted something really exciting and cool and independent in this location."

Hook Seabar, it turned out, was a perfect fit.

The room is light and bright, with quirky nautical motifs including a whale mural painted by artist Paul Morstad. Dhaliwall, who is probably best known to Vancouverites from her appearance on season three of *Top Chef Canada*, has created a menu that covers everything from poke and sushi to classic faves such as fish 'n' chips and inventive dishes like the whole *branzino* with harissa. "I'm not all things for all people, but I'm trying to be as accessible as possible," she says. "It's all Ocean Wise for sure, and we use local salmon and ling cod, and other seafood when it's available."

And she loves peppering her food with international flavours. "There's a lot of different ethnic influences in Vancouver, and people aren't afraid to try things," she says. "The different cultures and foods, and being able to experience them, are the best thing about this city."

¾ cup cream cheese, room
  temperature
¼ cup mascarpone, room
  temperature
¼ cup full-fat mayonnaise
1 cup grated semi-hard cheese such
  as cheddar, Gruyère, Jack
  or Edam (divided)
¼ cup grated Parmesan
1 green onion, thinly sliced
1 small poblano or jalapeño pepper,
  roasted, peeled, seeded and
  cut into ¼-inch dice

Juice of 1 lemon
½ tsp Tabasco sauce, or to taste
½ tsp Worcestershire sauce,
  or to taste
½ tsp kosher salt
½ lb fresh Dungeness or rock
  crabmeat, picked of shells
  or cartilage, chilled
1 Tbsp unsalted butter
½ cup panko crumbs
¼ cup heavy (36%) cream
1 lemon, halved
Grilled bread, chips or crackers,
  to serve

Dungeness Crab Dip

SERVES 6 TO 8

Creamy, cheesy, gooey and utterly irresistible: Kayla Dhaliwall's crab dip will make you the star at your next party. Don't be tempted to skip the panko topping. The buttery crunch is what puts this appie over the top.

In a stand mixer fitted with a paddle attachment, combine cream cheese and mascarpone and mix on medium speed for 3 to 5 minutes, until smooth. Scrape down sides of bowl.

Add mayonnaise, ½ cup grated semi-hard cheese and the Parmesan and mix for 40 seconds on low speed until blended. Add green onion, roasted pepper, lemon juice, Tabasco, Worcestershire and salt, and mix for another 30 seconds on low speed.

Remove bowl from mixer. Using a spatula or wooden spoon, gently fold in crabmeat. Place in an airtight container and keep chilled until you're ready to finish the dish.

Preheat oven to 400°F.

Heat butter in a sauté pan over medium heat, add panko crumbs and lightly toast.

Scrape crab dip into a saucepan, add heavy cream and warm gently over medium heat for 4 to 6 minutes, stirring constantly.

Pour the dip into a shallow casserole dish. Sprinkle with the remaining ½ cup semi-firm cheese, then top with buttered panko crumbs. Bake for 12 to 15 minutes, until hot and bubbling. You can roast the lemon halves in the oven as well.

Serve the dip immediately with grilled bread, chips or crackers and roasted lemon.

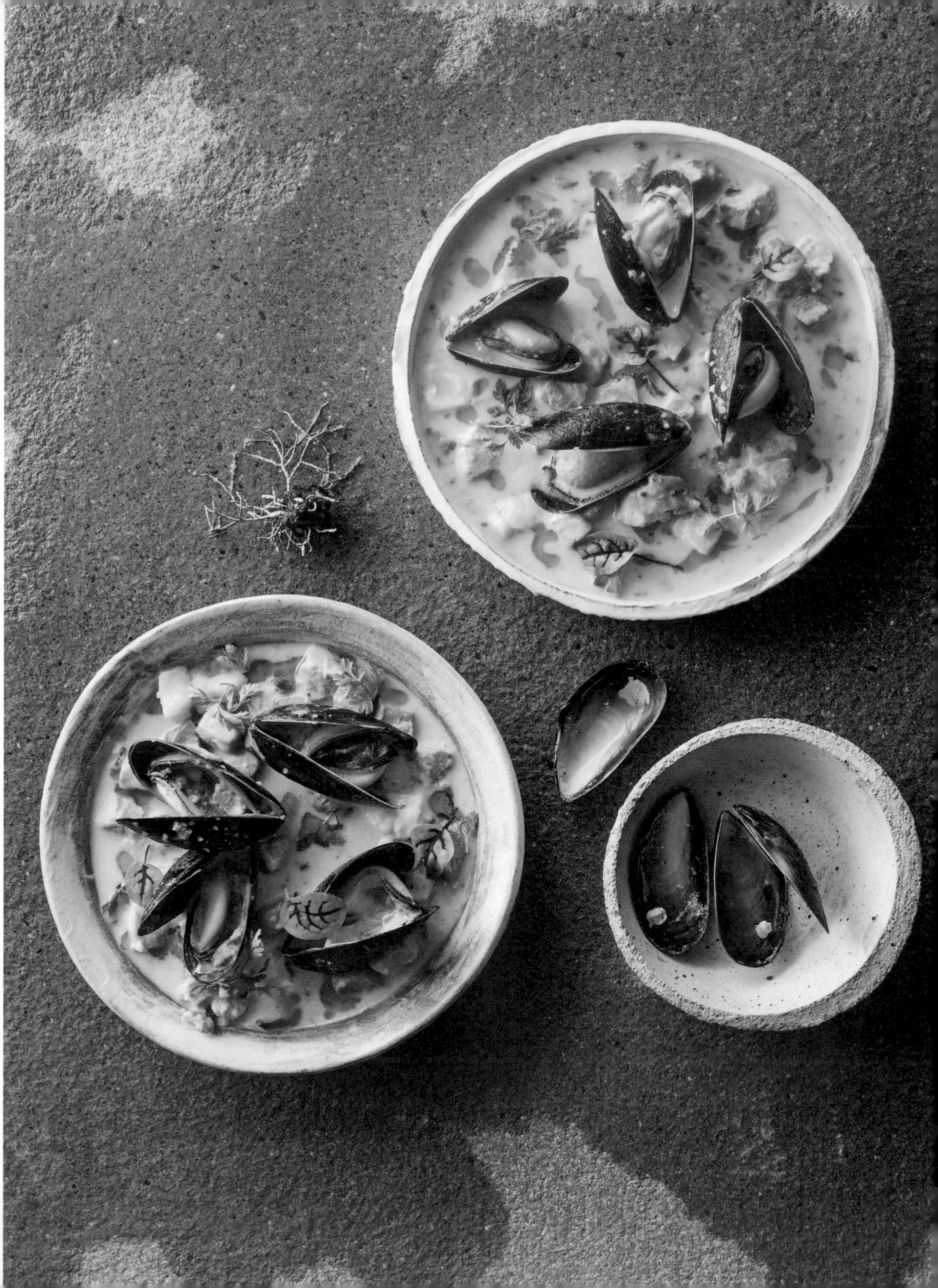

5 slices bacon, cut into ¼-inch dice
1 shallot, finely chopped
2 cloves garlic, finely chopped
½ cup good-quality dry white wine
1½ cups mashed potato
4 cups high-quality fresh fish stock
1 cup heavy (36%) cream
½ lb fresh skinless fin fish, such
  as halibut, ling cod or snapper,
  deboned and cut into bite-sized
  pieces

12 live mussels, scrubbed and
  debearded
8 medium prawns, peeled and
  deveined
½ Tbsp kosher salt, or to taste
2 Tbsp finely chopped fresh
  chives
12 sprigs fresh chervil (optional)

West Coast Chowder

SERVES 4

Seafood chowder is probably the most iconic of all B.C. West Coast dishes. This creamy but light version from Hook Seabar is made gluten free with mashed potatoes to thicken it rather than a floury roux. It's also versatile: if you can't find mussels, replace them with clams; if you love scallops or crabmeat, just add them in.

Put bacon in a stockpot and render over medium heat until firm and crisp. Add shallots and garlic and cook for 30 seconds, until softened. Pour in wine and deglaze.

Add mashed potato and fish stock. Simmer for 3 to 4 minutes, stirring occasionally, until mixture has emulsified.

Add cream, fish, mussels and prawns. Cover and simmer 1 to 2 minutes, until shells are opened. Discard any unopened mussels. Season with salt—taste and adjust seasoning as necessary.

To serve, remove the mussels and prawns and set aside. Divide broth and fish between four bowls, then arrange mussels and prawns on top and garnish each plate with chopped herbs.

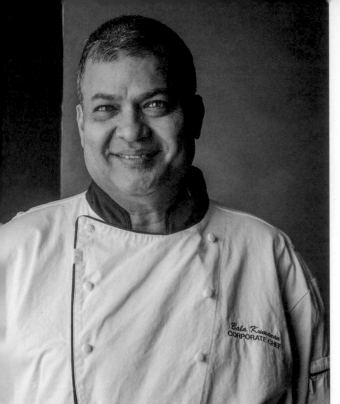

BALA KUMANAN

Hy's Steakhouse & Cocktail Bar Whistler

"PEOPLE THINK A steakhouse is easy," says Hy's corporate chef Bala Kumanan. "Everything is cooked *à la minute*, and when a customer is paying for a premium experience, it has to be perfect every time."

Since Hy Aisenstat opened his first steakhouse in Calgary in 1955, Hy's Steakhouse & Cocktail Bar Whistler has been known for a clubby atmosphere, old-school cocktails and perfectly cooked cuts of beef. Oh—and that gooey, chewy, utterly irresistible cheese toast. Good luck ordering just one basket. In the intervening years, food fashions have come and gone, but Hy's kept serving its wedge salads and steak tartare and filet à la Hy's. And while other restaurants may have parked their gueridons, Hy's kept tossing Caesar salads tableside and setting bananas Foster alight.

Now the classic steakhouse is back in style, big time, and for its endurance, we can thank the Swiss- and French-trained Kumanan. Based here on the West Coast, he oversees the menus at all the Canadian locations, including the one in Whistler, with its comforting leather banquettes and warm wooden panelling. What a joy it is to step into its calm, welcoming embrace after a day on the slopes, to be served a perfectly made cocktail and to dig into a steak done exactly the way you like.

The menu is tweaked at least once a year, but the classics are the classics. And, Kumanan points out, as important as the food is the ambience and the service customers expect when they're enjoying a fine-dining experience. "Hy's is almost sixty-five years old, and we continue to deliver excellence. That is key to our longevity," he says.

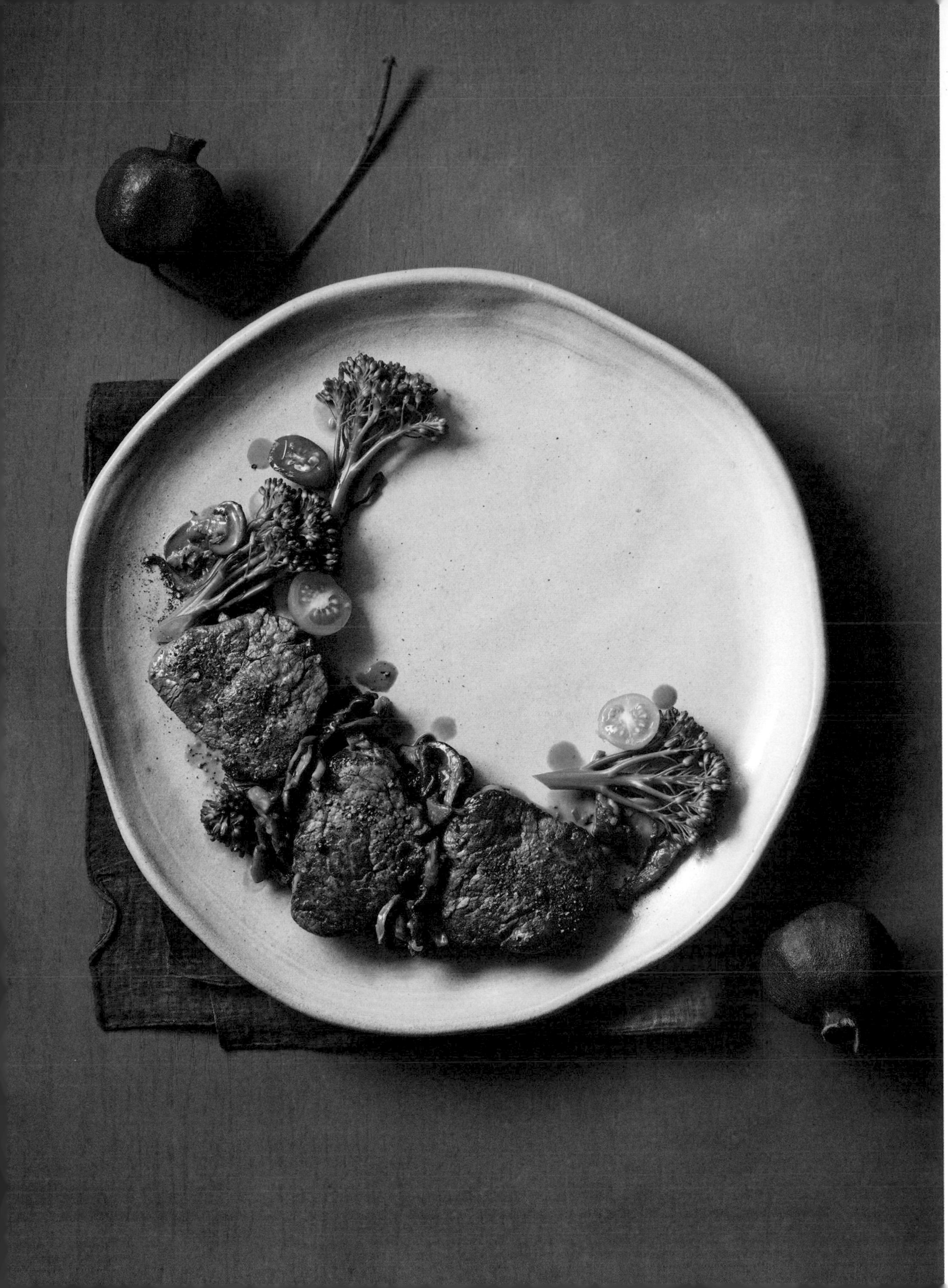

À LA HY'S SAUCE

2 Tbsp unsalted butter

2 shallots, finely chopped

8 oz oyster mushrooms, sliced

8 oz fresh shiitake mushrooms, sliced

8 oz button mushrooms, sliced

6 Tbsp brandy

4 cups veal stock

½ cup heavy (36%) cream

1½ tsp chopped fresh thyme

Salt and freshly ground black pepper,
to taste

STEAK

4 (8-oz) prime-grade filet mignon steaks,
each cut into 3 medallions

Salt and freshly ground black pepper,
to taste

4 Tbsp clarified unsalted butter

Rice, salad or potatoes (roasted, baked
or mashed), to serve

Sautéed broccolini or other vegetables,
to serve

Filet à la Hy's

SERVES 4

This classic signature dish is rich with cream, mushrooms and a splash of brandy that has been briefly set alight for flair and flavour.

À LA HY'S SAUCE Melt butter in a heavy-bottomed, flame-proof saucepan over medium heat, add shallots and cook for 5 to 10 minutes, until translucent. Add the 3 types mushrooms and cook for 10 to 15 minutes, until excess moisture has evaporated and bottom of pan begins to brown.

Pour in brandy to deglaze. To flambé, move pan away from stove and place it on a heatproof surface far from anything flammable. Carefully light brandy with a barbecue lighter or a long fireplace match. When flames subside, add veal stock and return to heat.

Cook over low heat for about 1 hour, until only 1 cup of sauce is left. Add cream and cook for another 10 to 15 minutes, until sauce is thick enough to coat the back of a spoon. Add thyme and season with salt and pepper. Keep warm.

STEAK Season each medallion with salt and pepper. Heat a frying pan over high heat, add 1 tablespoon of butter and sear 3 medallions to your preferred doneness, about 1 minute per side for medium rare, 3 minutes per side for well done. Repeat with remaining batch of medallions until they are all cooked. (Avoid overcrowding the pan to ensure a good sear.) When the medallions are cooked, let them rest for a few minutes before serving.

Place 3 medallions on each plate and spoon sauce on top. Serve with rice, salad or potatoes and sautéed broccolini or other vegetables.

2 cups pulp-free orange juice

2 Tbsp banana liqueur

¼ cup granulated sugar

½ cinnamon stick

8 scoops good-quality vanilla ice cream

4 bananas (not too ripe)

¼ cup (½ stick) unsalted butter

¼ cup packed brown sugar

½ cup dark rum

Bananas Foster

Impress your guests with this classic flambéed dessert that is simply ablaze with drama. Besides, what's not to love about caramelized bananas and ice cream?

Combine orange juice, banana liqueur, granulated sugar and cinnamon stick in a small saucepan and cook over medium heat, until reduced to 1 cup. Remove cinnamon stick and set aside.

Place 2 scoops of ice cream into each of 4 bowls and put them in the freezer until ready to serve.

For full theatrical effect, you will want to prepare this dish in front of your guests. Place a butane burner on a heat-resistant surface and make sure there is nothing flammable within reach. Have all your ingredients ready in small bowls or ramekins as you will have to work quickly and carefully.

Peel each banana and cut it in half, then split each half lengthwise—you should have 16 pieces of banana in total.

Light the burner, bring flame to medium heat and place a medium frying pan over the flame. Add butter and brown sugar and cook until butter has melted and sugar is fully dissolved. Add bananas, turning them carefully as they start to caramelize.

Remove the pan from the burner and place it on a heatproof surface far from anything flammable. Add rum to pan and carefully light it with a barbecue lighter or a long fireplace match. As soon as flame starts to dim, add sauce and cook for another minute. Gently place 4 pieces of banana in each bowl of ice cream.

Return pan to heat and cook sauce for another 2 to 3 minutes, until syrupy. Spoon sauce over each bowl and serve immediately.

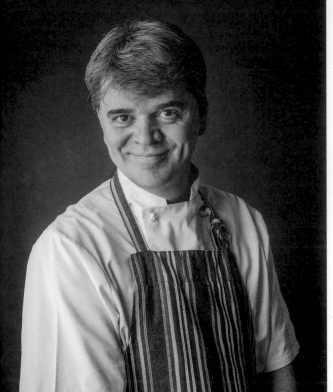

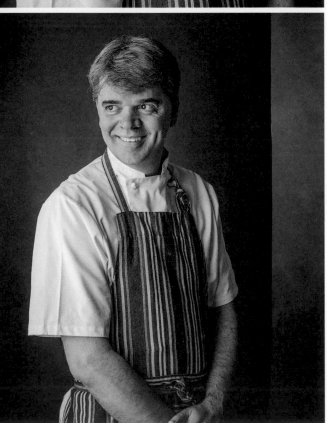

JAMES WALT

Il Caminetto

JAMES WALT KNOWS he's a lucky guy. "We've got three beautiful valleys and amazing seafood, spectacular produce and a wine country that's evolving at an impressive rate," he says. "For me, it doesn't get much better. We're spoiled."

For twenty years, he turned all that fresh, local fare into inspired modern dishes as executive chef at Araxi, the elegant Whistler restaurant that is as well known for its lavish winemakers' dinners as it is for its sophisticated farm-to-table fare. Then, in 2017 came an offer he couldn't refuse.

Toptable Group, the company that owns Araxi (page 28), asked Walt to become executive chef of its newly acquired Il Caminetto, the lushly romantic Tuscan-themed restaurant previously owned by the legendary Umberto Menghi. It would be a perfect fit for a guy who'd once been the executive chef at the Canadian embassy in Rome. "Il Caminetto opened in 1981, the same year as Araxi," Walt says. "I love Italian food and I'm pretty stoked about this."

At Il Caminetto, his approach is to take traditional regional Italian dishes and reimagine them with local ingredients and an elevated presentation. Even so, he says, "I'm so farm to table, but I don't want to change things such as the olive oils, chilies, lemons or San Marzano tomatoes. I don't want to invent pastas for the sake of inventing something new. I'd rather do true Bolognese pasta using boar, for instance."

At the same time, Walt continues to keep his hand in at Araxi, The Cellar by Araxi and Bar Oso. But Il Caminetto has a special place in his heart—after all, a love of ingredient-driven food is something he shares with most Italians.

"Things taste the way they taste for a reason. I want to achieve that," he says. "It's kind of a passion project." And here in his mountain hideaway, he has access to (almost) everything he needs. "The geography," he says, "doesn't get any better."

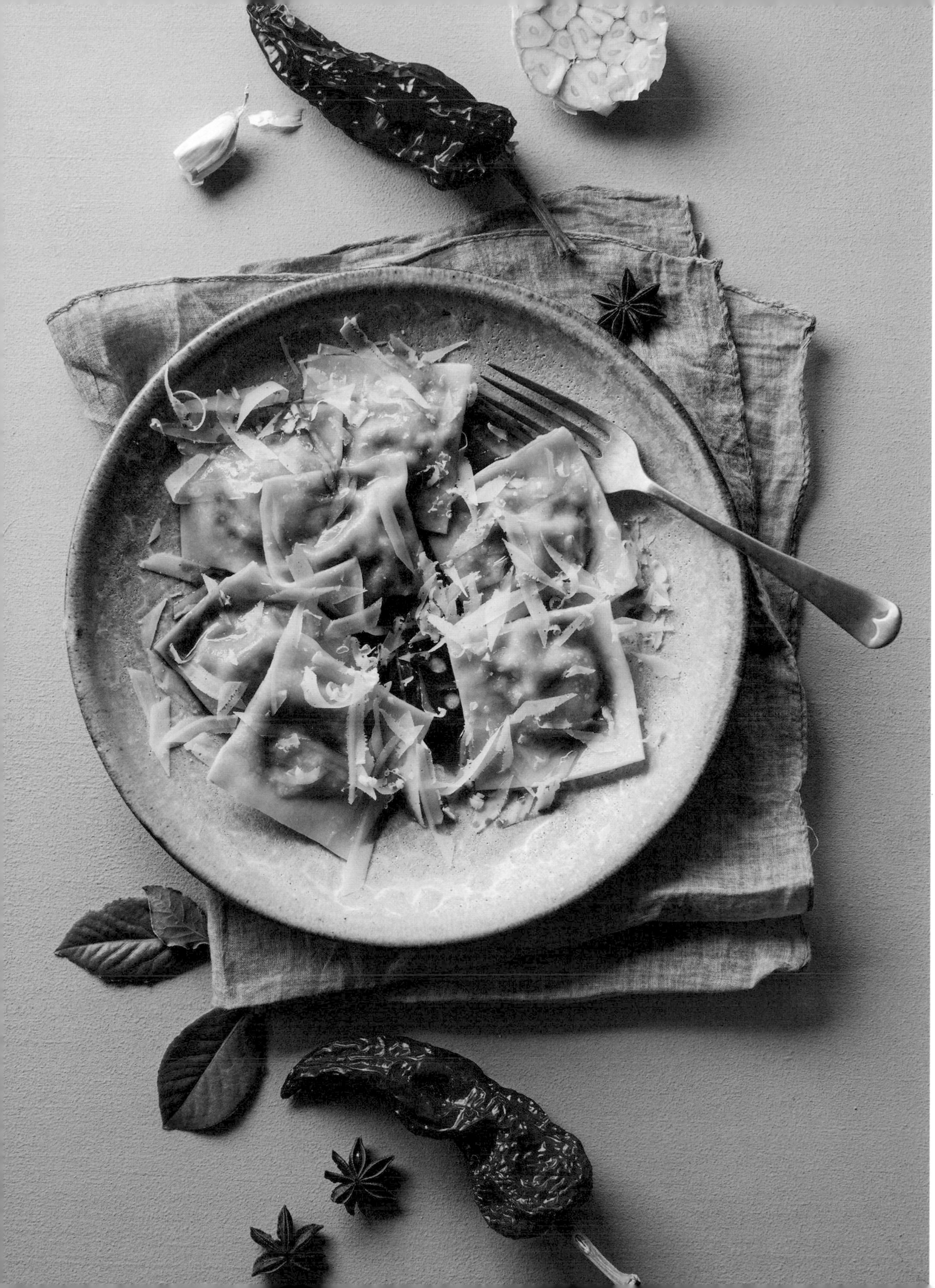

BEEF FILLING
¼ cup canola or grapeseed oil (divided)
4 (6-oz) beef cheeks, cleaned of sinew
  and connective tissue
Sea salt and freshly ground black
  pepper, to taste
3 large shallots, cut in half
2 cloves garlic, chopped
1 carrot, cut into quarters

1 stalk celery, cut into quarters
1 star anise
1 Tbsp tomato paste
1½ cups ruby port
1 bay leaf
5 cups veal or chicken stock
¼ cup extra-virgin olive oil, for drizzling
½ cup grated pecorino, to serve

PASTA DOUGH
4 large eggs
3 large egg yolks
1 Tbsp extra-virgin olive oil
4 cups Italian "00" flour, plus
  extra for dusting
1 tsp kosher salt

EGG WASH
1 large egg, lightly beaten
1 Tbsp cold water

Slow-Cooked Beef Ravioli

SERVES 4 (MAKES 12)

The Sea to Sky corridor is home to several ranches of pasture-raised, organic beef, perfect for the rich, hearty filling in James Walt's ravioli. These are quite large and offer a dramatic presentation; if you prefer a smaller ravioli, just use a smaller cutter instead.

BEEF FILLING Preheat oven to 325°F.

Heat 2 tablespoons oil in a Dutch oven over medium heat. Season beef cheeks with salt and pepper. Working in batches, sear beef cheeks for 4 to 5 minutes, until golden brown on all sides. Transfer beef to a plate and set aside. Pour off the fat and wipe the pan clean.

Heat the remaining 2 tablespoons oil in the pan over medium heat. Add shallots, garlic, carrots, celery and star anise and cook for 8 to 10 minutes, until vegetables have coloured and softened. Stir in tomato paste and cook for 2 to 3 minutes. Pour in port and cook for another 8 to 10 minutes, until wine has reduced by half.

Gently stir in beef and bay leaf, pour in stock and bring to a boil. Cover with a lid and braise in oven for 2½ to 3 hours, until beef is fork tender.

Using a slotted spoon, transfer beef to a bowl and set it aside to cool slightly. Strain braising liquid through a fine-mesh sieve into a clean pot. Using a spoon, skim off any fat from the surface and discard. Set pan on medium-low heat and cook for 20 to 25 minutes, until juices reduce to a sauce-like consistency.

When beef cheeks are cool enough to handle, using your hands or a fork, gently separate or pull apart the braised meat. Reserve 1 cup of beef sauce for later, and pour the remainder over the beef and mix well. Place in the fridge to cool.

PASTA DOUGH Combine eggs, yolks and oil in a large bowl and mix gently with a fork, just enough to break the yolks. Place flour and salt in a food processor and blend for 10 seconds to aerate. With motor running, slowly pour in egg mixture and process just until combined.

Turn dough out onto a clean work surface. Bring dough together with your hands and knead for 5 to 7 minutes, until smooth. Wrap dough in plastic wrap and set aside to rest for 30 minutes. (Tightly wrapped, it will keep refrigerated for up to 2 days.)

Lightly dampen a clean dish towel with cold water. Following the instructions on your pasta machine, divide the dough in half and roll out each one into a thin sheet, roughly the thickness of a dime. Using a sharp knife, cut pasta into 24 (3-inch) squares. Dust each square with flour, arrange the pasta in a single stack and cover with the damp dish towel.

ASSEMBLY Lightly dust a baking sheet with flour and fill a small bowl with water. In another small bowl, combine egg-wash ingredients and mix well.

Place a pasta square on a clean work surface. Spoon 2 teaspoons of filling onto the centre of the pasta. Using a pastry brush, lightly brush pasta edge with egg wash. Place a second square over the first to completely enclose filling. Press edges tightly from centre to outer edge to force out any air and create a tight seal. Place finished ravioli on the baking sheet and repeat with remaining pasta. Set aside. (Any leftover filling can be frozen in an airtight container for up to 2 weeks.)

Bring a large saucepan of salted water to a boil. Carefully lower pasta into pan and cook for 5 minutes.

Meanwhile, heat reserved beef sauce in a large sauté pan over low heat.

Using a slotted spoon, transfer ravioli to the pan and toss gently with the sauce. Spoon into 4 warm bowls and drizzle with olive oil. Serve with grated pecorino.

SALSA VERDE

8 tomatillos, peeled and cut into quarters

1 avocado, peeled and pitted

1 green onion, sliced

1 clove garlic

½ jalapeño pepper, seeded and deveined

2 Tbsp chopped fresh cilantro leaves

1 Tbsp sea salt

Juice of 1 lime

¼ cup grapeseed oil

CRAB SALAD

1 lb fresh Dungeness crabmeat, picked of shells or cartilage

¼ cup extra-virgin olive oil

Grated zest and juice of 1 lime

1 Tbsp finely chopped fresh chives

6 ripe peaches, pitted and cut into sixths

1 cup organic salad leaves

Crab Salad with Peaches and Salsa Verde

SERVES 4

Two of the best ingredients from B.C. are the local Dungeness crab and sweet peaches from the Okanagan Valley. They team up in this salad that is pure summer perfection on a plate.

SALSA VERDE Combine all ingredients in a food processor and process at high speed until smooth. Set a fine-mesh sieve over a clean bowl and strain the mixture. Discard the solids. Store in an airtight container in the fridge for up to 2 days. (It loses its colour and flavour if stored for longer.)

CRAB SALAD Fill a large bowl with ice. In a smaller bowl set over the ice, combine crabmeat, oil, lime zest and juice and chives and mix gently. On 4 chilled plates, place 9 peach wedges in a row along the centre. Top each with crabmeat. Drizzle liberally with salsa verde, top with salad leaves and a little more salsa. Serve immediately.

Kissa Tanto

JOËL WATANABE IS getting used to defying people's expectations. When he and his business partner Tannis Ling opened their modern Chinese bistro Bao Bei in early 2010, people expected mainstream Chinese food. Instead they got quirky pan-Asian dishes with French influence. Their follow-up was even more puzzling to some: Japanese-Italian fusion? Wait, what?

"I was trying to avoid making any statement of what kind of food we were going to do," Watanabe admits. "But it just makes sense aesthetically and culturally. Both cultures are very clean and ingredient driven." Besides, he adds, "It's the paramount goal to be delicious. If it's not delicious, what's the point?"

Delicious it is. And not just the food—the room itself is a mid-twentieth-century Tokyo-jazz-club-esque confection of teal blue and lipstick pink with brass accents in an old mah-jong parlour. Gorgeous cocktails like My Private Tokyo (amaretto, plum wine, vermouth, lemon and egg white) are shaken up behind a sexy bar. The wine and beer lists are filled with global surprises.

But it's the food that propelled it to the number-one spot on *enRoute*'s 2017 list of best new restaurants in Canada: the whole fried fish, so crisp and tender at once; the daily fish crudo; the pasta with butter-roasted mushrooms. Flavours come together in surprising ways that once tasted, seem so right that you wonder how it could have been any other way. And everything is prepared with the sort of meticulousness that you would expect from the former raw-bar chef at Araxi (page 28).

"Kissa Tanto for me is a culmination of my life. It's my serious ownership of a restaurant," says Watanabe, who has been working in restaurants since he was seventeen. "I always give my all, but this is even more."

GNOCCO FRITTO

1½ tsp active dry yeast

½ tsp granulated sugar

6 Tbsp lukewarm water (105°F to 110°F)

2 cups all-purpose flour, plus extra for dusting

1 tsp kosher salt

2½ Tbsp rendered beef fat or lard

4 cups vegetable oil, or as needed, for deep-frying

BURNT SOY SAUCE

4 green onions, cleaned and trimmed

1 cup Japanese soy sauce

CARNE CRUDA

3 oz high-quality tenderloin or eye of round, cut into ¼-inch cubes

1 Tbsp Burnt Soy Sauce (see here)

1 Tbsp grassy, high-quality extra-virgin olive oil

Salt, to taste

1 Tbsp chopped Asian pear

1 tsp *arima sansho* (pickled Japanese peppercorns, similar to Sichuan peppercorns)

1 radish, thinly sliced

1 Tbsp sunflower sprouts

1 Tbsp sliced green onions

1 Tbsp finely grated Parmesan

Carne Cruda

SERVES 2

Japanese flavours make a classic beef tartare exciting and new—and the crisp crackers known as gnocco fritto *offer a wonderful textural contrast.*

GNOCCO FRITTO In a large bowl, combine yeast, sugar, and water and mix well.

In a separate bowl, combine flour and salt and mix well. Using your hands, rub fat (or lard) into flour, until it resembles a coarse crumb. (Mixing with your hands helps melt the fat and distribute it evenly.) Gradually add flour mixture to water mixture and knead for 4 to 5 minutes to make a dough. Cover with a cloth and rest in warm place for 1½ hours, until doubled in size.

Roll out dough on a lightly floured surface to ¼-inch thickness. Cut into 2-inch squares (or whatever shape you prefer).

In a deep-fryer or deep saucepan, pour in oil to a depth of 3 inches and heat over medium-high heat until it reaches 340°F. Carefully lower dough into oil, in small batches, and fry for 30 seconds, until crispy and golden. Turn occasionally. Using a slotted spoon, remove from oil and transfer to a plate lined with paper towels to drain. Set aside.

BURNT SOY SAUCE Preheat a barbecue or a cast-iron grill plate to medium-high heat. Arrange green onions and grill for 2 minutes, until charred all over. Transfer to a high-speed blender (such as a Vitamix), add soy sauce and blend until smooth. Keep in a covered container in the fridge for up to 3 weeks.

CARNE CRUDA In a medium bowl, combine beef, burnt soy sauce and oil. Season with salt and mix well.

Place a 3-inch ring mould in the centre of a serving plate and add crudo. Remove ring and garnish with Asian pear, *arima sansho*, radish, sunflower sprouts, green onion and Parmesan. Serve with gnocco fritto.

DASHI

1 cup water

½ cup bonito flakes

1 (3-inch) piece kombu (dried seaweed), wiped clean with a damp cloth

White soy sauce or regular Japanese soy sauce, to taste

TOSA JOYU DIPPING SAUCE

1 cup Japanese soy sauce

⅓ cup water

⅓ cup sake

⅓ cup mirin

1 (3-inch) piece kombu (dried seaweed), wiped clean with a damp cloth

2 cups bonito flakes

¾ cup Dashi (see here)

1¼ cups lemon, lime or yuzu juice, or a combination (yuzu juice is available at Fujiya)

FRIED FISH

4 L vegetable oil, or as needed, for deep-frying

1 (2- to 2¼-lb) fresh whole white fish such as sea bass or bream, cleaned and patted dry

3 cups potato starch

Salt, to taste

¼ cup grated daikon radish, to serve

Whole Fried Fish with Tosa Joyu Dipping Sauce

SERVES 4

This showstopper will never leave the Kissa Tanto menu. Just imagine how impressive it would be at your next dinner party! It does require deep-frying a whole fish, though, so be careful and follow instructions closely.

DASHI Bring water to a boil and remove from heat. Add bonito flakes and kombu and set aside for at least 45 minutes. Strain. Season with soy sauce.

TOSA JOYU DIPPING SAUCE Place soy sauce, water, sake and mirin in a small saucepan and bring to a boil. Add kombu and simmer for 30 minutes. Remove from heat, remove kombu and add bonito flakes. Let sauce sit overnight, then strain and chill.

Mix in dashi and citrus juice. Keep chilled until ready to serve.

FRIED FISH Pour oil into a large stockpot deep enough to accommodate the whole fish with a little extra room. Heat oil over medium-high heat until it reaches a temperature of 350°F.

Score fish in a 1-inch diamond pattern cut to the bone. Dust fish with potato starch until completely coated. Carefully lower fish into hot oil and deep-fry for 3 minutes, until just crispy and golden brown. Carefully remove from oil and transfer to a plate lined with paper towels to drain. Season with salt.

In a dipping bowl, form a small mountain of daikon and surround with dipping sauce. Serve fish on a platter with the dipping sauce.

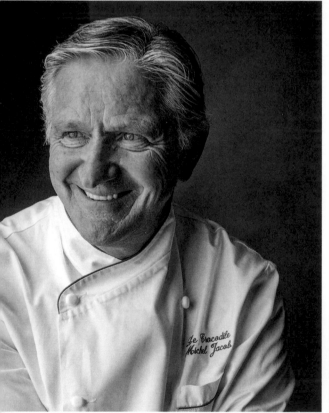

MICHEL JACOB

Le Crocodile

IN VANCOUVER, RESTAURANTS come and go. But not Le Crocodile. For thirty-five years, its flawless *escargots maison* and *tarte à l'oignon* have assured us that, no matter what happens, all is right with the world. It's never too trendy, always just perfect. "As we say in France, if you're in, you're already out," says chef-owner Michel Jacob. "The number-one reason we are still open after thirty-five years is because of the consistency." Well, that and the fine food, exceptional wine list and Jacob's gracious hospitality.

He came to Vancouver from his native Alsace in 1980 and opened Le Crocodile three years later, naming it in honour of a famous three-Michelin-starred restaurant in his hometown of Strasbourg. Since then he's seen the Vancouver food scene undergo a remarkable transformation from staid and provincial to sophisticated, vibrant and gloriously global. "Now I think we're the equivalent of Montreal, if not ahead," he says. He played a huge part in that change, not just by elevating the city's quality of dining, but by mentoring so many of its best chefs, including Ned Bell (page 176), who has said that apprenticing at Le Crocodile was "like going to Harvard."

Its discreetly attentive service has made it as much a favourite with celebrities as with its passionately loyal regular clientele. "We have people who've come through the door for the past twenty-five years, and we already know what they will be eating," Jacob says. "They don't even need a menu." And somehow, in a city that seems to have thrown in the towel (a trendy unbleached linen one, *bien sûr*) on fine dining, Le Crocodile remains one of the few go-to special occasion spots.

"I am very fortunate to be fulfilling my passion. It's a luxury to be able to make a living out of what you love to do."

Butter, for greasing
1 sheet frozen puff pastry, thawed
½ cup sour cream
2 Tbsp whipping (33%) cream
Pinch of ground nutmeg
Salt and freshly ground black pepper,
    to taste
2 onions, thinly sliced on a
    mandoline
3 oz back bacon, cut into thin strips

Tarte Flambée

"Think of this popular snack as Alsatian pizza," Michel Jacob says. If you prefer, you can replace the bacon with smoked salmon or mushrooms. Use all-butter puff pastry if you can find it.

Preheat oven to 500°F. Grease a baking sheet or line it with parchment paper.

Roll pastry into a ⅛-inch-thick square or rectangle, then cut in half.

In a small bowl, combine sour cream, whipping cream and nutmeg. Season with salt and pepper and mix until very smooth.

Spread mixture evenly over pastry dough. Scatter onions on top, then add bacon. Bake for 10 minutes and serve immediately.

4 large red-skinned potatoes
6 spears asparagus
4 quail eggs
¼ cup extra-virgin olive oil
¼ cup fresh lemon juice
2 Tbsp white wine vinegar
1 Tbsp Dijon mustard

Salt and freshly ground black
   pepper, to taste
1 Tbsp very thinly sliced radishes
1 Tbsp chopped onions
4 fresh basil leaves, finely chopped
1 small English cucumber, sliced
Cooked meat from 4 lobster claws

Lobster and Potato Salad in a Lemon-Mustard Vinaigrette

SERVES 4

Simple yet oh-so-rich and decadent. The citrusy vinaigrette balances the richness of the lobster meat, while the potatoes provide a pleasantly starchy platform for all the deliciousness. Instead of lobster, you could also use poached prawns or cooked crabmeat.

Place potatoes in a large saucepan, cover with water and bring to a boil. Cook for 20 minutes, until tender. Drain and place potatoes in the fridge for 1 hour, until cooled. Slice into thin slices.

Bring a small saucepan of water to a boil, add asparagus and cook for 4 minutes. Drain, then transfer to a bowl of ice water. Cut into 1-inch-long batons.

Bring a small saucepan of water to a boil, add quail eggs and cook for 4 minutes. Drain, then transfer to a bowl of ice water. Carefully peel them and cut in half.

In a small bowl, whisk together oil, lemon juice, vinegar and mustard. Season with salt and pepper.

Place sliced potatoes, asparagus, radishes, onions and basil in a large bowl. Drizzle with a little more than half the vinaigrette and gently work together to create a sauce.

Divide cucumber slices between 4 plates, then top with potato salad. Arrange lobster meat and quail eggs on top and either drizzle with the remaining dressing or dot it around the salad.

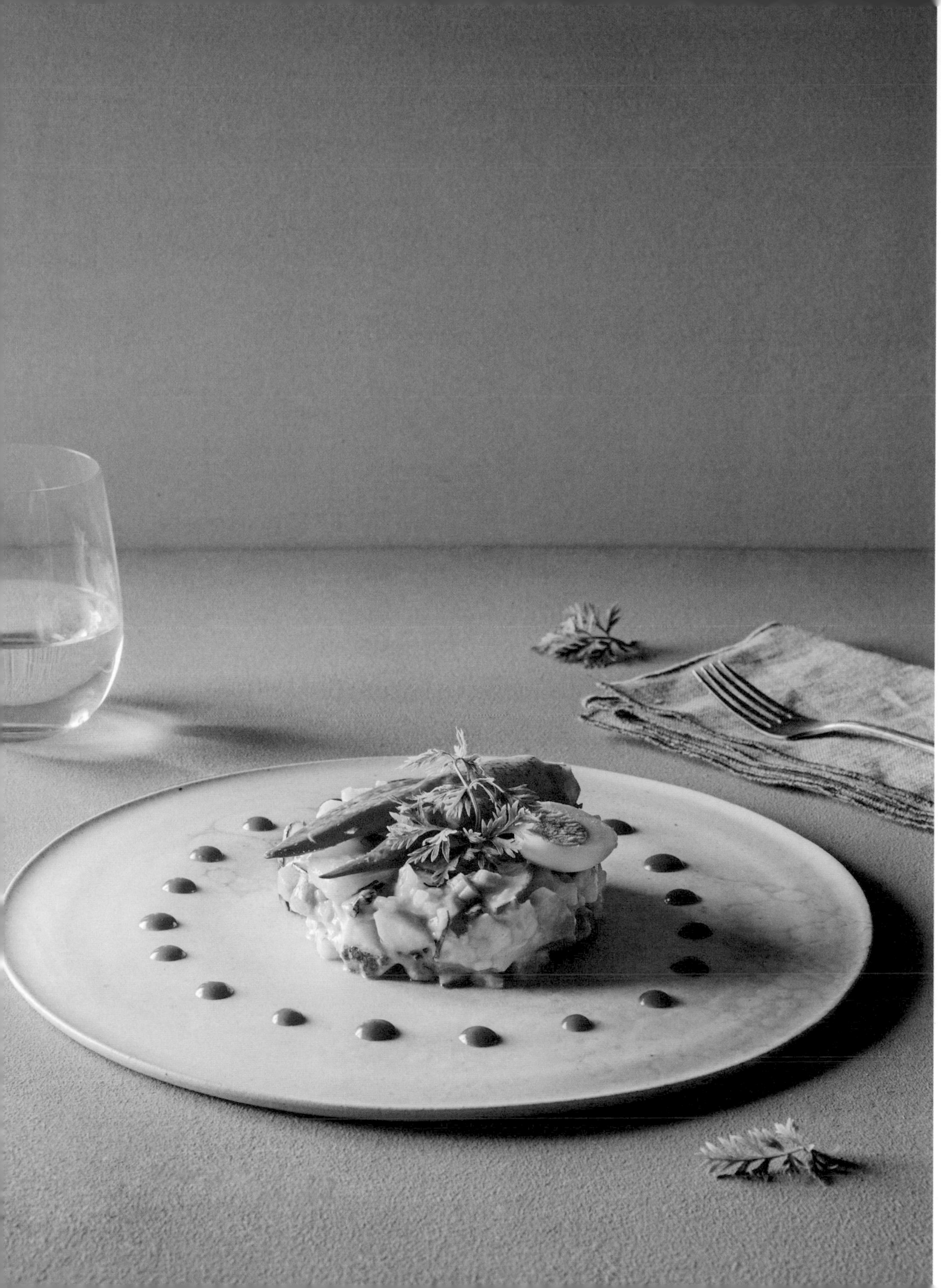

Maenam

ANGUS AN IS restless. He keeps opening new eateries—a noodle bar here, a fried chicken joint there, a Thai street food place next—as if running *Vancouver* magazine's 2016 Restaurant of the Year wasn't enough to keep one chef busy. "With these little restaurants—when I step away from Maenam and plan them—I feel more inspired," he insists with a laugh.

Well, thank goodness for that. Maenam opened in 2009 after An closed his critically acclaimed modernist experiment Gastropod. He took his cue from one of his mentors, David Thompson, the Michelin-starred chef of London's Nahm who'd once cooked for the Thai royal family. No one was doing great modern Thai in Vancouver, An realized, and he saw an opportunity to offer something unique.

"Our recipes are very authentic in spirit. We pride ourselves on using B.C. ingredients when in season. That plus a modern approach to cuisine are what define Maenam," he says. "Some of my favourite dishes are the simple ones—like the hot-and-sour *matsutake* [pine mushroom] and clam soup—because they resemble the location of where we are in the world."

Maenam turned out to be just what Vancouver was craving: the fragrant complexity of Thai food served in a chic room and well paired with wine, beer and ingredient-driven craft cocktails. "We wanted to make sure that we're not just an ordinary ethnic restaurant." Over the years, the awards and accolades have rolled in: Best new restaurant. Best Thai. Best Asian. Canada's Top 100. Simply, the best.

And now this endlessly inventive chef is ready to have some fun with whole crabs and roast ducks, and exciting new flavours. "The first couple of years we were conservative. We didn't even consider having a tasting menu until 2013. We still have safe bets on the menu, but we're more playful now."

PICTURED ON P.158

FRIED SHALLOTS AND GARLIC

Vegetable oil, for deep-frying

6 large shallots, finely sliced lengthwise

8 cloves garlic, sliced

DRESSING

⅔ cup chicken stock

¼ cup palm sugar

¼ cup soy sauce

¼ tsp ground white pepper

1 Tbsp tamarind concentrate (not paste or block; available at Asian markets)

½ cup sesame seeds (divided)

¼ cup Fried Shallots (see here)

SALAD

1 lb roasted duck meat or barbecue duck

12 lychees, peeled and torn into pieces

4 cups fresh cilantro leaves

½ cup Fried Shallots (see here)

½ cup Fried Garlic (see here)

¼ cup sliced green onions

½ cup toasted small peanuts

Roasted Duck Salad

SERVES 4

Duck is one of the most popular meats in Asian cultures. Here, it adds a deep, rich, meaty note to a salad brightened with sweet, sour and salty flavours plus a pleasantly crunchy texture.

FRIED SHALLOTS AND GARLIC Fill a small saucepan 3 inches deep with vegetable oil and heat over medium-high heat until it reaches a temperature of 350°F. Gently lower shallots into saucepan and deep-fry for 2 minutes, until golden. Using a slotted spoon, transfer shallots to a plate lined with paper towels and drain. Repeat process with garlic and set aside.

DRESSING Heat stock in a small saucepan over medium-high heat. Add sugar and simmer, until dissolved. Add soy sauce, white pepper and tamarind concentrate and stir. Remove from heat.

Toast the sesame seeds in the oven until golden. Using a mortar and pestle, grind ¼ cup of the sesame seeds to a paste and then transfer to the mixture in the saucepan. Repeat with ¼ cup fried shallots, transfer to the saucepan and mix well.

SALAD Preheat oven to 300°F. Place duck meat in the oven to warm up for 15 minutes, until heated through.

In a medium bowl, combine the rest of the ingredients. Toss with half the dressing.

Slice or shred the duck meat into bite-sized pieces and toss with remaining dressing. Add to the bowl of salad, transfer to a serving plate and garnish with remaining ¼ cup toasted sesame seeds. Serve.

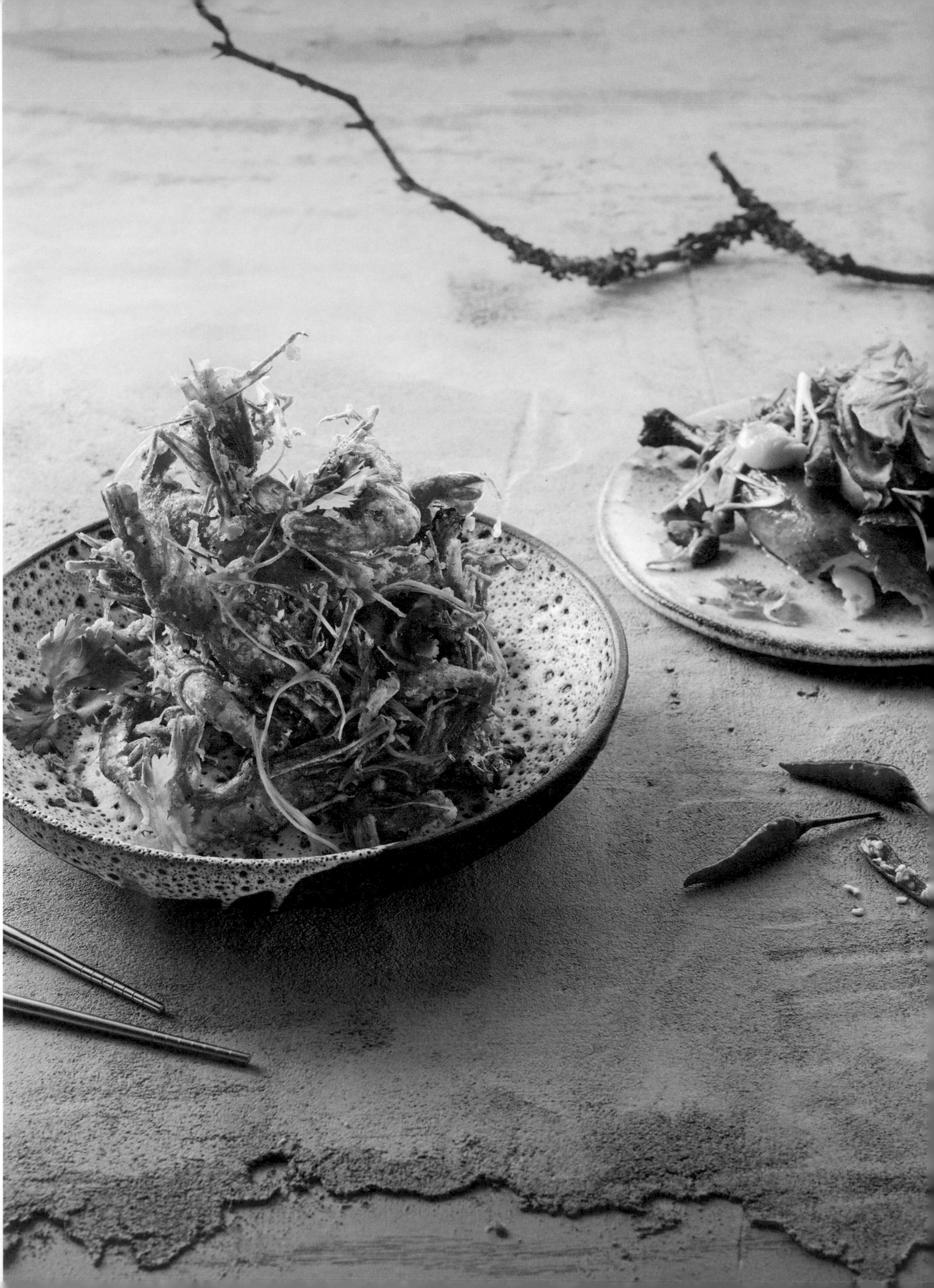

2 lbs live B.C. spot prawns

2 cups cornstarch

1 cup water

1 Tbsp freshly ground black pepper, plus extra to taste

1 Tbsp kosher salt, plus extra to taste

4 cups vegetable oil or as needed for deep-frying, plus 2 Tbsp for frying paste

3 cloves garlic

2 bird's-eye chilies

2 fresh cilantro roots or stems

2 Tbsp fish sauce

Pinch of ground white pepper

Fresh cilantro leaves

Green onions, finely sliced

Black Pepper Stir-Fried Spot Prawns

SERVES 4

Spot prawns are the rock star of the West Coast seafood world. Buttery sweet and only available for a few short weeks a year, local chefs snap them up as soon as the first prawn boats dock at Fisherman's Wharf in Richmond. If you can't find them, use the best whole prawns you can find.

If you've purchased live prawns, submerge them for a few seconds in cold unfiltered tap water, then remove them immediately—this is the easiest and most humane preparation method.

In a bowl, combine cornstarch, water, 1 table-spoon black pepper and 1 tablespoon salt. Stir until the slurry is well combined and thick like heavy cream.

Pour enough oil into a deep saucepan or deep-fryer to fully submerge the prawns—adding more oil, if necessary—and heat to a temperature of 350°F. Dredge prawns in the slurry and carefully lower them one at a time into the oil, taking care not to splash hot oil. Deep-fry for 2 to 3 minutes, until golden and crispy. (Do not overcook.)

Using a mortar and pestle, combine garlic, chilies and cilantro roots (or stems). Add salt and grind to a paste.

Heat 2 tablespoons oil in a wok over medium-high heat and add paste. Fry for 2 minutes, until golden and aromatic. Add crispy prawns. Stir in fish sauce and season with white and black pepper. Remove from heat.

Fold in cilantro leaves and green onions and toss. Serve immediately.

KAZUHIRO HAYASHI

ALAN FERRER

Miku / Minami

FUNNY WHAT A flicker of flame can do to a piece of fish. It lightly caramelizes that slice of tuna or salmon or mackerel, making it taste deeper and sweeter, adding another layer of texture so it's even more melt-in-your-mouth delicious. *Aburi oshi* sushi, or "flame-seared pressed sushi," they call it, back in its home of Osaka, Japan.

Seigo Nakamura—the founder of Miku—figured Vancouver would love *aburi*, too. In 2008, he opened Miku next door to the cruise ship terminal; three years later, he opened Minami in Yaletown. Miku is bright and modern, decorated with stylized red, blue and gold fish. Minami, on the other hand, is muted in soft earth tones and filled with greenery. Both have found a loyal following. Since then countless restaurants have added *aburi*-style sushi to their repertoires.

"We introduced salmon *oshi* to Vancouver," says Alan Ferrer, who is both Minami executive chef and corporate kitchen chef for both restaurants. (He shares the workload with Kazuhiro Hayashi, who is corporate executive sushi chef and executive chef at Miku.) The salmon *oshi* features sliced sockeye on top of pressed rice, daubed with a special umami-rich sauce, then lightly torched and garnished with rings of jalapeño. So. Good.

It's not the only thing to eat on the menu, of course. Minami has a slightly stronger focus on meat and cooked dishes like octopus and fritters, but both offer a plethora of rolls, nigiri, sashimi and other dishes. Many can be ordered *aburi* style, if you fancy a little fire with your fish. Or simply order the *shokai* menu, and chef will create a feast of artfully elevated bites that pay homage to the power and beauty of the flame.

SUSHI RICE

2 cups sushi rice

3 cups water (or as rice-cooker instructions or package directions suggest)

½ cup Japanese rice vinegar

6 Tbsp granulated sugar

¼ cup kosher salt

CRAB FILLING

1 cup fresh snow crabmeat, picked of shells or cartilage

½ cup Japanese mayonnaise

ASSEMBLY

4 pieces nori seaweed

1 small Japanese cucumber, cut into 4 long strips

8 oz sashimi-grade red tuna, thinly sliced

3 Tbsp soy sauce

Aburi Sushi Bites

MAKES 4 ROLLS

This sushi extravaganza comes from Minami, where they are happy to sizzle things with a kitchen torch. If you are reluctant to risk your eyebrows, you can always skip the bacon-and-scallop topping, and you don't need to torch the roll if you don't want to. You can pick up sushi mats and ingredients at Asian markets and some grocery stores, but the folks at South China Seas are happy to show you how to use them.

SUSHI RICE Place the rice in a colander and rinse under cold running water, until water runs clear. Set aside for 30 minutes. Add rice and 2 cups water to a rice cooker and cook until tender. (Alternatively, place in a saucepan and bring to a boil, then cover and reduce heat to low. Cook for 20 minutes.) Let rice rest for 10 minutes, keeping the lid closed to help prevent rice from becoming overly sticky or getting mushy. Use a wooden spatula to fluff the rice.

Meanwhile, combine rice vinegar, sugar and salt in a bowl and mix until fully dissolved. Once the rice is cooked, add sushi vinegar and mix gently and evenly. Set aside to cool to room temperature.

CRAB FILLING Squeeze crabmeat using a clean cloth until most of the juice comes out. Combine with mayonnaise and mix well.

ASSEMBLY Cover a sushi rolling mat (*makisu*) with plastic wrap. Place a sheet of nori on top of the plastic on the mat. Place a handful of prepared sushi rice across the nori and gently pat it evenly over the seaweed.

TOPPINGS AND GARNISH

4 oz thick-cut bacon, cut in ½-inch-wide chunks
6 sashimi-grade scallops (20/30 size), 1 inch in diameter
6 raw spot prawns, peeled but tails on
Salt, to taste
Juice of ¼ lemon
2 Tbsp salmon roe, for garnish (optional)

About an inch from one edge, place 3 tablespoons of crab mixture and a cucumber strip along the length of the roll. Using the covered sushi mat, roll the rice around the filling and press lightly to seal.

Remove the mat and plastic wrap and top the roll with sliced red tuna. Place the covered sushi mat over the roll and squeeze lightly to shape the roll. Cut into 6 equal pieces. Brush each with soy sauce.

Using a kitchen torch, lightly sear the top of the roll (optional).

TOPPINGS AND GARNISH In a small frying pan over medium-high heat, add bacon and pan-fry for 10 minutes, until golden. Transfer to a plate lined with paper towels and drain.

Season scallops and spot prawns generously with salt. Using a kitchen torch, lightly sear the outside of the scallops and spot prawns. (Alternatively, sear them quickly in a hot pan.)

Divide the toppings equally between the rolls, securing with a skewer. Squeeze lemon on each piece of scallop and garnish plate with salmon roe (if using).

WASABI CRÈME FRAÎCHE

2 Tbsp crème fraîche (or 1 Tbsp
    sour cream mixed with 1 Tbsp
    heavy (36%) cream)
1 tsp soy sauce
1 tsp wasabi paste

TARTARE

1 Tbsp dried *wakame* (seaweed)
4 oz sashimi-grade sockeye salmon,
    coarsely chopped
1 Tbsp chopped cucumber
1 Tbsp chopped celery
1 Tbsp chopped green onions
1 Tbsp ponzu sauce
1 tsp sesame oil

GARNISH

Root vegetable chips
½ ripe avocado, cubed
1 radish, shaved
Baby greens

B.C. Sockeye Salmon Tartare

SERVES 4

This Miku recipe makes a wonderful appetizer to share, though if you're feeling greedy, it would be a nice dish for one. Make sure to purchase top-quality salmon as you will be serving it raw. Ingredients like wasabi and wakame *are available at Asian markets and some supermarkets.*

WASABI CRÈME FRAÎCHE In a small bowl, combine all ingredients and mix until smooth.

TARTARE Rehydrate *wakame* in cold water for 2 minutes. Drain excess water and place on paper towel to dry. Coarsely chop.

In a small bowl, combine *wakame* and remaining ingredients and gently mix.

ASSEMBLY Place a 3-inch ring mould on a plate and spoon tartare mixture in evenly. Spoon wasabi crème fraîche on the edge of the tartare, then garnish with vegetable chips, avocado, radish and baby greens. Serve.

My Shanti

IT'S A LONG WAY to My Shanti, and we're not talking about its location in South Surrey.

For Vikram Vij, it's just the latest stop on a remarkable journey that began in his childhood home of India and took him to Canada's West Coast, where he became a nationally celebrated chef, sommelier, cookbook author and television personality. Vij's, the award-winning restaurant he co-owns with his business partner Meeru Dhalwala, is legendary in Vancouver as one of the few places celebrities and food writers will line up for. But My Shanti is his most personal project yet.

"It's very beautiful, it's very distinctive," he says. "It's the chaos of India—the colours, the spices, the visuals." Unlike Vij's, which he describes as modern Indian, My Shanti is more traditional—and regionally inspired. "It's based on my travels to India, where I went to people's homes and learned how they cook," he says.

Each fragrant dish represents a different region of India: there's a Goan Pork Vindaloo and Keralan Duck Biryani; there's Gunpowder Prawns from Bombay and goat from Bangalore. These are flavours to fall in love with, and that's just what Vancouver has done. Shortly after it opened in 2014, My Shanti was named or nominated to just about every best new restaurant list going.

But why South Surrey? The suburb is booming as Vancouverites venture farther afield in search of housing that is actually affordable—and Vij knows those real-estate refugees will want the same exceptional cuisine they have in the city. After all, he's one of them, having bought a house here in 2017. "We have to stop saying it's not Vancouver. It *is* Vancouver," he says.

And Vancouver is something Vij knows well. After all, he and Dhalwala were two of the main architects of the city's vibrant food scene.

"Meeru and I were just at that cusp of where dining changed," he says. "The city has given us the respect of allowing us to be who we are. It's not just that people are open to it, people love it."

½ cup ghee or cooking oil

4 tsp cumin seeds

1 (3-inch) cinnamon stick

5 black cardamom pods, lightly pounded (optional)

10 cloves

1 lb red onions, thinly sliced

6 lbs goat meat, bone-in, cut into 1½-inch cubes with bone attached

1 Tbsp kosher salt

9 cloves garlic, chopped

2 Tbsp finely chopped ginger

8 tomatoes, puréed (about 4 cups)

6 cups water

1 tsp freshly ground black pepper

2 tsp ground nutmeg

2 Tbsp ground coriander

1 tsp ground turmeric

1 Tbsp paprika (optional)

2 tsp ground cayenne pepper (optional)

2 cups plain yogurt (minimum 2% milk fat), room temperature, stirred

Naan or steamed rice, to serve

Vikram's Bone-In Goat Curry

SERVES 6 TO 8

Goat is an exotic meat to many North Americans, but it is hugely popular in other parts of the world—in fact, it's the world's most widely consumed red meat, and becoming more so here. It's lean, sustainable and delicious, with a flavour halfway between beef and lamb, and a sturdy partner for bold spices. Halal butchers and some independent mainstream ones carry it; phone ahead to be sure that it's available and ask the butcher to cut it into cubes for you. This recipe will take about three hours to cook.

Heat ghee (or oil) in a large saucepan over medium-high heat for 1 minute. Add cumin, cinnamon, cardamom (if using) and cloves and allow cumin seeds to sizzle for 30 seconds. Stir in onions and sauté for 7 to 8 minutes, until edges turn crispy and brown.

Stir in goat meat and salt, then cook, stirring regularly, for 10 minutes. (The meat will release some of its juices during this time.) Reduce heat to medium, cover and cook for 35 minutes, stirring occasionally. (Note: Add ½ cup of water if the meat sticks to the pan.)

Add garlic and ginger and stir well. Add tomatoes and water, cover and cook for 1 hour.

In a large bowl, combine pepper, nutmeg, coriander, turmeric, paprika and cayenne (if using) and yogurt. To prevent yogurt from curdling, stir 3 to 4 tablespoons of the hot curry mixture into yogurt. Pour yogurt into the pan of curry and stir well. Cover and cook for another 20 to 45 minutes, until goat is tender and cooked. Remove from heat and serve with naan or rice.

1 Tbsp canola oil

1 large onion, puréed (about 1 cup)

2 lbs ground lamb

3 Tbsp finely chopped ginger

3 Tbsp finely chopped garlic

1½ Tbsp finely chopped jalapeño peppers

1½ tsp kosher salt

2 Tbsp paprika

1 tsp crushed red pepper

1 large egg , beaten

12 (12-inch) metal skewers

Chutney, to serve

Grilled Lamb Kabobs

SERVES 6

Vibrant with spice, but not overpoweringly so, these kabobs are a savoury and satisfying way to start a feast. Note that you will need twelve (twelve-inch) metal skewers for this—wooden skewers aren't sturdy enough to do the job. At My Shanti, Vij mixes the lamb with wild boar meat and serves the kabobs with coconut and mint chutneys; you could do the same if you like. He recommends serving a Cabernet Franc from France's Loire Valley alongside.

Heat oil in a heavy-bottomed frying pan over medium heat. Add onion and sauté for 8 to 10 minutes, stirring frequently, until browned. Remove from heat and transfer to a bowl. Set aside to cool for at least 15 minutes.

In a large bowl, combine lamb, ginger, garlic, jalapeño peppers, salt, paprika, crushed red pepper, sautéed onion and half the egg. (You can use the rest of the egg for another dish.) Using your hands, mix well until thoroughly combined. Cover with plastic wrap and refrigerate for 30 minutes, until meat is firm enough to shape and place onto skewers.

Preheat a barbecue or cast-iron grill plate to high heat. (If you're cooking indoors, remember to turn on the stovetop fan, since cooking the meat will emit smoke.)

Divide meat into 12 equal parts. Wrap a portion around a skewer, forming a 1- × 8-inch kabob. Repeat with the remaining portions. Place kabobs on the grill and cook for 4 to 5 minutes, turning often, until well done but not charred or blackened. Pierce the meat with a knife to be sure it's completely cooked inside.

Using an oven mitt or a dish towel, carefully grasp the hot skewer with one hand, and with the other, use a fork or knife to push the cooked meat off the skewer. Place 2 kabobs on each plate. Serve with chutney.

WILLIAM LEW

Notch 8

THE FAIRMONT HOTEL Vancouver, with its distinctive green copper roof and château-style architecture, is among Vancouver's most iconic buildings. Completed in 1939, it was one of the grand railway hotels dreamed up by Canadian Pacific Railway president William Cornelius Van Horne to encourage people to ride his trains west. So when the restaurant was rejuvenated a couple of years back, it seemed like a good idea to pay homage to that epic rail history.

"Notch 8" is the final notch available to a train engineer. It's where the terms "a notch above" and "top notch" originated. Pretty lofty goals for a young chef, but William Lew is up to the challenge. After a stint at the Fairmont Pacific Rim, where he led the drive to create Canada's first all-Ocean-Wise sushi bar, Lew was ready to flex his creative culinary muscles at Hotel Vancouver. What he created was a menu of whimsical dishes that "connect the west to the rest of Canada."

For instance, there's the dish he calls Over the Rocky Mountains, which features "the things that are grown and live around that environment." Birch syrup–glazed bison, wild-rice chips that look like jagged peaks, walnut powder for the snowcaps—all are arranged to look like the Rocky Mountains. "It's taking what makes B.C. beautiful and putting it on the plate," he says. He brings that sense of whimsy to the super-popular afternoon teas as well, especially the themed ones such as the Mad Hatter's Tea or the one designed around vintage board games.

But whether he's assembling finger sandwiches or arranging smoked seafood in a glass terrarium, sustainability is always at the forefront of Lew's mind. That means local, organic, Ocean Wise and otherwise eco-friendly ingredients when possible, which isn't always easy at a grand, historic hotel. Still he tries, adding, "We are 'Super, Natural British Columbia,' but we can only sustain that if we all try and believe in that message."

2 Tbsp vegetable oil
1 fennel bulb, coarsely chopped
1 onion, coarsely chopped
1 leek, white and light green parts
    only, chopped
6 stalks celery, coarsely chopped
4 cloves garlic, crushed
3 slices peeled ginger
3 sprigs fresh thyme

3 L fish stock
4 cups clam nectar
¼ cup fish sauce
¾ cup dried shiitake mushrooms
1 bay leaf
½ cup bonito flakes
1 (3-inch) piece kombu (dried seaweed),
    wiped clean with a damp cloth
2 sprigs fresh tarragon

SMOKED OYSTER AIOLI
2½ oz canned smoked oysters
1 cup mayonnaise
Grated zest of 1 lemon
Smoked sea salt, to taste

Tidal Pool (Cedar-Smoked Seafood Bowl)

SERVES 4

This entrée is similar to a seafood hotpot with wild B.C. fish, shellfish, clams and mussels in a sea water stock. All seafood should be fresh, local and Ocean Wise if possible. If you like, serve it as they do at the Hotel Vancouver, in a beautiful glass bowl or aquarium.

SEA WATER STOCK Heat oil in a stockpot over medium heat and add fennel, onions, leeks, celery, garlic, ginger and thyme. Sauté for 10 minutes, until softened.

Pour in fish stock, clam nectar and fish sauce. Add mushrooms, bay leaf, bonito and kombu. Cook for 1 hour, until reduced by half. Stir in tarragon and simmer for another 5 minutes.

Strain out solids and discard. Cool stock and set aside until needed. This will make about 8 cups. It can be stored for up to 6 months in the freezer.

SMOKED OYSTER AIOLI Place smoked oysters, mayonnaise and lemon zest in a blender or food processor and process until smooth. Season to taste with smoked sea salt. Transfer to a small squeeze bottle and keep chilled until needed.

SEAFOOD

1 (2-oz) package dried *wakame* (seaweed)

Vegetable oil, for frying

4 (2-oz) salmon fillets

4 (2-oz) sablefish fillets

4 (2-oz) albacore tuna loins

5 cups Sea Water Stock (see here) (divided)

12 live mussels, scrubbed and debearded

20 live clams, scrubbed

12 watermelon-radish balls, made with
½-inch melon baller

8 scallops

20 side-stripe shrimp

4 oz Dungeness crabmeat, picked of
shells or cartilage

12 smoked oysters

1 oz roe (mix of Northern Divine caviar,
trout roe, salmon roe, etc.)

Fronds from 1 fennel bulb

Baby shiso leaves (optional)

SEAFOOD Put *wakame* in a bowl, add cold water and set aside for 3 minutes, until rehydrated. Strain and squeeze out excess water. Set aside.

Heat a frying pan over medium-high heat and add enough vegetable oil to cover the pan lightly. Working in batches, quickly sear salmon, sablefish and tuna for 2 minutes on each side, until firm and cooked on the outside but still slightly translucent inside. Remove from heat and set aside.

Bring 4 cups of sea water stock to a boil in a large saucepan. Add mussels, clams and watermelon-radish balls, cover and cook for 5 to 10 minutes, until shells start to open. Add scallops and shrimp and cook for another 2 to 3 minutes, until shellfish are fully opened. Remove pot from heat.

ASSEMBLY Divide seafood and watermelon-radish balls between 4 bowls, reserving some shrimp for garnish. Add 1 cup of sea water stock to each bowl. Garnish with *wakame* and drizzle smoked oyster aioli overtop. Add crab and a couple of shrimp, arranging them, if you like, to look like the shoreline at low tide. Finish each dish with roe, fennel fronds and baby shiso leaves (if using). Serve immediately.

SCONES

3 cups all-purpose flour

2 Tbsp baking powder

1 cup granulated sugar

½ tsp kosher salt

1 cup (2 sticks) unsalted
  butter, cut into cubes

2 large eggs

1 cup heavy (36%) cream

1 cup raisins

Clotted cream or butter, to serve

Raspberry jam, to serve

EGG WASH

1 large egg

2 tsp whole milk

Pinch of salt

VARIATIONS:

For a berry scone, replace raisins
with 1 cup of berries (B.C. blueberries,
raspberries or a combination of both).
Frozen berries are easier to handle and
won't bleed in the pastry. For a chocolate chip scone, replace raisins with
1 cup chocolate chips.

The Fairmont Hotel Vancouver Scones

MAKES 12 LARGE

These are a favourite at the hotel's afternoon tea and so easy to make at home. Executive pastry chef D'Oyen Christie recommends making them in large batches. Simply make the recipe as outlined, roll and cut out the scones, brush them with the egg wash and then freeze them. Pop them straight into the oven and have just-baked scones whenever you want.

In a large bowl, combine flour, baking powder, sugar and salt and mix well. Using your fingertips, blend in butter until a fine crumb.

In separate bowl, mix eggs and cream together, then stir in raisins.

Add liquid ingredients to dry ingredients. Knead lightly until you have a soft dough, but do not overwork. Transfer to a floured work surface and roll to 1½-inch thickness. Cut out to your preferred shape and size and place on a baking sheet lined with parchment paper.

In a small bowl, combine egg-wash ingredients and mix well. Brush mixture on top of the scones. Allow to rest for 30 minutes at room temperature.

Preheat oven to 325°F.

Bake for 20 to 25 minutes until golden brown. Serve with clotted cream or butter and raspberry jam.

Ocean Wise

IT'S TACO TUESDAY at the Vancouver Aquarium Café, and the special is tender shrimp in a crispy wonton shell. The shrimp are wild caught and sustainably harvested—this is, after all, the home of Ocean Wise—and the taco is just the latest variation on the dish Ned Bell first made famous more than a decade ago when he was executive chef at Murrieta's in Calgary.

Back then, sustainability wasn't top of mind for most chefs—or diners. The grandfather of sustainable seafood lists, Monterey Bay Aquarium's Seafood Watch program, launched in 1999; the Vancouver Aquarium's Ocean Wise followed six years later.

"Fifteen years ago there wasn't a lot of work being done because there weren't a lot of questions being asked," says Bell, who became the Aquarium's Ocean Wise executive chef in 2016. "When the Ocean Wise program launched in 2005, we were already cooking that way, but it was not a sustainability issue, it was a quality ingredients issue."

Growing up in fertile Okanagan farm country, Bell had always believed in the importance of knowing the people who grew your food. But it was only once he became executive chef of YEW seafood + bar at Four Seasons Vancouver that he realized just how dire the situation was for our oceans and the creatures that live in them. He led the hotel to become 100 percent Ocean Wise, Canada's first luxury property to do so. He started a foundation, Chefs for Oceans. He cycled across Canada to raise awareness. He canned sustainable tuna to raise money. He wrote a cookbook, *Lure: Sustainable Seafood Recipes from the West Coast*.

Today he focuses his talents on special events and collaboration dinners across the country and spends the rest of his time spreading the word about sustainability. "As a conscious consumer, I truly live an Ocean Wise life," he says.

PLUMS

2 lbs plums, pitted and cut into
  quarters (divided)

2 sprigs fresh rosemary, leaves coarsely
  chopped, plus extra for garnish

2 Tbsp canola oil

1 shallot, finely chopped

¾ cup honey

1 cup good-quality Pinot Noir

½ cup plum or red wine vinegar

1 tsp sea salt

SALMON

4 (5-oz) salmon fillets, skin on

Sea salt and freshly ground black
  pepper, to taste

1 Tbsp canola oil

2 Tbsp unsalted butter

½ lemon

Salmon with Sweet-and-Sour Pinot Noir Plums and Rosemary

SERVES 4

The Pinot Noir intensifies the fruit flavours—and is delicious to sip. Pick one you love to drink, preferably from B.C., so you can serve the rest of the bottle with the finished salmon dish.

PLUMS In a small bowl, combine half the plums and all of the rosemary and set aside for at least 10 minutes.

Meanwhile, heat oil in a small saucepan over medium heat, add shallots and sauté for 1 minute until fragrant. Add remaining half of plums, honey, wine, vinegar and salt and bring to a boil. Reduce heat to medium-low and simmer for 20 to 30 minutes. Add rosemary-infused plums and cook for another 5 minutes.

SALMON Preheat oven to 400°F.

Use paper towels to pat salmon dry and season with salt and pepper. Heat oil in a heavy-bottomed, ovenproof frying pan over medium heat until heated through. Carefully lay fish in pan skin-side up and cook for 30 seconds. Roast in oven for 2 to 3 minutes.

Remove from oven. Flip fish skin-side down and return to the stovetop over medium heat. Add butter to pan and squeeze some lemon juice over each fillet. Baste for a minute by spooning melted butter over fish.

Divide salmon between 4 plates and top with plums and wine sauce. Garnish with rosemary leaves and serve with remaining wine.

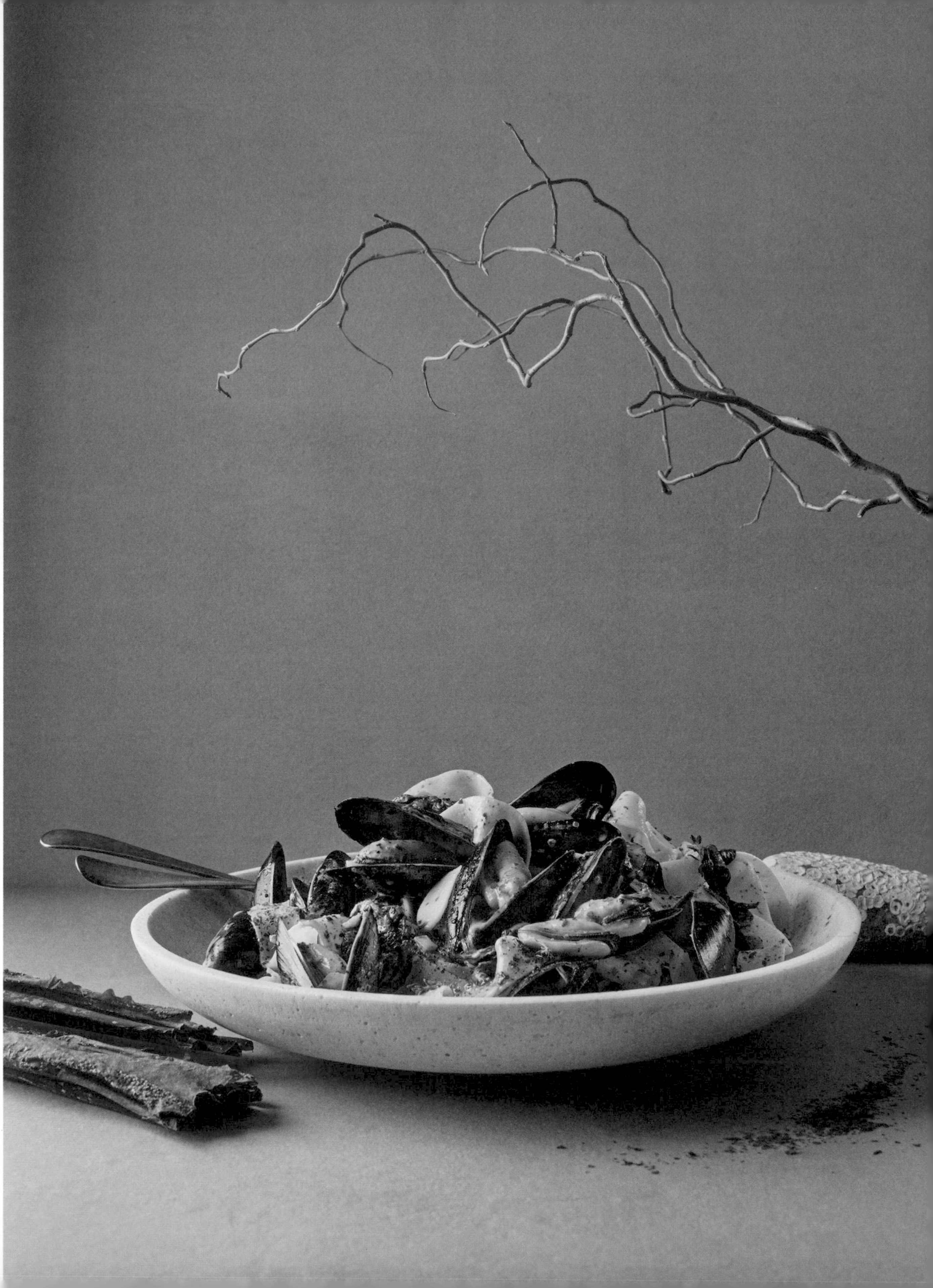

KELP CREAM

½ Tbsp canola oil

½ shallot, finely chopped

1 small clove garlic, finely chopped

1 bird's-eye chili, seeded and finely chopped

1½ cups whipping (33%) cream, plus extra if needed

1 cup fresh kelp or ⅓ cup dried bull or winged kelp, rinsed (if dried, soak in warm water for 10 minutes)

Grated zest of ½ lime

½ tsp sesame oil

Sea salt, to taste

MUSSELS AND PAPPARDELLE

3 lbs live mussels

1 lb dried pappardelle or fettuccine

2 Tbsp extra-virgin olive oil

2 Tbsp unsalted butter

2 cloves garlic, finely chopped

1 shallot, finely chopped

¼ cup white wine

3 Tbsp sliced fresh basil

3 Tbsp dried crushed bull or winged kelp (see headnote)

Grated zest and juice of 1 to 2 lemons

1 tsp crushed red pepper (optional)

Mussels and Kelp Pappardelle

SERVES 4

This pasta dish is rich, creamy and full of umami, thanks to the kelp in the bright-green cream sauce and garnish. Ask your fishmonger to source fresh curly kelp for you. You can find dehydrated bull or winged kelp at health food stores. Once added to the sauce, it rehydrates to a spinach-like texture in less than a minute.

KELP CREAM Heat oil in a large saucepan over medium heat, add shallots and garlic and sauté for 30 seconds, until fragrant. Add remaining ingredients except salt, bring to a simmer over medium heat and cook for 5 minutes. Remove pan from heat and cool lightly.

Transfer mixture to a blender or food processor and process until smooth. Strain purée through a fine-mesh sieve. Thin out, if desired, with a little extra cream. Season to taste with salt. (Can be made ahead and refrigerated.)

MUSSELS AND PAPPARDELLE Put mussels in a colander and rinse under cold running water. Discard any that are open and won't close when tapped or that have broken shells. Scrub off any debris and pull off beard. Keep chilled until needed.

Bring a large saucepan of salted water to a boil over high heat and add pasta. Cook until al dente, according to manufacturer's instructions.

Meanwhile, heat oil and butter in a large frying pan over medium-high heat. Add garlic and shallots and sauté for 5 minutes, until tender and translucent. Pour in wine and bring to a boil.

Add mussels, cover and cook 2 minutes, just until the shells open up. Discard any that don't open. Add kelp cream and cook for another 2 minutes, until warmed through. Stir in basil, dried kelp, lemon zest and juice and crushed red pepper (if using).

Drain pasta and stir it into pan of mussels. Transfer to a large serving bowl and serve family style.

MARK PERRIER

Osteria Savio Volpe

MARK PERRIER DESCRIBES his Fraserhood restaurant as "a true neighbourhood spot. Warm, generous, honest and fun." It's certainly all that. But it's also the sort of place where you'd be happy to cross a couple of bridges and make your way through heavy traffic just for a taste of the house-made pasta and—seriously—a kale salad so good, it makes you think this whole kale thing isn't a hoax after all.

The name translates in Italian to something like "tavern of the wise fox." The food is Italian, but not any Italian you likely know. After all, Perrier himself isn't Italian and has never been to Italy. But he has worked in top Italian kitchens and cooks the way Italians do: by using the best local ingredients, simply, to celebrate their good, honest flavours.

He began his career in fine dining, including roles at West and CinCin Ristorante, and a stint at the two-Michelin-starred Le Gavroche in London. When he opened Cibo Trattoria in 2009, *enRoute* magazine named it the best new restaurant of the year. Two years working as a butcher for Two Rivers Specialty Meats followed, and then in 2015, the realization of his dreams of opening Osteria Savio Volpe, which went on to earn a top ten spot on *enRoute*'s list.

Here pork, chicken, veal and fish roast succulently over a wood fire, kissed by sweet smoke. The pasta is made from scratch every day and tossed with long-simmering sauces like Perrier's favourite Sunday *sugo*. Vegetables are served at the peak of freshness. A small, well-edited wine list offers delightful surprises.

"Every day that we are blessed to be open and busy is a highlight for me," he says. "I love that this city allows me to cook the food that I want. No compromises." Sounds like something a wise fox would say.

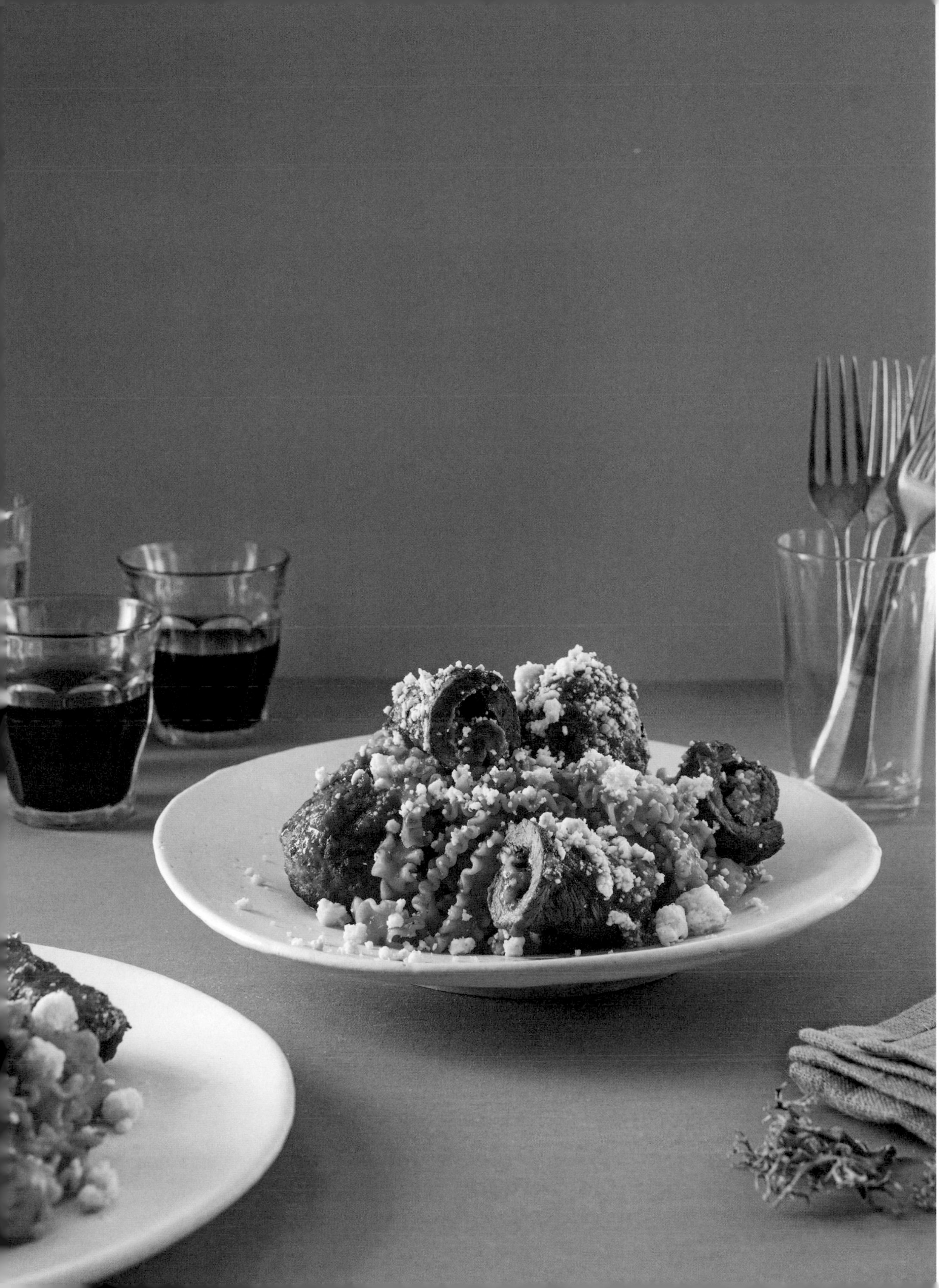

ROASTED PORK BONES

2 lbs pork neck bones

1 cup water

MEATBALLS

1 to 2 Tbsp extra-virgin olive oil

1 onion, finely chopped

2 cloves garlic, finely chopped

1 cup bread crumbs

¾ cup whole milk, or as needed

1 large egg

8 oz ground beef

8 oz ground pork

4 oz ground veal

Pinch of ground nutmeg

½ cup chopped fresh parsley

¼ cup grated Parmesan

¼ cup grated pecorino

¼ cup dried currants, soaked in hot water

¼ cup pine nuts, lightly toasted

BRACIOLE

1 (18-oz) beef outside round (sometimes called rouladen), cut into 6 slices (ask your butcher)

2 Tbsp lard, room temperature

Salt and freshly ground black pepper, to taste

2 cloves garlic, finely chopped

¾ cup chopped fresh parsley

½ cup grated aged provolone

½ cup grated Parmesan, pecorino or Grana Padano cheese

Mafaldine with Sunday Sugo, Braciole and Meatballs

SERVES 6

Mafaldine, which is also known as reginette, *Italian for "little queen," is a ribbon-shaped dried pasta that is about a half inch wide with wavy edges on both sides. If you can't find it, use another dried pasta that can stand up to a sturdy sauce, such as ziti, rigatoni or spaghetti. This recipe also comprises several steps—if time is of the essence, you could always leave out the braciole or the meatballs or both. After all, every part of this dish is richly delicious.*

ROASTED PORK BONES Preheat oven to 400°F.

Place neck bones in a roasting pan and roast for 2 hours, until golden. Pour water in roasting pan and deglaze, scraping up drippings. Set aside.

MEATBALLS Heat oil in a frying pan over medium heat, add onion and garlic and sauté for 10 minutes, just until softened and translucent. Remove from heat and set aside to cool.

Preheat oven to 400°F. In a large bowl, soak bread crumbs in enough milk to moisten. Mix in egg until well combined. Gently add meats and mix well. Add the remaining ingredients, being careful not to overmix. Form meat into golf-ball-sized rounds and arrange on a baking sheet. Roast for 15 minutes, until evenly browned.

BRACIOLE Place slices of meat between 2 sheets of wax or parchment paper and pound with a meat mallet, until ¼ inch thick. Smear lard over each slice. Season with salt and pepper, then sprinkle with remaining ingredients. Roll and tie with butcher's string, sealing the ends as best you can.

SUGO AND PASTA

1 quantity Braciole (see here)

2 cups red wine

1 quantity Roasted Pork Bones (see here)

2 Tbsp lard

6 cloves garlic

½ cup diced pancetta

2 large onions, diced

1 (4-inch-square) piece raw pork skin

Pinch of crushed red pepper

2 Tbsp tomato paste

2 (796-mL) cans whole tomatoes, passed
through a food mill

1 quantity Meatballs (see here)

1 lb *mafaldine* or other sturdy dried pasta

Ricotta salata, crumbled, or grated
Parmesan, to taste

SUGO AND PASTA Preheat oven (or reduce oven heat) to 250°F.

Heat a frying pan over medium-high heat and brown the seasoned braciole. Transfer braciole to a plate. Pour wine into pan. Cook for 15 to 20 minutes, until wine is reduced by half. Stir in deglazing liquid from the pork bones.

Melt lard in a large Dutch oven over low heat, add garlic and slowly cook for 5 minutes, until golden. Add pancetta and onions and cook for 30 minutes, until deeply caramelized. (Do not rush this stage.)

Add pork skin and crushed red pepper to the pan and cook for 4 to 5 minutes. Stir in tomato paste and cook for 5 minutes until the paste turns a brick-red colour. Add roasted pork bones and reduced wine mixture and bring to a boil. Add canned tomatoes and reduce to a simmer. Add braciole, cover and place in the oven to cook for 1½ hours.

Add meatballs, partially cover the pan and cook in the oven another 30 minutes until braciole is tender and meatballs are cooked through. Remove from oven and allow meatballs and braciole to cool in the sauce. Remove string from braciole before serving.

Remove pork bones and pork skin. Pick meat from neck bones and add back to sauce. Dice pork skin and add to sauce.

Bring a large saucepan of salted water to a boil and cook pasta following package directions. When pasta is nearly cooked, add a ladle of pasta water to the *sugo*.

Drain pasta and add to pot. Finish cooking pasta in the sauce. Top with the ricotta salata (or Parmesan) and serve.

1 (2½- to 3-lb) whole rabbit or chicken

Salt and freshly ground black pepper, to taste

2 fresh bay leaves

1 sprig fresh rosemary

2 sprigs fresh thyme

4 cloves garlic (divided)

1 cup extra-virgin olive oil, or as needed (divided)

½ cup all-purpose flour, or as needed

½ cup diced pancetta

1 onion, finely chopped

½ cup dried porcini mushrooms, rehydrated and chopped, liquid reserved

1 cup white wine

2 (398-mL) cans Italian plum tomatoes

2 cups chicken stock, or as needed

Fresh pine mushrooms (as many as you can afford, Chef says)

1 clove garlic, chopped

½ bunch fresh parsley, chopped

Crusty bread, to serve

Rabbit Cacciatore with Pine Mushrooms

SERVES 4

"Cacciatore" means hunter in Italian, and this is one dish well worth hunting down. If you can't find rabbit, you can always make it with chicken instead. If you have leftovers, shred the meat and mix with the sauce, then toss with a sturdy, bite-sized pasta such as fusilli.

Cut the rabbit (or chicken) into sections, chopping through the bones with a heavy knife when necessary. You should have 2 legs, 2 shoulders, 2 bellies, 1 neck, 2 rib and 2 loin sections. Season with salt and pepper.

Using a mortar and pestle, pound the bay leaves, rosemary, thyme and 3 cloves of garlic into a paste and add ¼ cup oil. Rub herb paste over rabbit. Place in fridge to marinate for at least 6 hours or overnight.

The next day, lightly dust the rabbit sections with flour. Heat ¼ cup oil in a large frying pan and sear rabbit pieces in batches until golden, adding more oil as necessary. Remove from pan.

Add pancetta and onion to pan and cook for 10 minutes, until onion is soft and begins to caramelize. Add porcini mushrooms and cook for 2 to 3 minutes. Add wine and deglaze pan.

Reduce heat slightly, then add porcini liquid, tomatoes and rabbit. Add chicken stock until rabbit is half submerged. Bring to a low simmer, partially cover and braise for 40 minutes, until rabbit is tender. Add more chicken stock as needed.

Heat 2 tablespoons oil in a frying pan and sauté the pine mushrooms with garlic and parsley. Place on top of the servings of rabbit. Serve with plenty of bread to soak up the sauce.

WESLEY YOUNG

PIDGIN

"PIDGIN" IS THE coming together of two languages to create a third, wholly new one. At PiDGin, it's East and West, Gastown and Chinatown, old and new all joining to create a whole new way of dining.

"With each dish we get to play with things that aren't traditionally put together," says co-owner Brandon Grossutti. "That's partially why we're called PiDGin—it's two new things coming together. It's uniquely Vancouver. In Vancouver culture, we're as comfortable having dim sum as we are a traditional English breakfast as we are a bowl of dal."

Chef Wesley Young adds, "It has to make sense in your mind as well. I want resonance more than dissonance. Our atmosphere is very convivial, and everything should fall into place with that."

He joined the team in 2016 after years spent cooking in Western fine-dining establishments. Now, with its exuberant fusion fare, PiDGin gives Young the opportunity to be creative with the Asian ingredients he grew up eating and the big, bold, complex, chili-and-yuzu-flecked flavours he loves.

The best way to understand this new language of food is to take the quick course of its many components—that is, to enjoy the tasting menu. No, scratch that: the best way to experience PiDGin is by starting with one of the fantastic cocktails created by an inventive bar, like the juicy watermelon-and-tequila One-Eyed Samurai. Or maybe a sake flight—they have fourteen by the glass. Or maybe a Japanese whisky. Or any selection from the globe-trotting wine list.

Doesn't matter; the food and drink bring East and West together quite tastily. "This city is such a tapestry of cultures and foods," explains Grossutti. "We just want to express what Vancouver is on a plate."

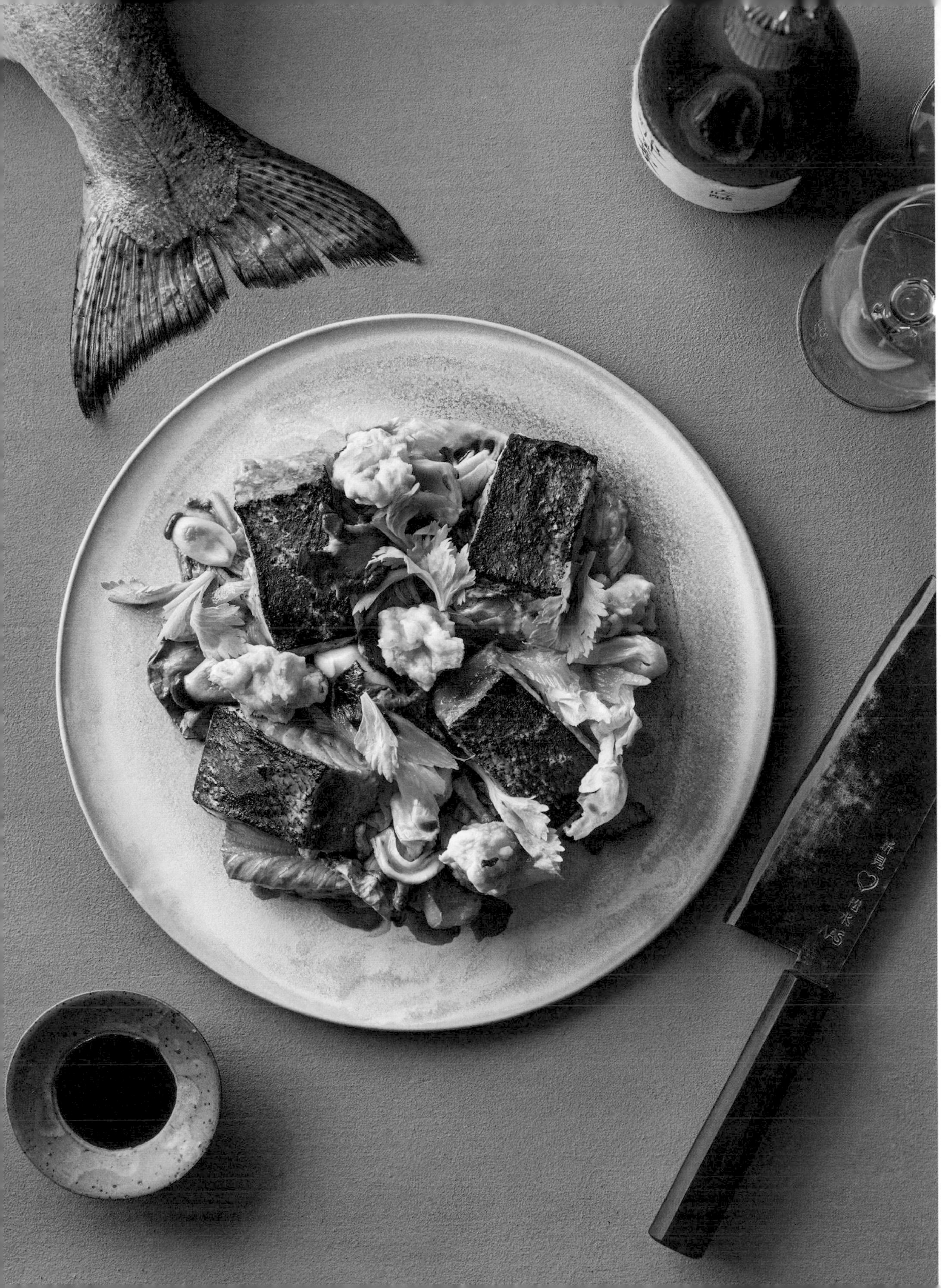

SAKE KASU–CURED SALMON

¼ cup sake *kasu*
1½ Tbsp mirin
1½ Tbsp sake
1½ tsp granulated sugar
Pinch of salt
1 (6-oz) spring salmon fillet, skin on

DASHI

4 cups water
1 (6-inch) piece kombu (dried seaweed), wiped clean with a damp cloth
¼ cup bonito flakes

PICKLED CELERY

1 stalk celery, thinly sliced on the bias, about ⅛ inch thick
¼ cup granulated sugar
¼ cup white wine vinegar
2 Tbsp water
2 tsp soy sauce
Pinch of salt

TEMPURA SAUCE

6 Tbsp Dashi (see here)
¼ cup soy sauce
2 Tbsp mirin

Sake Kasu–Cured Salmon with Braised Lettuce, Pickled Celery and Tempura

SERVES 2 AS AN APPETIZER

Sake kasu is the lees of sake making, and the not-so-secret ingredient used by many Vancouver chefs. The best place to find it is on Granville Island at Artisan SakeMaker, the brewery of Masa Shiroki. At PiDGiN, Chef Wesley Young uses it to add subtle depth of flavour to that favourite of West Coast dining, salmon. The tempura, pickles and sauce elevate this dish to the extraordinary.

SAKE KASU–CURED SALMON In a bowl, combine all ingredients except the salmon and whisk together. Spread the marinade generously over the salmon. Cover and place in the fridge at least six hours or overnight. Brush excess marinade off the salmon and bring to room temperature for about an hour.

DASHI In a large saucepan over medium-high heat, bring the water and kombu to a simmer, then add bonito flakes. Reduce heat to low and wait for the bonito to sink down to the bottom. Remove from heat and strain through a fine-mesh sieve. Cool down and set aside until needed. Leftover dashi can be stored in the fridge for up to 5 days and used for another recipe.

PICKLED CELERY Put celery into a bowl or glass jar. In a small saucepan, combine the rest of the ingredients and cook over medium-high heat, stirring frequently, until it reaches a simmer and sugar is fully dissolved. Pour over celery. Leave for 4 hours to pickle.

TEMPURA SAUCE In a bowl, combine all ingredients and set aside until needed. This will keep for up to 5 days in the fridge.

PRAWN AND ARTICHOKE TEMPURA

2 Tbsp all-purpose flour

2 Tbsp cornstarch

Pinch of salt, plus extra to taste

¼ cup ice-cold soda water, or as needed

2 oz spot prawns (about 4) or side-stripe shrimp (6), peeled, deveined and finely chopped

1 canned artichoke heart, finely chopped

Canola or vegetable oil, for deep-frying

Shichimi togarashi, to taste

Fresh lemon juice, to taste

ASSEMBLY

2 tsp canola oil

¼ head butter lettuce, coarsely chopped

3 Tbsp Tempura Sauce (see here), plus extra for drizzling

1 Tbsp unsalted butter

PRAWN AND ARTICHOKE TEMPURA In a bowl, combine flour, cornstarch and salt and whisk in enough soda water to form a thin batter.

In a separate bowl, combine spot prawns (or shrimp) and artichokes. Stir in enough batter to bind everything together.

Pour oil into a small saucepan 2 inches deep and heat to a temperature of 350°F.

Using a teaspoon, scoop up some of the tempura mixture. With a second spoon, carefully push the tempura off the first spoon into the hot oil and take care not to splash hot oil. Fry for 2 to 3 minutes, until golden. Repeat with the remaining batter.

Using a slotted spoon, transfer tempura to a plate lined with paper towels to drain. While tempura is still hot, season it with salt, *shichimi togarashi* and a little lemon juice.

ASSEMBLY Preheat oven to 350°F.

Place the salmon in a baking dish skin-side down and bake for 6 to 10 minutes, until firm and opaque on the outside but still slightly translucent inside.

If you like, flip the fish and using a kitchen torch, sear skin for a few seconds until it is blackened. Alternatively, if you don't have a torch, you could pop it skin-side up under a very hot broiler for about 30 seconds.

Heat oil in a frying pan over medium heat. Add pickled celery and butter lettuce and sauté for a few seconds until lettuce is wilted but still has texture. Stir in tempura sauce and butter. Remove from heat.

Place pickled celery-lettuce mixture on a plate and top with salmon. Arrange fritters around salmon and drizzle tempura sauce on top. Serve immediately.

WATERMELON TEQUILA
1 large seedless watermelon
1 (750-mL) bottle blanco tequila

SIMPLE SYRUP
1 cup granulated sugar
1 cup water

WATERMELON GRANITA
Remaining Watermelon Purée (see here)
Simple Syrup (see here)

ASSEMBLY
1 oz Watermelon Tequila (see here)
1 oz sake
1 oz fresh lemon juice
2 tsp Simple Syrup (see here)
2 dashes orange blossom water
1 large egg white
1 quantity Watermelon Granita (see here),
    for garnish (optional)

One-Eyed Samurai Cocktail

SERVES 1

Named for the famous strongman Date Masamune of Japan's Edo period—who did, indeed, have just one eye—this is a refreshing yet complex cocktail made even better with a watermelon granita garnish.

WATERMELON TEQUILA Put watermelon flesh in a blender and purée. In a glass jar or pitcher large enough to hold 8 cups, mix 3 cups of purée with tequila. (Reserve the remaining pulp for the granita.) Place in the fridge and infuse for 8 to 12 hours, then strain out the pulp through a fine-mesh sieve. Leftover watermelon tequila will store in the fridge for up to 2 weeks.

SIMPLE SYRUP Mix sugar and water in a small saucepan over medium heat. Bring to a simmer, stirring, until sugar is fully dissolved. (It can be stored in the fridge for up to 2 weeks.)

WATERMELON GRANITA Strain remaining watermelon purée through a fine-mesh sieve, then measure remaining juice. Add a quarter of that amount of simple syrup. For example, if you have 2 cups watermelon juice, add ½ cup simple syrup. Pour into a large baking pan and freeze for 2 hours, drawing a fork through the granita every 30 minutes or so to break it into crystals.

ASSEMBLY Place all ingredients except granita in a cocktail shaker without ice and shake vigorously to create a voluminous foam. (This is called a dry shake.) Add ice and shake again. Strain into a chilled coupe glass. Garnish with a spoon filled with watermelon granita beside or on top of the glass.

Royal Dinette

EVEN WHEN SHE was a child, Eva Chin knew that food connects people and the land. It's a lesson the chef learned growing up on her family farm in Hawaii, and one that's been reinforced as she's travelled the world cooking and staging at restaurants that range from Maaemo in Norway to Arcane in Hong Kong.

It's a mindset that fits perfectly with the tradition established by David Gunawan (page 102), the chef who opened Royal Dinette in 2015. Like other Vancouver chefs, he emphasized local ingredients but took it one step further: in an attempt to draw attention to the problem of food waste, he often featured misshapen "ugly duckling" vegetables, offcuts of meat and what would normally be treated as food scraps. Turned out, those ugly duckling foods were packed with flavour.

At Royal Dinette, the ingredients may be as local as they come, but in Eva Chin's hands, the flavours arrive from all over the world in dishes such as heirloom carrots with crispy chicken skin and sprouted grains or B.C. ling cod with mustard seeds and a mushroom dashi. Meanwhile, bar manager Kaitlyn Stewart—the 2017 winner of the prestigious Diageo World Class competition—shakes up inventive drinks made with fresh, local ingredients. Cedar-smoked rye or jalapeño-infused pisco, anyone?

You might not expect to find this sort of handcrafted artisanal fare amid the glass towers of downtown's business district, but it turns out that it's just what people were hungry for. Now this bright and cheerful room, with its subtly retro vibe and farm-fresh fare, has indelibly changed the downtown dining scene, and for the better.

PICTURED ON P.194

COFFEE SYRUP
1 cup granulated sugar
1 cup water
2 Tbsp Tim Hortons ground coffee

COCKTAIL
1 oz Bulleit rye
½ oz Amaro Montenegro
½ oz Tim Hortons Coffee Syrup (see here)
½ oz fresh lime juice
2 dashes Angostura bitters
Ginger beer

Views from the Drink

SERVES 1

When bar manager Kaitlyn Stewart was competing in the Diageo Reserve World Class Canada competition in 2017, she had to create a cocktail representing the host city, Toronto. This was it: flavoured with Timmy's and garnished with a statuette of the Six's hometown hero, Drake. Kaitlyn went on to win not just the Canadian competition, but the global one, giving her the title of World's Best Bartender.

COFFEE SYRUP Place sugar and water in a small saucepan and bring to a simmer, stirring until sugar is fully dissolved. Remove from heat, stir in ground coffee and steep for 10 minutes. Strain through a fine-mesh sieve and refrigerate until needed.

COCKTAIL Combine all ingredients, except ginger beer, in a cocktail shaker with ice. Vigorously shake for 7 to 10 seconds. Strain into a Collins glass over crushed ice and top with ginger beer.

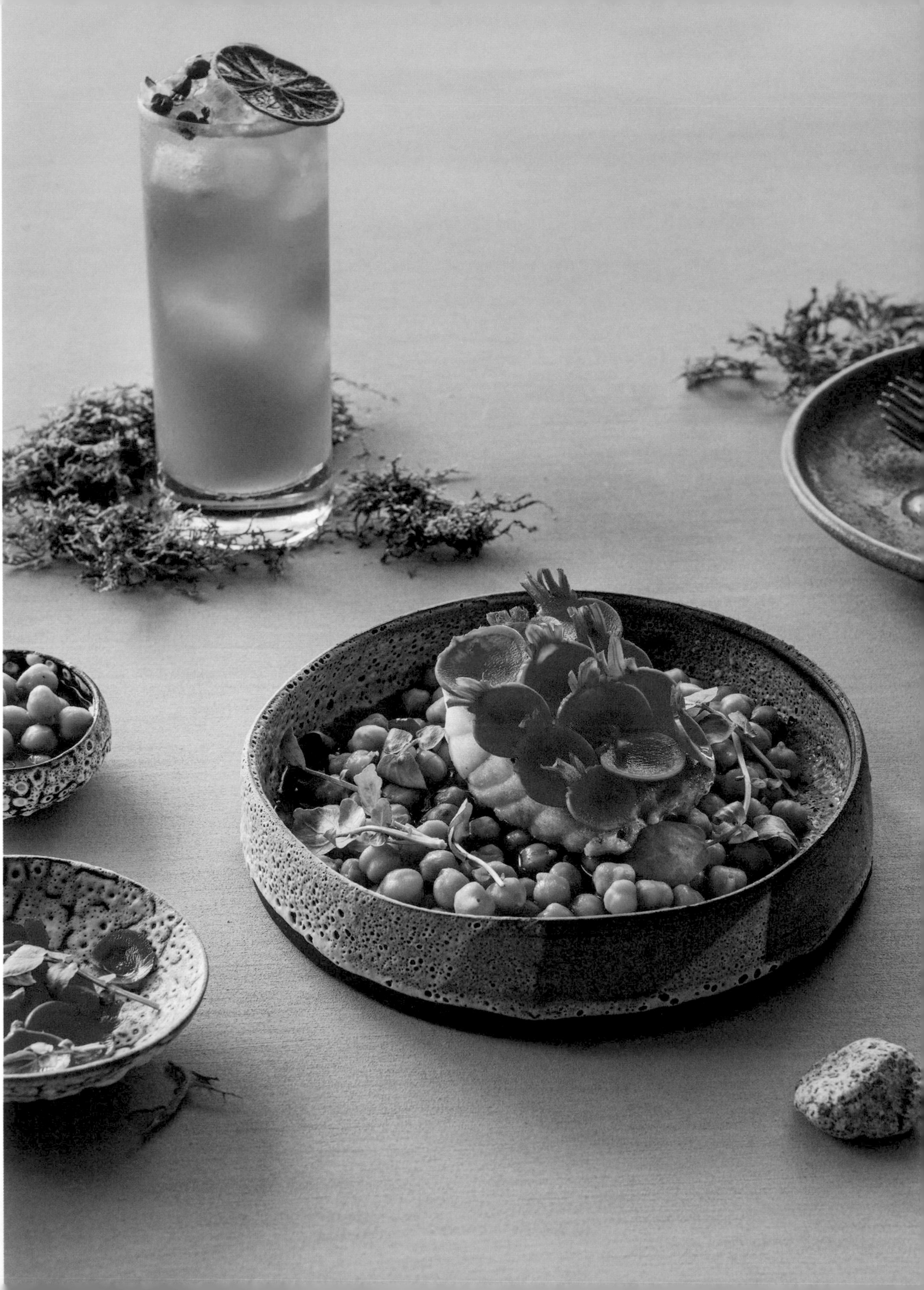

CHICKPEAS

1 cup dried chickpeas, soaked
   overnight in water,
   or 2 (540-mL) cans chickpeas
⅓ cup extra-virgin olive oil
2 shallots, finely chopped
2 cloves garlic, finely chopped,
   plus 1 clove, finely grated (divided)

1 sprig fresh thyme
1 bay leaf
1½ to 2 cups water, or as needed
1 Tbsp red wine vinegar
3 Tbsp chopped roasted red bell peppers
1 tsp smoked paprika
Salt and freshly ground black pepper,
   to taste

LING COD

4 (4-oz) skinless ling cod fillets
Salt, to taste
2 Tbsp grapeseed oil
2 Tbsp unsalted butter
12 to 20 slices *jah choy* (fermented
   radish, available at Asian markets)
   (optional)
Sprigs of watercress, pea shoots or
   other greens, for garnish (optional)

Ling Cod with Chickpeas and Fermented Radish

SERVES 4

This dish makes the most of humble ingredients—ling cod and chickpeas—spicing them up with earthy, smoky flavours. Versatile and easy to cook, ling cod is a sustainable fish native to the northeastern Pacific. Start it the night before you plan to serve it, although in a pinch you could always replace the dried chickpeas with canned ones. If you do use dried chickpeas, try the ones from Vancouver-based GRAIN (eatgrain. ca), which sources single-farm organic pulses from Saskatchewan.

CHICKPEAS Drain chickpeas and discard soaking liquid. (If using canned, drain the liquid in the can and rinse the chickpeas in a colander.)

Heat oil in a large saucepan over medium heat. Add shallots and chopped garlic and sauté for 10 minutes, until shallots are softened. Add thyme and bay leaf.

Add chickpeas and pour in enough water to cover. Bring to a boil, then reduce heat to medium-low and simmer for 1 hour, until the chickpeas are just tender. (If using canned chickpeas, simmer for only 20 minutes or so.) Set aside to cool.

Stir in vinegar, grated garlic, red peppers and smoked paprika. Season with salt and pepper to taste.

LING COD Pat fish dry with a paper towel, then season with salt.

Heat oil in a frying pan over medium-high heat. Add fish, reduce heat to medium and cook for 2 minutes. Flip the fish, add butter and melt until foamy. Drizzle butter over the fish and baste for 3 minutes, until fish is just cooked through.

Divide the chickpeas between 4 plates, then arrange fish on top of chickpeas. If you like, garnish each piece with a few slices of fermented radish and/or a sprig or two of watercress, pea shoots or other greens. Serve immediately.

Tacofino

THERE WAS A time—and it was not so long ago—that a visit to Tofino meant a pilgrimage to the orange food truck parked in the Live to Surf parking lot. Now, luckily, Tacofino has come to us, with two trucks and four bricks-and-mortar locations in Vancouver and one in Victoria, as well as the original truck in Tuff City, to satisfy all our fish taco and Diablo cookie needs.

"Tacofino is a growing collection of beautiful spaces where we serve delicious, fresh and affordable food and drinks, while making people feel like they're at the beach—or at least, very near to one," explains Kaeli Robinsong, who co-founded Tacofino with her husband, Jason Sussman. The duo, named two of *Western Living* magazine's Foodies of the Year in 2015, are also parents of young children; clearly, keeping busy is what keeps them going.

She describes the food as "Mexi-Cali cuisine with an environmental and nutritional conscience." That means Ocean Wise seafood and local ingredients when possible, as well as zesty margaritas and thirst-quenching micheladas and plenty of tortillas topped with everything from chorizo and braised pork al pastor to cauliflower, squash, steak, vegetable scrapple and, of course, fish.

"Our fish taco put us on the map, but I still love our nachos," she says. "There's nothing better than sharing a good plate of nachos, and I feel like we got them right."

½ cup canola oil, plus extra for greasing

1½ cups all-purpose flour

1 cup cocoa powder

1 tsp baking soda

½ to 1 tsp ground cayenne pepper

1 tsp ground cinnamon

1 cup chocolate chips

2 large eggs

1 cup firmly packed brown sugar

1 cup granulated sugar

3 Tbsp finely grated ginger or ginger juice

1 Tbsp pure vanilla extract

1 tsp kosher salt or granulated sugar, for sprinkling

Chocolate Diablo Cookies

MAKES 12 LARGE

Chocolate and spice and everything nice—that's what these cookies are made of. These are huge and cakey, with a thrill of heat running through them. Totally irresistible.

Preheat oven to 375°F. Lightly grease 2 baking sheets with oil or line with parchment paper.

In a large bowl, sift together flour, cocoa, baking soda, cayenne and cinnamon and mix well. Stir in chocolate chips.

In a separate medium bowl, whisk eggs. Add both sugars, ½ cup oil, ginger (or ginger juice) and vanilla. Add flour mixture and stir until combined.

Using a ¼-cup measure, scoop 6 portions of dough onto each baking sheet, evenly spaced 2 inches apart. Using the bottom of the measuring cup, flatten cookies slightly. Sprinkle dough with salt or sugar.

Bake one pan at a time in centre of oven for 11 to 13 minutes, until cookies start to crack but are still fudgy in the middle. Cool on wire racks, then serve.

CHICKEN STOCK (SEE NOTE)

Bones from 2 free-range chickens

2 whole dried ancho chilies

4 L water

TORTILLA SOUP

1 Tbsp vegetable oil

1 cup chopped onion

8 cups Chicken Stock (see here)

5 Tbsp fresh lime juice

Salt, to taste

GARNISH

Roasted chicken meat, shredded

Ripe avocado, sliced

Aged white cheddar, grated

Sour cream

Fresh cilantro leaves

Corn chips

Lime, cut into wedges

Hot sauce (preferably Valentina)

NOTE:

It's best to make your own stock from scratch, but if you're in a rush, you can use a good-quality store-bought chicken stock instead. When you make the soup, sauté the onions, then add 1 tablespoon ancho chili powder and cook for 1 minute, until fragrant. Add 4 litres of chicken stock and simmer for 15 minutes.

Tortilla Soup

MAKES 4

Jason Sussman and Kaeli Robinsong worked together to develop their take on the classic Mexi-Cali soup. It gets added heat from ancho chilies, plus satisfying layers of texture with chicken, cheese, avocados and crunchy corn chips. It's a meal in a bowl that will have you craving more.

CHICKEN STOCK Place bones and chilies in a pot and cover with water. Simmer for at least 6 hours, then strain. Pick out the ancho chilies and peel them. Discard the stem and most of the seeds, and chop up the chilies before returning them to the stock.

TORTILLA SOUP Heat oil in a large stockpot over medium heat, add onions and lightly sauté for 10 minutes, until softened. Pour in stock and bring to a boil over high heat. Reduce heat to medium-low and simmer for 15 minutes. Add lime juice aand season with salt to taste.

Ladle soup into 4 bowls and garnish each bowl with chicken meat, avocado, cheddar, sour cream, cilantro and corn chips. Serve with more corn chips, lime wedges and hot sauce.

Thierry Café

WHERE TO START? Perhaps with a jasmine macaron or citrus madeleine, or maybe a slice of deep, rich chocolate tart or a cream-layered *mille feuille*. Hmm. Would it be so wrong to have one of each?

Walking into Thierry Café is like entering a chocolate box filled with sweet, pretty, utterly irresistible things. Display cabinets circle round, tempting you with all the treasures of a classic French patisserie from tarts to tuiles. And there, standing behind all the magic, is Thierry Busset, a classically trained French pastry chef who came to Canada in 2000 and, luckily enough for the city's sweet tooths (sweet teeth?), never left.

He'd been working at the Michelin-starred Le Gavroche in London when he heard about Vancouver and thought it seemed like a nice place to visit and just maybe make a few croissants and *canelés*. He brought with him a tradition of making everything from scratch, even the candied orange peel, as well as his famous recipe for apple tart. "The apple tart is pretty much me," he says. "Marco Pierre White put it in his book, but it has been a family recipe forever. What makes it different is the way I slice it and put the apple on top."

In Vancouver, he would meet Toptable Group's founder Jack Evrensel and begin a seventeen-year career with one of Vancouver's leading restaurateurs. His journey would take him to Ouest and then to CinCin Ristorante (page 84), where he added Italian treats like tiramisu to his repertoire. But all the time, he knew that what he really wanted was to open his own pastry shop. In 2011, all the stars and sablés aligned, and he opened Thierry Café.

Now Vancouver has a little slice of French heaven on Alberni Street, where people can enjoy coffee and croissants, sandwiches and even a glass of wine. Close your eyes, and you can imagine you're on the boulevards of Paris. As for Busset, he's happy to be right here. "Me, I enjoy pretty much everywhere I go," he says, "but Vancouver I love."

VANILLA ICE CREAM
2 cups whole milk
½ cup heavy (36%) cream
1 vanilla bean, split lengthwise
6 large egg yolks
⅔ cup granulated sugar

RASPBERRY COULIS
1 lb frozen raspberries
⅓ cup granulated sugar

OLIVE OIL–ROASTED CHERRIES
3 Tbsp extra-virgin olive oil
2 lbs fresh cherries (about 8 cups),
    cut in half and pitted
1 cup Raspberry Coulis (see here)
Splash of kirsch

Vanilla Ice Cream with Olive Oil–Roasted Cherries

SERVES 4

Adding raspberry coulis to the cherries boosts the intensity of the cherry flavour, so vibrant against the rich creaminess of a classic vanilla ice cream. If you don't have time to make your own ice cream, you can, of course, use a purchased one.

VANILLA ICE CREAM Place ice cream machine bowl in freezer at least 24 hours before churning.

In a small saucepan, combine milk and cream. Scrape in vanilla seeds. Bring to a boil and immediately remove from heat.

In a heatproof bowl, whisk egg yolks and sugar until pale yellow. Pour 1 tablespoon of hot cream mixture into yolk mixture and whisk. Carefully whisk in another 2 tablespoons of hot cream, then slowly add rest, whisking constantly. Return to the pan and heat over medium heat, until temperature reaches 170°F (be careful not to go above 180°F or the mixture will curdle).

Strain through a fine-mesh sieve, then cool in fridge overnight.

Pour cooled mixture into an ice cream maker and freeze according to the manufacturer's instructions.

RASPBERRY COULIS Defrost the raspberries and mix with the sugar. Purée in a blender or food processor until smooth, then strain through a fine-mesh sieve. It can be stored for up to 3 months in the freezer.

OLIVE OIL–ROASTED CHERRIES Heat oil in a frying pan over medium-high heat. Add cherries and heat for 10 minutes, until warmed through but not too softened.

Add in raspberry coulis and a splash of kirsch and bring to a simmer. Pour into a serving dish.

TO SERVE Remove ice cream from freezer and set aside for 10 minutes. Transfer to bowls and serve with olive-oil roasted cherries.

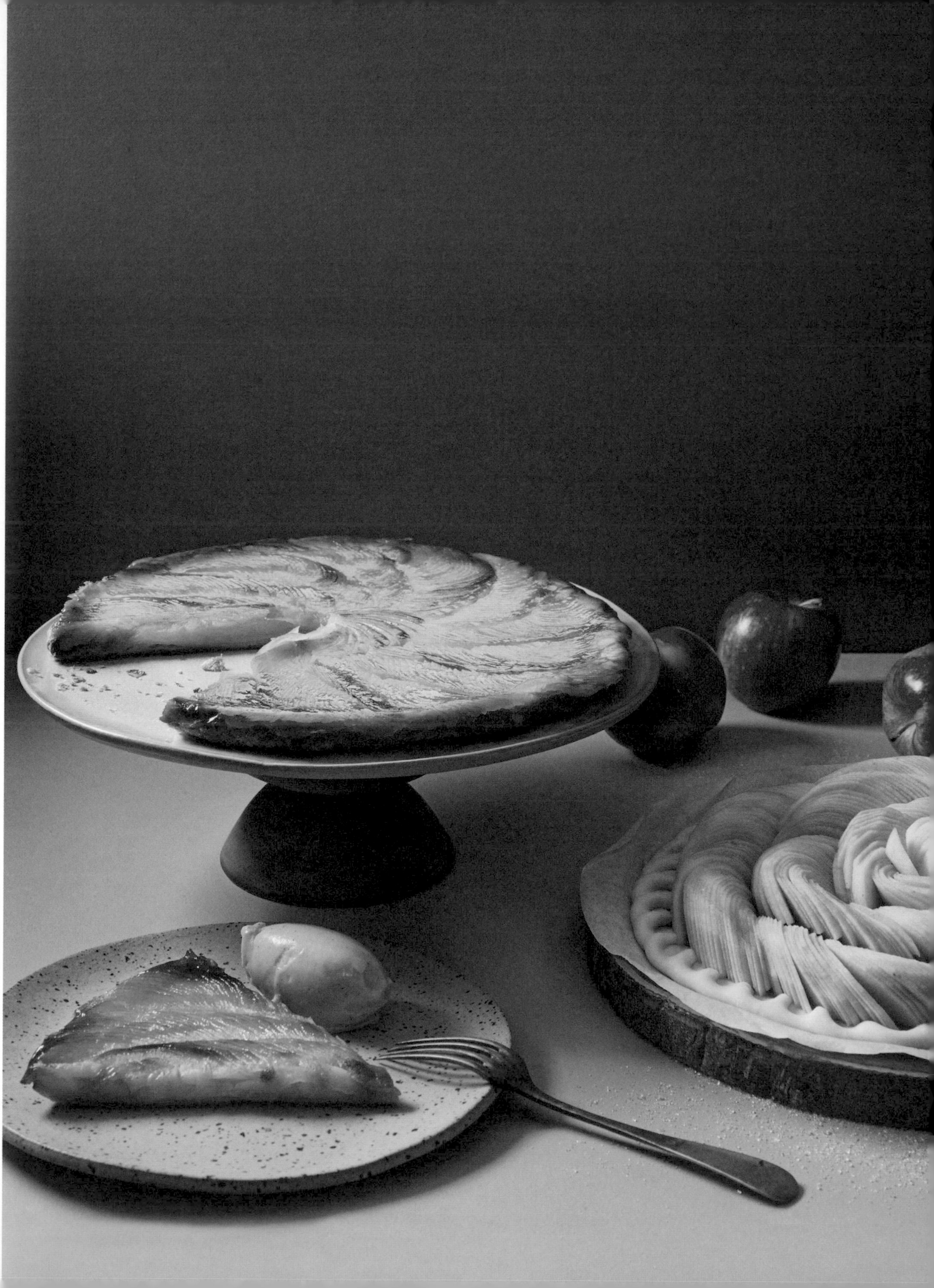

QUICK PUFF PASTRY

2 cups all-purpose flour, plus extra for dusting

1 cup (2 sticks) cold unsalted butter, cut into cubes

½ tsp kosher salt

½ cup ice-cold water

APPLES

10 cooking apples such as Golden Delicious, peeled, cored, cut in half and thinly sliced

¾ cup granulated sugar

⅔ cup (1⅓ sticks) unsalted butter, melted

1 to 2 Tbsp Grand Marnier

Apple Tart

SERVES 6

This is the tart Chef Thierry Busset made famous: crisp and caramelized, sophisticated and just plain delicious. Here he offers a cheater's version of puff pastry—no laminating it around a block of butter—but if you are completely pressed for time, you could always use a good-quality frozen puff pastry instead.

QUICK PUFF PASTRY Pour flour on a clean counter and make a well. Place butter and salt in the centre. Using your fingertips, gently work butter into the flour, until cubes of butter have broken into pea-sized pieces and the dough is grainy. Gradually add ice-cold water until incorporated, taking care to not overwork the dough. Roll dough into a ball, cover with plastic wrap and chill for 20 minutes.

Liberally dust the counter with flour and roll dough into a rectangle, about 16 × 8 inches. Fold it into 3 like a letter and give it a quarter turn. Roll this piece of dough back out into another 16- × 8-inch rectangle. Fold it into 3 again. These are your first 2 turns. Wrap this piece in plastic wrap and chill for another 30 minutes.

Give the chilled dough 2 more turns, as previously noted above. Wrap and chill for another 30 minutes. Dough is now ready.

Preheat oven to 375°F. Line a rimless baking sheet with parchment paper.

On a floured surface, roll out puff pastry ¼ inch thick. Cut it into a 12-inch-diameter circle. Place the dough on the prepared baking sheet. Fold outside 2 inches inward over your finger to create an edge. (Or, if you prefer, you can cut the dough into small rectangles for individual tarts.) Set aside in the fridge until ready to bake.

APPLES Fan apples out onto puff pastry starting from the outside and working your way in, making sure to pack them tightly. Once surface of puff pastry is totally covered with apples, sprinkle with sugar and top with melted butter.

Bake for 30 minutes, until golden brown and starting to caramelize. Remove from oven and sprinkle Grand Marnier over entire tart. Cover tart with a sheet of parchment paper and place another rimless baking sheet on top. Carefully flip so that the tart is on the second pan, with pastry-side up. Bake for another 10 minutes until puff pastry is golden brown.

Set baking sheet on a wire rack and cool slightly. Flip tart back over onto serving plate and peel parchment gently off the top.

Thomas Haas Chocolates & Pâtisserie

ON A BUSY Saturday, if the lineup at his North Shore location gets too long, the soft-spoken Thomas Haas might pop out from the kitchen at the back to pass around his famous Sparkle cookies. On weekdays, kids drift over from the school across the street to search for the chocolates he has left in well-known hiding places. Anytime at all, there's a steady stream of customers yearning for his salted caramels and croissants, galettes and Danishes, macarons and prettily painted truffles.

Modestly, the German-born pastry chef describes his sweet little slice of paradise as "a contemporary patisserie and chocolate shop with a distinct European flair." He leaves out the bit about how no Vancouver party would be complete without Thomas Haas chocolates, or how people order them from all over the world or how he was named one of the top ten chocolatiers in North America, back when he worked in New York.

"My most memorable moments are the daily interactions with happy customers, many of whom have been loyal to us and our creations for years," he says, then slips in slyly, "Supplying the White House and two presidents of the United States with our chocolates for over eight years was one of our best-kept secrets."

Until he opened his second location in Kitsilano, his double-baked almond croissant, with its shatteringly crispy exterior and sweet almond cream filling, was one of the few foodstuffs that would entice Vancouverites across the bridge to North Van. Now, luckily, he also sells his chocolate bars at Whole Foods, *viennoiseries* at select cafés and chocolates online. The more Thomas Haas, the better a place this world will be.

RHUBARB COMPOTE

2 cups finely chopped rhubarb

1 Tbsp fresh lemon juice

¼ cup granulated sugar

Pinch of salt

½ vanilla bean, split lengthwise

CRÈME BRÛLÉE

2 cups heavy (36%) cream

½ cup whole milk

1 vanilla bean, split lengthwise

5 large egg yolks

½ cup granulated sugar, plus extra to brûlée

Rhubarb Crème Brûlée

SERVES 8

The tartness of rhubarb is a perfect foil for the creamy sweetness of the custard in this updated classic dessert. You will need a kitchen torch to create the sugar crackle on the top.

RHUBARB COMPOTE In a saucepan, combine rhubarb, lemon juice, sugar and salt. Scrape in vanilla seeds and cook over low heat for 20 minutes, until rhubarb softens and mixture thickens. Remove from heat, then set aside to cool.

In 8 (6-oz) ramekins, add enough rhubarb compote to cover the bottoms in a single layer. Put ramekins in the freezer for 20 to 30 minutes, until compote sets.

CRÈME BRÛLÉE Combine cream and milk in a saucepan over low heat. Scrape vanilla seeds into pan and bring to a simmer.

In a separate bowl, whisk yolks and sugar together until pale. Very slowly stir in hot cream mixture until well blended. (Avoid overmixing— this will incorporate too much air into the custard.)

Preheat oven to 300°F. Set a kettle of water to boil.

Remove ramekins from the freezer and arrange them in a deep baking dish. Pour custard into the ramekins, filling each three-quarters full.

Fill baking dish with boiling water until it reaches halfway up the outside of the ramekins and bake for 1 hour, until set. (Jiggle dish slightly and if the centre is not moving anymore, the custard is done.) Carefully remove from the baking dish and chill overnight before serving.

Sprinkle 1 generous teaspoon of sugar over each custard, then caramelize using a kitchen torch.

CHOCOLATE HAZELNUT CHANTILLY
1 cup chopped *gianduja* (see Note)
2 cups heavy (36%) cream

NOTE:
Gianduja is an Italian sweet chocolate and hazelnut confection from Turin, Italy. It is sold both as a candy and as a spread for baking. Spreadable *gianduja* is available at some gourmet stores and baking supply shops.

PASTRY CREAM
2 cups whole milk
6 large egg yolks
½ cup granulated sugar
⅓ cup cornstarch
⅓ cup (⅔ stick) unsalted butter, room temperature
½ cup praline paste (see Note)

NOTE:
Praline paste is made by creating a brittle of sugar and toasted hazelnuts, letting it harden, and then grinding it until it forms a paste. It is sometimes available at gourmet markets, baking supply stores or online. If you can't find it, replace with hazelnut or almond butter and ¼ cup sugar.

CHOUX PASTRY
⅔ cup water
½ cup whole milk
1½ tsp granulated sugar
½ cup + 2 Tbsp (1¼ sticks) unsalted butter
Pinch of salt
1¼ cups all-purpose flour
7 large eggs

ASSEMBLY (OPTIONAL)
Chocolate pieces, to decorate
Chopped hazelnut, to decorate

Hazelnut Praline Eclair

MAKES 24

Eclairs are having a moment. They are little logs of light-as-air choux pastry filled with cream, and they are easier to make than you might think. You will need a pastry bag with a large star tip, though. And be sure to make the chocolate hazelnut Chantilly the night before you fill your eclairs.

CHOCOLATE HAZELNUT CHANTILLY Put gianduja in a bowl. Bring cream to a boil, then pour into the bowl and stir until smooth. Cool the mixture at least 6 hours and preferably overnight.

PASTRY CREAM Bring milk to a simmer in a medium saucepan.

In a separate bowl, whisk yolks, sugar and cornstarch together until smooth.

When milk comes to a boil, pour it very slowly into yolk mixture while stirring constantly. Pour mixture back into saucepan and bring just to a boil; the mixture should reach 170°F and be thickened.

In another bowl, combine butter and praline paste. Pour in hot custard mixture and whisk until everything comes together. Set the bowl in a larger bowl of ice water and continue whisking until it cools down. Put plastic wrap overtop, right on the surface of the custard, and chill for at least 2 hours before using.

CHOUX PASTRY Preheat oven to 350°F. Line a baking sheet with parchment paper.

In a medium saucepan, combine water, milk, sugar, butter and salt. Bring to a simmer over medium heat, then add flour. Stir until dough comes away from the sides and bottom of pan and cook for 1 minute. Remove from heat.

In a stand mixer fitted with a paddle attachment, mix dough until it cools down slightly. Slowly add eggs, one at a time. Beat until smooth and glossy. The dough should form a soft peak.

Transfer batter into a piping bag with a large star tip, then pipe into 5-inch-long lines on prepared baking sheet. Bake for 30 to 40 minutes, until almost doubled in size. Be careful not to open the oven door too early on (this might deflate the eclairs). Set aside and cool completely.

ASSEMBLY Trim tops of eclairs, then pipe and fill with pastry cream. Whip up praline Chantilly and pipe on top of eclair in a spiral pattern. Decorate with chocolate and hazelnut pieces (if using) before serving.

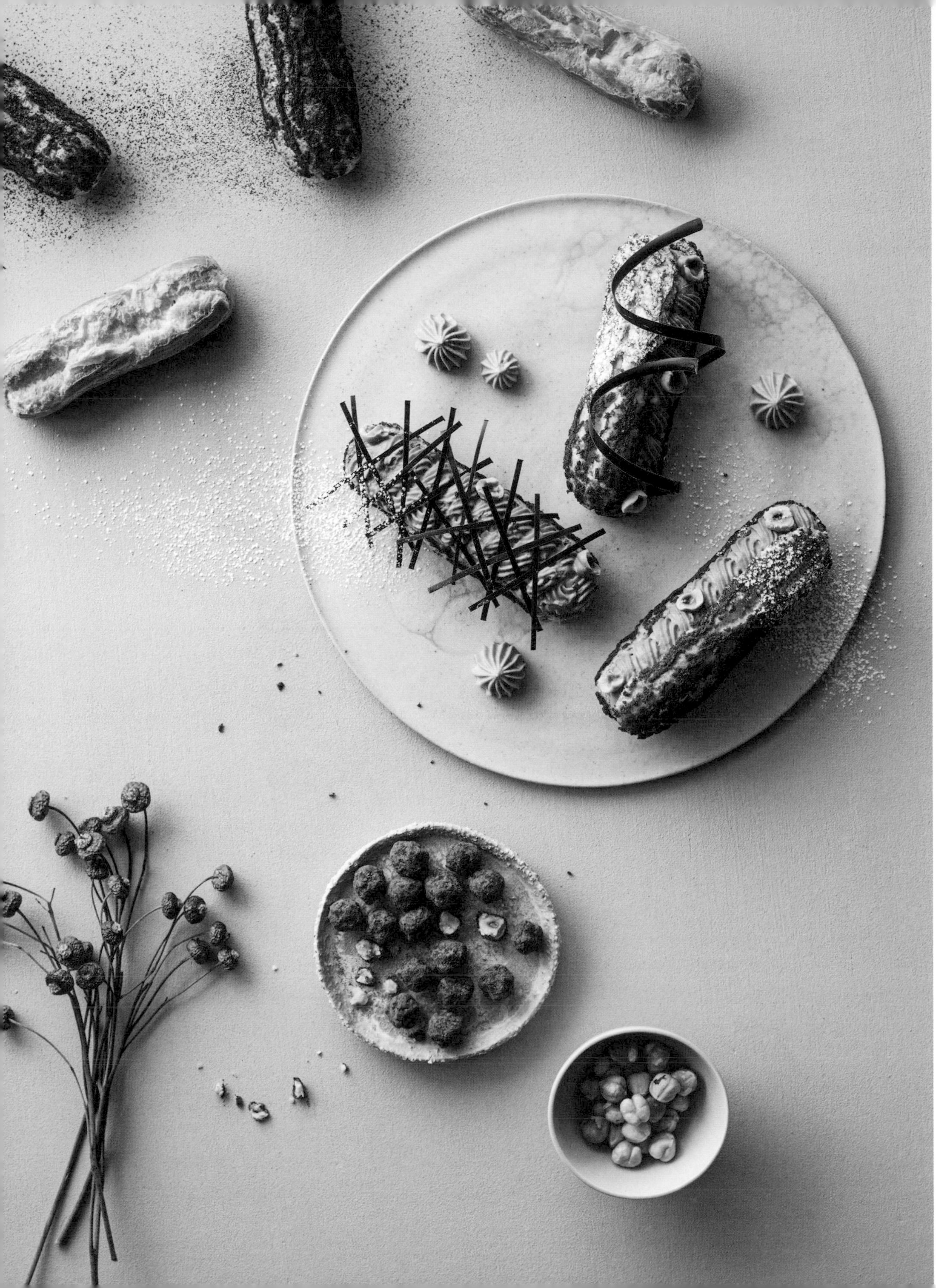

CLEMENT CHAN

Torafuku

THE NAME MEANS "Lucky Tiger," and lucky is just how Clement Chan feels these days. "The most exciting thing for me was to take a small truck business and turn it into a restaurant and maintain our clientele," he says.

He first learned to cook from his grandmother, helping her roll wontons and dumplings in her Szechuan restaurant. Later, as a professional cook, he spent years working at high-end restaurants around the city and winning awards along the way. Then a decade or so ago, he started travelling, mostly to Asia. "That opened my eyes a little more," Chan says. "That's when I partnered up to open Le Tigre."

By 2012, his Le Tigre food truck had hit the road, and hungry Vancouverites were lining up for the big, bold flavours of his modern Asian street food, the wonderfully messy Kickass Rice Bowl, Crack Salad and Po Pork Bun. Three years later, he decided to create a bricks-and-mortar version of the truck and, with his business partner Steven Kuan, opened Torafuku on Main Street, on the rapidly gentrifying border of Chinatown. "We wanted it to be a little more high-end, but still affordable," he says.

The decor was simple and modern. Cocktails, beer and wine were added to the menu, and favourite dishes were fancied up, just a little. Take that signature rice bowl, now rebranded Kickass Rice 2.0 and made into an *aburi*-style sushi roll topped with torched pork belly, crunchy sesame seeds and crumbled nori. But he never stopped making food designed to grab your taste buds' attention.

And what about those names? Rabbit Food. Get in My Belly. Flaming Lambo. Taco 'Bout Awesome. "The whole concept was to make people read the menu—but also to make it fun," he says with a laugh. "I just do a riff on meals that inspire me."

1 cup dried shiitake mushrooms

1 cup dried wood ear mushrooms

4 Japanese eggplants, peeled and cut in half lengthwise

3 Tbsp canola oil, plus extra for drizzling (divided)

Salt and freshly ground black pepper, to taste

1 white onion, finely chopped

10 oz king oyster mushrooms, stems removed and finely chopped

1 bunch kale, stems removed and leaves finely chopped

2 cups grape tomatoes, cut in half

2 cups shredded green cabbage

13 oz *konnyaku* (konjac), finely chopped (see Note)

1 Tbsp finely chopped garlic

1½ cups chopped fresh basil

1 package round wonton wrappers

Soy sauce, to taste

Sesame oil, to taste

Sliced green onions, to taste, for garnish

NOTE:
Konjac is a tuber-like vegetable often used in Asian cooking, especially in Japan. It is sometimes called an elephant yam, although it is not technically a yam at all. It is the corm of a lily-like flower and is typically made into noodles called *shirataki* or into *konnyaku*, which is sold in a greyish block. Both are available in the fridge section at Fujiya.

Lucky Dumplings

MAKES 24

The lucky one is you—you get to eat these tender dumplings stuffed with all sorts of savoury deliciousness. The key is to make sure the dumplings are well sealed so the filling doesn't burst out when they are cooking.

Preheat oven to 375°F.

Put shiitake mushrooms in one large bowl and wood ears in another. Pour 4 cups of boiling water into each bowl and set aside for 30 minutes, until softened. Drain and discard liquid. Remove stems, then coarsely chop the caps.

Place eggplants on a baking sheet, drizzle with oil and season with salt and pepper. Roast for 10 to 20 minutes, until soft.

Meanwhile, heat 1 tablespoon oil in a large frying pan over medium-high heat, add mushrooms and sauté for 10 to 15 minutes, until soft. Season with salt and pepper. Set aside.

Wipe pan clean, heat another 1 tablespoon oil over medium-high heat, add onions and sauté for 10 minutes, until softened and translucent.

Remove eggplants from oven and set aside to cool. Mash, then drain out any extra liquid. Put them in a large mixing bowl, add all mushrooms (including king oysters), kale, tomatoes, cabbage, and konjac and mix well. Add garlic, basil and salt and pepper.

To make dumplings, place ½ tablespoon of filling in the middle of a wonton wrapper. Brush water around the edges of dumpling wrapper, then fold in half and crimp 5 to 6 times until sealed. Repeat until you run out of filling or wrappers.

Bring a large saucepan of water to a boil. Carefully lower dumplings into pan, working in batches of 6 pieces, and cook for 1 or 2 minutes, until they float to the surface. Using a slotted spoon or spider, transfer onto a plate or into a bowl. Drizzle with soy sauce and sesame oil and garnish with green onion. Serve immediately.

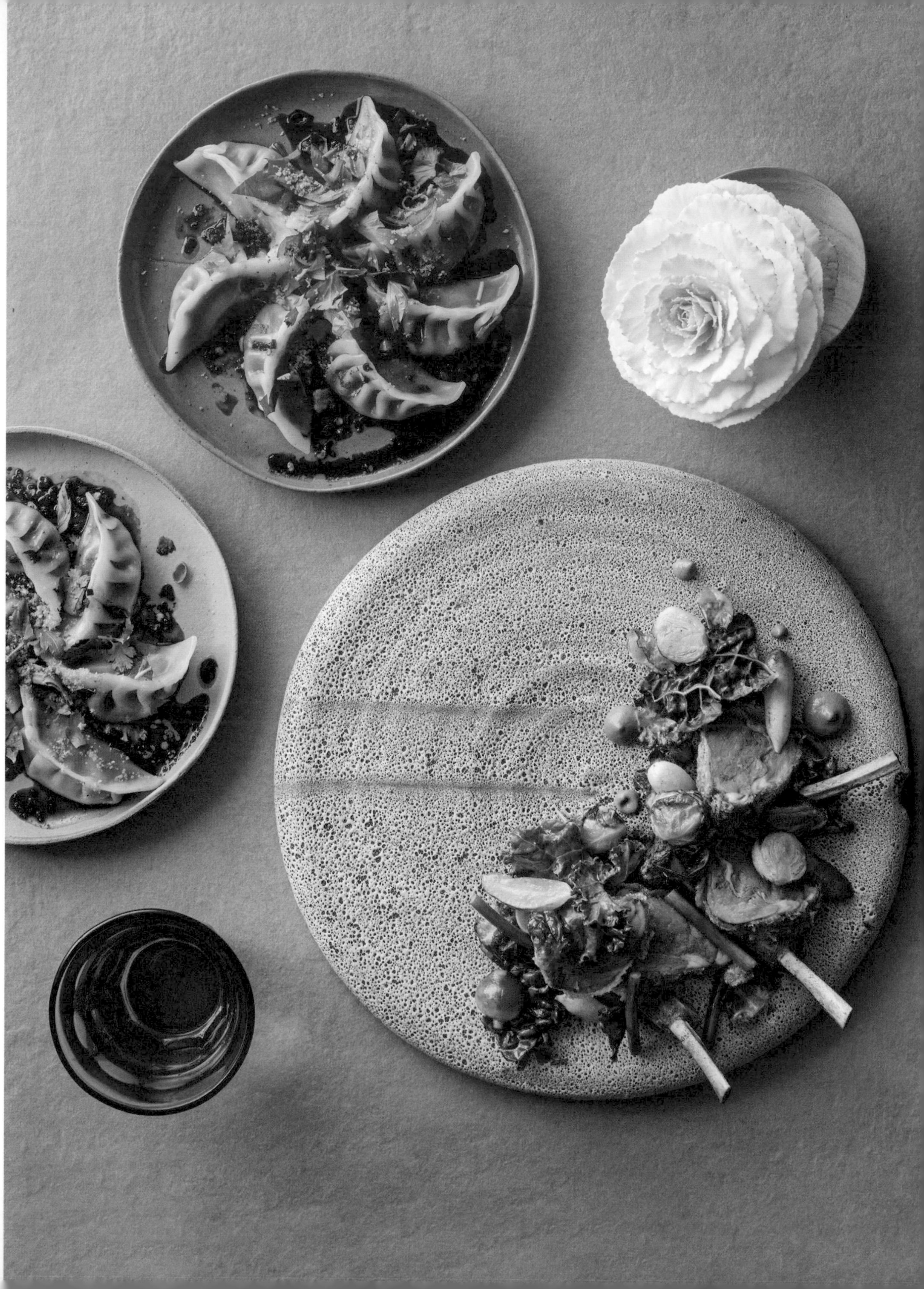

CHIMICHURRI

1 bunch fresh cilantro,
  leaves only, chopped
1 bunch fresh Italian parsley,
  leaves only, chopped
2 cloves garlic
2 Tbsp capers
½ to 1 cup rice vinegar
1 cup grapeseed oil

VEGETABLES

2 Tbsp vegetable oil
2 cloves garlic, chopped
10 Brussels sprouts,
  cut into quarters
6 baby red radishes, cut in half
1 bunch garlic scapes, cut into
  bite-sized pieces
Shaoxing cooking wine or
  vegetable stock, to taste
1 bunch green kale, stems
  removed and leaves chopped
2 Tbsp soy sauce
Salt and freshly ground black
  pepper, to taste

LAMB

1 cup sake *kasu* (see Note)
1 cup sake
1 (18- to 20-oz) rack of lamb,
  Frenched (ask your butcher)
  and sliced into chops
Salt and freshly ground black
  pepper, to taste

TEMPURA BATTER

1 cup gluten-free tempura flour
  (divided)
2 pinches *shichimi togarashi*
2 cups soda water
Vegetable oil, for deep-frying
Salt and freshly ground black
  pepper, to taste

NOTE:

Sake *kasu* is the lees
from sake production
and can be found at
Artisan SakeMaker
on Granville Island.

Rack 'Em Up

Clement Chan loves his funny, punny names for dishes, and this one is no exception. It's a flavourful and sophisticated appetizer that you may want to double or triple for a crowd.

CHIMICHURRI Place all ingredients except oil into a blender or food processor and process until well blended. With the motor still running, gradually add oil and blend until emulsified. Set aside.

VEGETABLES Heat oil in a large frying pan over medium-high heat, add garlic and sauté for 1 minute, until fragrant. Add Brussels sprouts and sauté for another 2 minutes, until light brown. Add radishes and garlic scapes and sauté for another 2 minutes.

Add a splash of Shaoxing wine (or stock) and kale, adding more wine if you need it. Season with soy sauce, salt and pepper. Set aside and keep warm.

LAMB Put sake *kasu* and sake in a blender and blend until smooth. Season lamb with salt and pepper, then coat with sake *kasu* paste.

Heat a frying pan over medium-high heat, then sear lamb chops for 2 minutes on each side, until browned. Set aside.

TEMPURA BATTER Place ½ cup tempura flour into a mixing bowl and stir in *shichimi togarashi*. Mix in soda water.

Pour oil into a deep-fryer or a deep saucepan and heat to a temperature of 375°F. Put remaining ½ cup gluten-free tempura flour in a shallow plate and dredge lamb. Dip lamb into tempura batter and shake off any excess. Carefully lower lamb into pan, taking care not to splash hot oil. Deep-fry for 3 minutes, until golden. Transfer to a plate lined with paper towels and set aside to rest for 30 seconds. Season with salt and pepper.

Smear chimichurri on a platter, arrange lamb chops randomly and fill gaps with vegetables. Serve immediately.

Two Rivers Specialty Meats

THE TWO RIVERS are the Lillooet River and Ryan Creek, which meet in Pemberton where Jason Pleym and Margot Millerd married. But they are also the twin streams of sustainability and flavour that flow through every chop, sausage and steak they sell.

It's hard to remember what dining in Vancouver was like before Two Rivers Specialty Meats came along. In just a decade, Pleym and Millerd made us care how ethically our meat was raised, how locally it was sourced and how compassionately it was harvested. Pleym also introduced us to cuts we'd never tasted before: flat iron, chuck eye, bavette and stiletto.

But until 2017, all of that delicious protein was only available to chefs and those who subscribed to the grocery delivery service Spud or bulk-ordered through the Two Rivers website. Then they opened "Two Rivers Specialty Meats—The Shop" in North Vancouver and changed everything all over again.

Here, in the Shop, meat is cut the old-fashioned way, hand-carved along muscle seams. That's because Pleym believes in doing things traditionally, the way that's authentic and real, even if it also happens to be the hard way. It goes back to when he and Millerd first opened Two Rivers in 2007 with nothing but her father's small herd of Pemberton Meadows Natural Beef to sell. It was too expensive to be ground into hamburger, like 95 percent of commercial beef is. And so Pleym taught himself how to cut meat. "The one beauty is that I didn't know what was expected, and that allowed us to change the process of butchering beef," he says.

But he did know what chefs wanted. James Walt at Araxi (page 28) was the first to buy his meat. Now Pleym's got nearly six hundred restaurant clients across B.C.—including himself, because in addition to the meat case and deli counter, the Shop features a licenced eat-in kitchen where dry-aged beef burgers and succulent ribs are grilled over charcoal.

"I've always had a keen interest in food and cooking," Pleym says. "Being able to work with people who can make food do those things—I love it."

½ lb bacon lardons
2 cups thinly sliced leeks, white
  and light green parts only
2 Tbsp unsalted butter (divided)
8 cups chicken stock
2 to 3 Tbsp extra-virgin olive oil
1 small onion, finely chopped

2 cups arborio rice
1½ cups white wine
½ cup grated Parmesan, plus
  extra for serving
Salt and freshly ground black
  pepper, to taste
Chopped fresh parsley, to taste

Leek Risotto with Bacon Lardons   SERVES 4 TO 6

Jason Pleym, owner of Two Rivers Specialty Meats, cuts rashers of bacon into quarter-inch chunks called lardons—they add a richly sweet, smoky flavour to a risotto that makes a terrific side dish. Be sure to soak and rinse the leeks ahead of time to remove any grit.

In a frying pan over low heat, add lardons and cook for 15 to 20 minutes, stirring occasionally, until fat is rendered and bacon is crispy. Using a slotted spoon, transfer bacon to a plate lined with paper towels.

Add leeks to pan, turn heat to medium and stir until well coated in bacon fat. Add 1 tablespoon butter and cook for 25 to 30 minutes, until very soft. Set aside.

Pour stock into a large saucepan and bring to a boil over high heat. Reduce heat to medium-low and set aside to simmer.

Heat oil in a large frying pan over medium heat. Add onion and sauté for 5 minutes, until softened and translucent. Add rice and stir well, until rice is well coated, slightly translucent and golden. Pour in wine and bring to a boil. Cook for 2 minutes, until the rice has absorbed the wine.

Add a ladle or two of stock, stirring and cooking until the rice has absorbed most of the liquid. Repeat until rice is almost al dente, about 18 minutes. Stir in leeks and lardons. Continue adding stock in small amounts for 7 minutes, until risotto is fully cooked.

Stir in Parmesan and remaining tablespoon butter, season with salt and pepper to taste and then scatter parsley overtop. Serve with more Parmesan.

2 to 3 Tbsp extra-virgin olive oil

3½ lbs beef "stiletto" (hind shank),
cut into 3 pieces

Salt and freshly ground black pepper,
to taste

2 fennel bulbs, chopped

1 onion, chopped

2 to 3 leek tops (the dark green part),
chopped

1 tsp fennel seeds

3 star anise

1 tsp black peppercorns

2 cups beef stock

1 (750-mL) bottle red wine

2 sprigs fresh thyme and/or rosemary

1 or 2 bay leaves (optional)

2 Tbsp cold unsalted butter

Chopped fresh Italian parsley, to taste

Braised Stiletto

SERVES 6

Jason Pleym has identified a new cut of beef called "stiletto," the hind shank, which is perfect for braising. If you can't find it, you could use any tough, flavourful braising cut you like. "Slow-cooking meats with stock and wine and vegetable creates the ultimate centre-plate experience," Pleym says. "The result is tenderness with rich, decadent flavours."

Preheat oven to 300°F.

Heat oil in a large Dutch oven over medium-high heat. Season beef lightly with salt and pepper and add to pot. Sear until browned on all sides. Transfer meat to a plate and set aside.

Add fennel, onion and leek tops to the pot and cook for 5 minutes over medium-high heat, until onion is soft and translucent. Stir in fennel seeds, star anise and peppercorns and cook for another 1 to 2 minutes, until vegetables are lightly browned and aromatic.

Pour in stock and wine and bring just to a boil. Return meat and any accumulated juices to the pot and stir in herbs. Cover and braise in oven for 4 to 4½ hours, until meat is tender.

Remove beef from pot and keep warm and covered while you finish the sauce. Strain cooking liquid through a fine-mesh sieve into a pot to remove any solids, and heat over medium-low heat, until reduced by half. Skim off any fat or impurities that float to the surface.

Season with salt and pepper, then whisk in cold butter just before serving. Cut stilettos in half and place on a serving dish. Pour the sauce over the beef and finish with parsley.

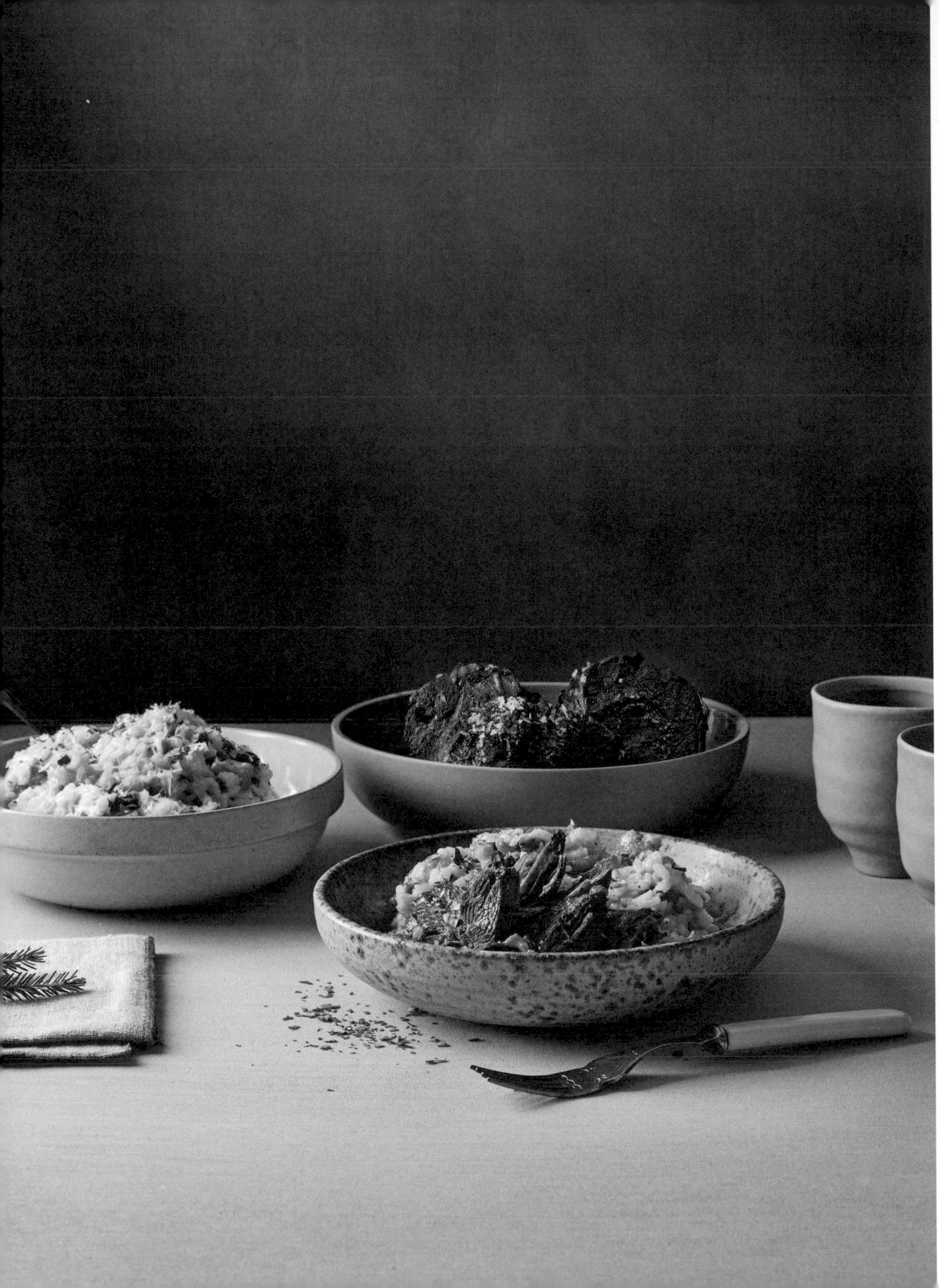

The Union

WHEN THE UNION opened in 2012 on the border between Chinatown and Strathcona, this historic neighbourhood was a bit of a wasteland, overshadowed by the viaducts and abandoned by the streetcar lines that used to run through here. Just a few short years later, it's one of the hippest parts of Vancouver—just like it was back in the day when Nora Hendrix used to work at Vie's Chicken and Steak House around the corner, where her grandson Jimi would hang out as a kid. Yes, *that* Jimi Hendrix. There's even a shrine to the famous rock star, who played his guitar in the area in the early 1960s.

All that goes to say: this hood has a seriously cool vibe, and the Union is a big part of it. Chef Lisa Henderson, who'd worked in Tofino, takes inspiration from the fresh, fragrant flavours of Thailand, the Philippines and Vietnam. Walk in the door, and you're hit by a wave of delicious aromas: mint and cilantro, lime and lemongrass, chilies and spices. Those same spices are at play in the dishes she chose for this book.

"These two recipes are quite the opposite from each other," she says. "The *som tum* salad is light and fresh and perfect for dinner parties—just add dressing a few minutes before serving. The massaman curry is a hearty, filling dish with some definite heat. Best of all, both dishes can be made ahead."

Those exotic flavours find their way into bar manager Rob Hoover's inventive cocktails, too, into drinks like the Tom Yum Collins or the selection of "bangas"—fresh cocktails made in a jar. Everything is prepared fresh, including the syrups and shrubs (drinking vinegars, which are very trendy in cocktail circles), the fruit purées and herbal waters.

The room has a bright, fresh industrial appeal, with reclaimed barnboard, exposed concrete and long community tables designed for good conversations with new friends—and for sharing Henderson's curries, noodle dishes and plates of chicken wings glazed with Asian spices. The ghost of Jimi would be cool with that.

DRESSING

2 cloves garlic, finely chopped

½ cup fresh lime juice

¼ cup grated palm sugar

¼ cup fish sauce

¾ tsp tamarind concentrate (not paste or block; available at Asian markets)

SALAD

1 (1- to 1½-lb) green papaya, cut in half lengthwise and seeds discarded

1 cup grape or cherry tomatoes

1 to 2 bird's-eye chilies, seeded and very thinly sliced

½ bunch fresh cilantro, leaves only, torn

10 fresh mint leaves, torn

½ to ¾ cup crushed toasted peanuts

Pinch of salt

1 lb cooked Ocean Wise shrimp meat

Banana leaves (optional)

Som Tum Salad (Green Papaya Salad)

SERVES 4

Bright, fresh and flavourful, this salad has layer upon layer of sweet, salty, sour and spicy flavours. Ingredients such as green cooking papaya, palm sugar, tamarind concentrate, fish sauce and banana leaves can be found in Chinatown as well as the big Asian markets such as T&T.

DRESSING Combine all ingredients in a bowl and whisk, until sugar has fully dissolved.

SALAD Using a vegetable peeler or sharp knife, remove the peel from the papaya. Using the large holes on a box grater or a food processor fitted with a grating attachment, grate papaya.

In a large bowl, combine papaya, tomatoes, chilies, cilantro, mint, peanuts and salt. Stir in dressing a little at a time to taste, just enough to delicately coat the papaya. Gently stir in shrimp meat. Line 4 plates with banana leaves (if using) and top with salad. Serve.

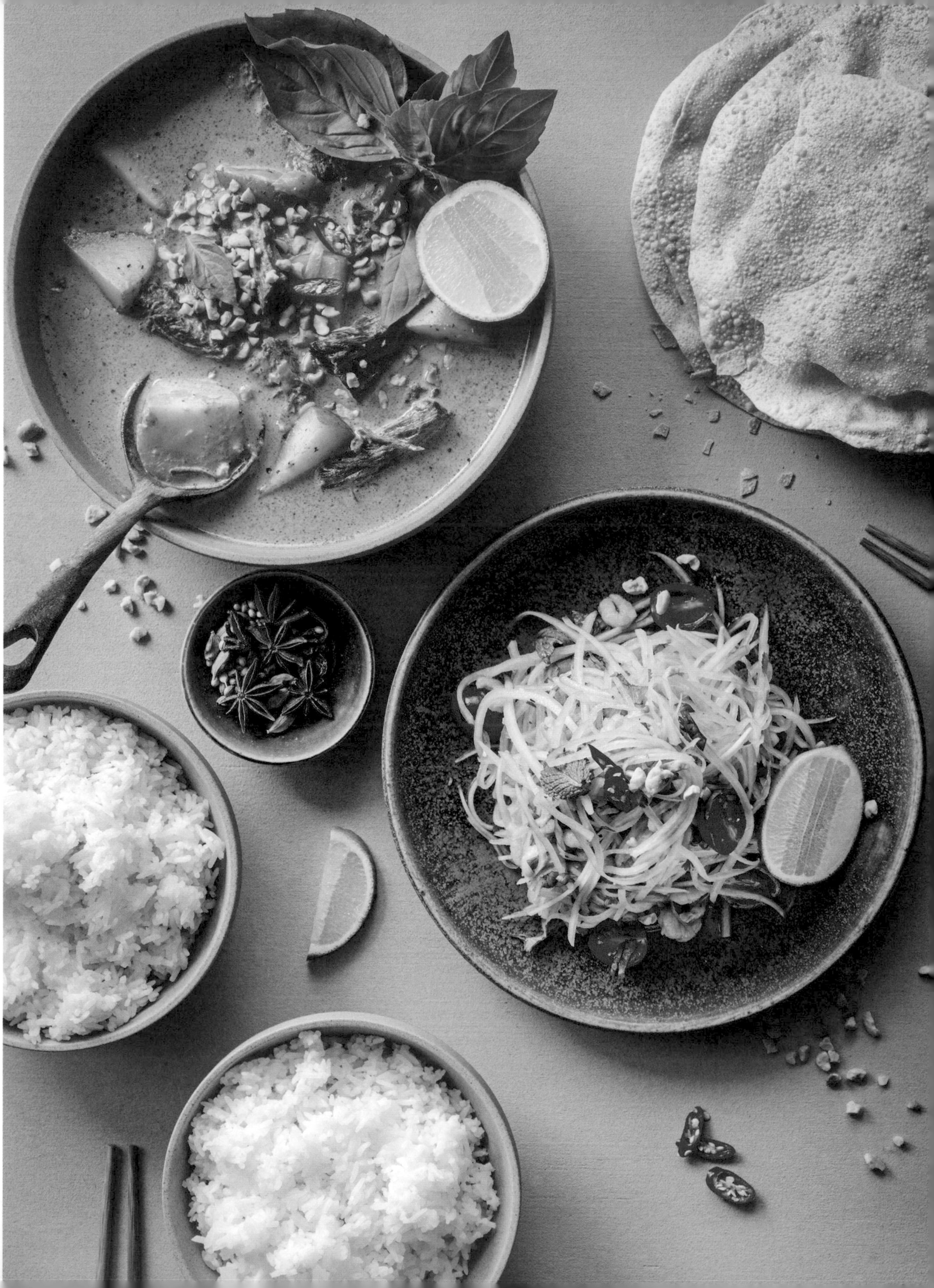

MASSAMAN CURRY PASTE

12 dried bird's-eye chilies

10 cloves garlic

3 stalks lemongrass, tough outer layers removed and thinly sliced

1 shallot, thinly sliced

1 (1½-inch) piece galangal, peeled and thinly sliced

1 Tbsp vegetable oil

6 green cardamom pods

6 cloves

1 (1-inch) piece cinnamon stick

2 Tbsp coriander seeds

2 tsp cumin seeds

½ cup coarsely chopped fresh cilantro root and/or stems

¼ cup salted dry-roasted peanuts

½ tsp ground nutmeg

½ tsp ground turmeric

½ tsp kosher salt

BEEF CURRY

1 cinnamon stick, broken in half

3 star anise

6 green cardamom pods

2 Tbsp vegetable oil

2 lbs quality braising beef (such as boneless short rib or chuck flat), cubed

2 (398-mL) cans coconut milk

3 Tbsp Massaman Curry Paste (see here)

2 Tbsp fish sauce

1 Tbsp tamarind concentrate (not paste or block; available at Asian markets)

2 Tbsp grated palm sugar or brown sugar

2 bay leaves

1 stalk lemongrass, tough outer layers removed, smashed with the back of a knife

3 makrut lime leaves (sometimes called kaffir lime leaves), rubbed between palms to release oils

1 yellow onion, sliced

1 bird's-eye chili, seeded and thinly sliced

5 to 6 small potatoes, cut into quarters

Steamed rice, to serve

Pappadums, to serve

Lime wedges, fresh Thai basil and crushed peanuts, for garnish (optional)

Massaman Beef Curry

SERVES 4

The list of ingredients may look daunting, but it's easy to make as long as you have everything ready to go. As a bonus, you'll have a lot of curry paste that you can freeze and then use at a moment's notice. Note that ingredients such as galangal, lime leaves, lemongrass and Asian spices are readily available in Asian markets.

MASSAMAN CURRY PASTE Preheat oven to 350°F.

Put chilies in a bowl, add warm water and soak for 15 minutes. Drain and pat dry.

In a bowl, combine chilies, garlic, lemongrass, shallots, galangal and oil and toss. Spread on a baking sheet and roast for 6 minutes, until fragrant and chilies are golden brown. Set aside to cool.

Combine cardamom, cloves, cinnamon, coriander and cumin in a small dry frying pan and toast over medium heat for 2 minutes, until fragrant. Set aside to cool. Gently crush cardamom pods, remove seeds and discard pods. Grind spices in coffee grinder or mortar and pestle.

Transfer spices to a food processor, add chili mixture and the rest of the ingredients and process to a smooth paste. Makes about 1 cup. It can be stored, covered, for up to 1 month in the fridge or 6 months in the freezer.

BEEF CURRY Preheat oven to 350°F.

Combine cinnamon stick, star anise and cardamom pods in a cheesecloth sachet.

Heat oil in a large frying pan over medium-high heat. Brown beef in batches and transfer to a Dutch oven or roasting pan. Add 2 tablespoons of the thick cream from the top of the coconut milk to the pan. Cook over medium heat for 20 seconds, until hot. Add curry paste. Cook for 1 minute, stirring, until aromatic. Add to Dutch oven and mix well.

Add remaining coconut milk, fish sauce, tamarind concentrate, sugar, cheesecloth sachet, bay leaves, lemongrass, makrut lime leaves, onion and bird's-eye chili. There should be enough liquid to cover the beef cubes—if necessary, add a little water. Cover Dutch oven or roasting pan with lid or foil and roast in oven for 1 hour.

Add potatoes and cook for another 30 minutes to 1 hour, until meat is fork tender. (The bigger the cubes of beef, the longer it will take.)

Serve with steamed rice and pappadums and garnish with lime wedges, Thai basil and peanuts.

Wildebeest

IN 2012, NOSE-TO-TAIL dining arrived in town on the back of a Wildebeest. Suddenly, we were all scarfing back sweetbreads and heart tartare, chugging sherry through marrow bones and asking for extra duck liver on our poutine.

Some things at Wildebeest have changed since then. For one thing, co-owner Josh Pape says, "We try to be exciting and bold in our flavour combinations, but we're not as offal driven as we were when we first opened." There are more non-meat dishes on the menu, and the restaurant has even hosted some pretty exciting vegetable-forward collaborative dinners.

Others things haven't changed so much. There's still the same stylish industrial-chic decor, the same inventive craft cocktail program and clever wine list, the same genial hospitality from Pape and fellow co-owner James Iranzad, who now own four restaurants (as Gooseneck Hospitality) around the city. Oh, yes—and the bone luge is still the signature dish.

And then there is Alessandro Vianello's hearty, flavourful, still mostly meat-driven food. He joined the team in 2016 after a career in fine dining in Vancouver and Italy, with a foray into casual with his highly rated food truck, Street Meet. He's now the development chef for the company and works alongside Wildebeest's chef de cuisine Ian McHale, nurturing his close relationship with local farmers and artisan producers to put the best products on the table. That could include goat, game, bison and even horse. "It's the playful and edgy side of casual fine dining," says Pape. And adds, "It's aging pretty well."

SHISHITO PEPPER PURÉE

2 Tbsp canola oil
1 cup shishito peppers
1 small shallot, kept whole
1 clove garlic
3 Tbsp whipping (33%) cream
2 Tbsp unsalted butter
Juice of 1 lime
Salt, to taste

SPOT PRAWN BISQUE

2 Tbsp canola oil
½ small white onion, chopped
2 cloves garlic, sliced
1 (1½-inch) piece ginger, peeled and chopped
1 lb spot prawn shells
1 tsp ground cumin
1 tsp ground coriander
1 tsp chili powder
1 tsp ground turmeric
1 tsp crushed red pepper
1 tsp freshly ground black pepper
1 (398-mL) can coconut milk
1 cup water or vegetable stock
Juice of 1 lime, to taste
Salt, to taste

PERCH

2 Tbsp canola oil (divided)
4 ocean perch or rockfish fillets
2 Tbsp unsalted butter
2 sprigs fresh thyme
16 garlic scapes
16 shishito peppers
Fresh cilantro leaves, for garnish

Pan-Roasted Ocean Perch

SERVES 4

The team at Wildebeest would like you to know they're not all meat, all the time. Just to prove it, there's this dish of tender perch, roasted and given a touch of heat with shishito peppers.

SHISHITO PEPPER PURÉE Heat oil in a large frying pan over medium-high heat. Add shishito peppers, shallot and garlic and sauté for 5 minutes, until softened. Remove from heat and cool slightly. Transfer to a blender, add remaining ingredients and purée until smooth.

SPOT PRAWN BISQUE Heat oil in a medium saucepan over medium-high heat. Add onions, garlic, ginger and spot prawn shells and cook for 15 minutes, until onions have softened and shells are bright coral pink. Add spices and sauté for 2 to 3 minutes, until spices are toasted and fragrant and prawn shells are well coated.

Reduce heat to medium-low and stir in coconut milk and water (or stock). Simmer for 1 hour.

Strain out solids and discard. Return bisque to a clean saucepan and simmer for 30 minutes, until reduced by half. Season with lime juice and salt to taste.

PERCH Heat 1 tablespoon oil in a large cast-iron or non-stick frying pan over medium-high heat. Place fish skin-side down in the pan and cook for 3 minutes. Add butter and thyme and baste fish for another minute, until cooked through and skin is crispy.

In a separate pan, heat remaining 1 tablespoon oil over medium heat, add garlic scapes and shishito peppers and sauté for 5 to 10 minutes, until golden brown.

Put a few dots of pepper purée on each of 4 plates, then add a few tablespoons of bisque in the centre of each. Arrange shishitos and scapes on the plates and top with seared perch. Garnish with cilantro.

VEAL SWEETBREADS
1 lb veal sweetbreads
4 cups whole milk
2 sprigs fresh thyme
1 clove garlic

PICKLED BLACK MISSION FIGS
2 Tbsp white wine
3 Tbsp extra-virgin olive oil
Salt, to taste
10 dried Black Mission figs, stems
    removed and cut into quarters

OLIVE TAPENADE
1 cup Castelvetrano olives, pitted
1 Tbsp grainy mustard
1 clove garlic
1 small shallot, chopped
3 Tbsp extra-virgin olive oil
2 Tbsp malt vinegar
Pinch of crushed red pepper

ASSEMBLY
3 Tbsp canola oil
1 cup all-purpose flour
4 slices sourdough bread
1 small shallot, cut into rings
Kosher salt, to taste
Microgreens or fresh parsley
    leaves, for garnish

Sweetbreads on Toast

SERVES 4

Although Wildebeest is no longer as focused on offal as it once was, this is still one of the most popular appetizers on the menu. Sweetbread is a pretty name for pancreas or thymus glands (don't think about it too closely), which have a delicately nutty flavour and velvety texture that make them a prized delicacy among gourmands.

VEAL SWEETBREADS Soak sweetbreads in cold water for at least 4 hours and up to 24 to remove any traces of blood.

Place all ingredients in a large saucepan and bring to a boil. Reduce heat to low and poach for 15 minutes. Remove sweetbreads from poaching liquid and set aside to cool.

Remove membrane and any veins or gristle from sweetbreads. (Be prepared—this could take some time.)

PICKLED BLACK MISSION FIGS In a bowl, combine wine, olive oil and salt and mix well. Add figs, then cover and refrigerate overnight to marinate.

OLIVE TAPENADE Combine all ingredients in a food processor and process until combined and slightly chunky.

ASSEMBLY Heat oil in a cast-iron or heavy-bottomed frying pan over medium heat. Put flour in a shallow bowl and dredge sweetbreads. Add sweetbreads to pan and sear for 5 minutes, until golden brown on all sides.

Toast bread.

Spread tapenade on toast, add sweetbreads and top with shallots and pickled figs. Season with salt and garnish with microgreens or parsley leaves.

ISABEL CHUNG

The Wildflower

THERE WAS A time when Isabel Chung thought
she would love the big city life. That was when she
was executive sous chef at the Fairmont Olympic in
Seattle. Then she came to Whistler and fell in love
with the mountains. "I've mellowed out a lot," she
says with a laugh. Now she lives in Pemberton, where
she finds culinary inspiration at some of B.C.'s best
farms. "The very best thing about living here is the
support for eating local," she says.

She brings all those tasty ideas back with her to
the Fairmont Chateau Whistler, where she oversees
all the restaurants and banquet facilities. But her
pride and joy is The Wildflower, the hotel's refined
casual Pacific Northwest restaurant. It has the feel
of an elegant steakhouse, she explains, but is still
approachable enough for families looking for a
relaxed meal after a day of boarding or biking.

"I want people to feel welcome," she says. "The
dining clientele is constantly evolving. These days, it's
younger people, people with families."

And so the menu offers refined dishes such as
rack of lamb and duck breast, but also features a
"Massive Meat Ball"—nine ounces of beef and pork
served with spaghetti and tomato sauce. "The food
is really comforting," she says. It's just the thing you
crave after a long day of exploring the wild mountain
country—or just browsing through the glorious Emily
Carrs at the Audain Art Museum.

One thing you will always find on her menus is
smoked salmon. She fell in love with hot-smoked fish
after she caught a huge salmon in Campbell River and
a neighbour helped her smoke it. It perfectly encapsulates her style of food: at once elegant and informal
and offering an authentic taste of the place she lives.

POTATO SALAD

1 lb fresh local baby potatoes, cut in half or quarters
2 Tbsp extra-virgin olive oil
½ tsp fresh thyme leaves
Pinch of salt, plus extra to taste
⅓ cup diced thick-cut bacon
½ lb green beans
1 shallot, finely sliced
1 Tbsp grainy mustard
1 tsp grated lemon zest
1 Tbsp chopped fresh Italian parsley

SPICE BLEND

1 Tbsp coriander seeds
1 Tbsp mustard seeds
1 clove
1 Tbsp black peppercorns
3 to 4 allspice berries
½ tsp fennel seeds
1 Tbsp smoked paprika
1 tsp garlic powder
½ tsp celery seeds

SALMON

Apple or cherry wood chips, soaked in water
4 (6-oz) salmon fillets
Kosher salt, to taste
Spice Blend (see here), to taste
¼ cup liquid honey

NOTE:

There will be extra spice—save it for the next time or try it on chicken or prawns. Any smaller amount becomes difficult to grind in an electric mill. Store in the fridge for up to 3 months.

Spiced Honey Smoked Salmon with Potato Salad

SERVES 4

This is the easiest smoked salmon ever—more of a grilled salmon with a nice, spicy rub. In the warmer months, Chef Isabel Chung likes to serve it with gnocchi and asparagus tips; in cooler months, with the potato salad below.

POTATO SALAD Preheat oven to 350°F.

In a medium bowl, combine potatoes, oil, thyme and salt and toss until well coated. Transfer to a roasting pan and roast for 30 minutes, until potatoes are cooked through and crisp on the outside. Remove from oven and set aside.

Add bacon to a frying pan and cook over medium-high heat for 10 minutes, until crisp and fat is rendered. Add green beans and shallots and cook for 2 minutes, until tender. Remove from heat.

Add green beans and bacon to pan of potatoes, and stir in mustard, lemon zest and parsley. Toss well, adjust seasoning and set aside.

SPICE BLEND Put coriander seeds, mustard seeds, clove, peppercorns, allspice berries and fennel seeds in a small frying pan and toast over medium heat for 2 to 3 minutes, until fragrant. Set aside to cool slightly.

Transfer toasted spices to a spice grinder or clean coffee grinder. Pulse until well ground but not reduced to dust. Transfer to a small bowl and add paprika, garlic powder and celery seeds. Stir until well combined.

SALMON Fire up a smoker or preheat barbecue to 325°F. Add wood chips and ensure that you have a good quantity of smoke in the cabinet. (Alternatively, grill the salmon over apple or cherry wood chunks.)

Pat salmon dry and season lightly with salt. Generously sprinkle spice blend over salmon until it is fully covered.

Smoke for 10 minutes for medium rare and until edges are just browned. Remove from smoker and drizzle with raw honey. Serve with potato salad.

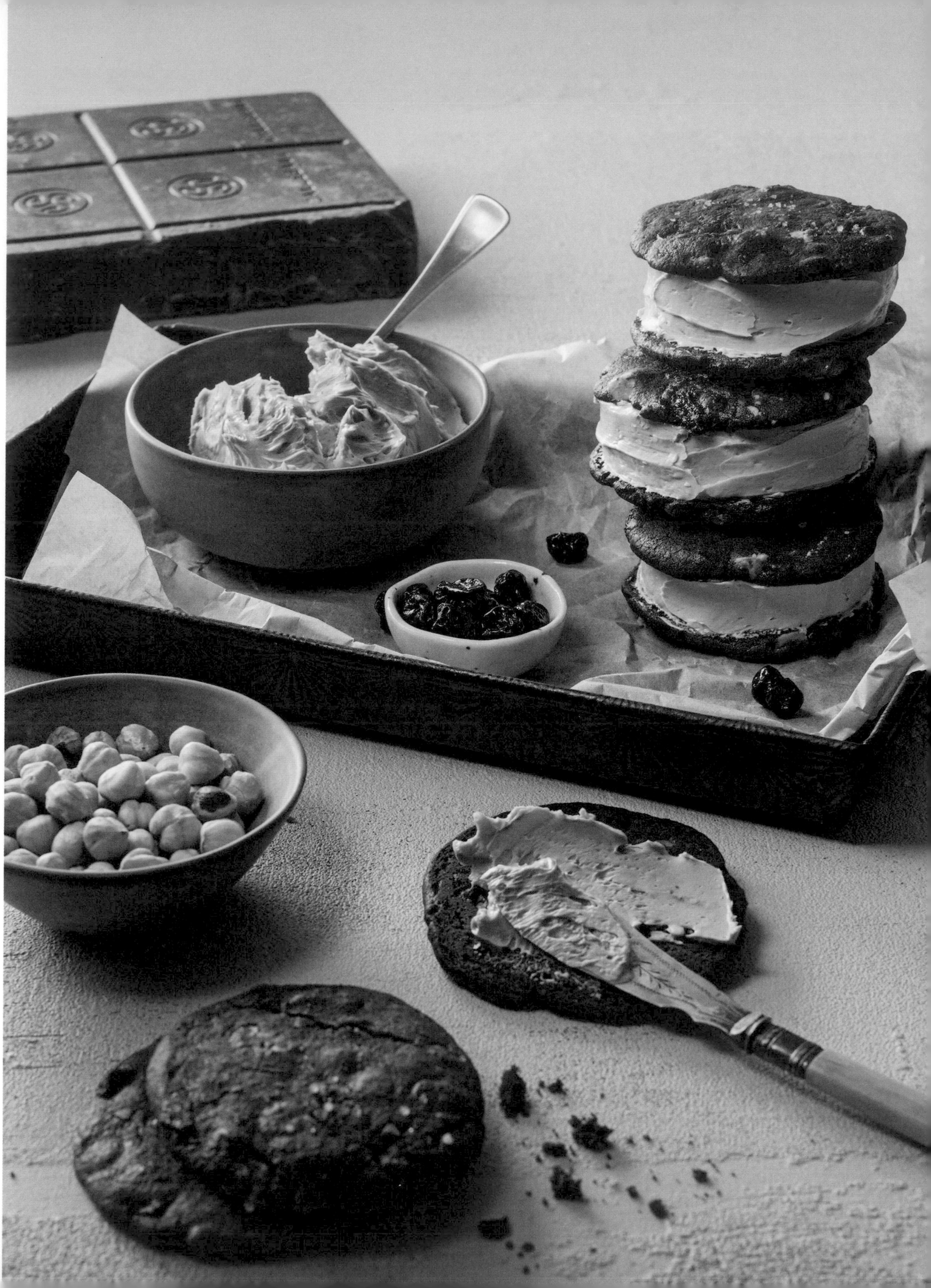

HAZELNUT CAPPUCCINO ICE CREAM
5 large egg yolks
⅔ cup granulated sugar
1 cup 2% milk
1 cup heavy (36%) cream
¾ cup cold espresso
¼ cup Frangelico liqueur

DARK CHOCOLATE, B.C. CHERRY AND HAZELNUT COOKIES
¾ cup (1½ sticks) unsalted butter, room temperature
⅔ cup packed brown sugar
⅓ cup granulated sugar
1 large egg
1 tsp pure vanilla extract
1½ cups all-purpose flour
⅓ cup cocoa powder
½ tsp baking soda
½ tsp fine sea salt
1 cup dark chocolate, cut into small chunks, or dark chocolate chips
½ cup dried B.C. cherries
½ cup toasted hazelnuts, lightly crushed
Flaky sea salt, for sprinkling

"Nuts about Cherries" Ice Cream Sandwich

MAKES 12 TO 24

Chewy, nutty, chocolatey and with the lusciously cool taste of ice cream—truly, can anything be better? If you don't have an ice cream maker (or are too lazy to get yours out of storage), you can always use slightly softened store-bought ice cream. Or, just enjoy the cookies on their own. We won't tell.

HAZELNUT CAPPUCCINO ICE CREAM Place ice cream machine bowl in freezer at least 24 hours before churning.

In a heatproof mixing bowl, whisk together egg yolks and sugar.

Combine milk and cream in a saucepan and bring to a simmer over medium heat.

While whisking, slowly pour cream mixture into egg yolk mixture. Return mixture to a clean saucepan over medium heat and stir constantly until slightly thickened and mixture coats the back of a wooden spoon. (It should reach a temperature of 170°F and no more than 180°F, or it might curdle.) Remove from heat.

Stir in espresso and Frangelico. Chill mixture overnight in a shallow container.

The next day, pour cooled mixture into an ice cream maker and freeze according to the manufacturer's instructions. Remove from machine and place ice cream in a freezer-safe container and freeze for 2 hours, until thick but still malleable.

DARK CHOCOLATE, B.C. CHERRY AND HAZELNUT COOKIES In a stand mixer fitted with a paddle attachment, cream butter and both sugars until light and fluffy. Beat in egg and vanilla extract.

In a separate bowl, sift together flour, cocoa powder, baking soda and fine sea salt.

Stir dry ingredients into wet ingredients and mix until well combined. Stir in chopped chocolate (or chocolate chips), cherries and hazelnuts. Chill for at least 30 minutes.

Preheat oven to 350°F. Line 2 baking sheets with parchment paper.

Drop cookie dough by the spoonful onto prepared baking sheets, evenly spacing them at least 1 inch apart. Flatten slightly with the back of a spoon and sprinkle very lightly with flaky sea salt. Bake for 10 minutes. (Cookies will still be soft to the touch.) Remove from oven and cool on wire racks to room temperature.

Place baking sheets in freezer and freeze cookies through before filling.

ASSEMBLY Remove cookies and ice cream from freezer. Generously layer ice cream between 2 cookies, then wrap in parchment paper or plastic wrap. Repeat with remaining cookies and ice cream. Return assembled cookies to freezer. Serve.

Metric Conversion Chart

VOLUME

IMPERIAL	METRIC
⅛ tsp	0.5 mL
¼ tsp	1 mL
½ tsp	2.5 mL
¾ tsp	4 mL
1 tsp	5 mL
½ Tbsp	8 mL
1 Tbsp	15 mL
1½ Tbsp	23 mL
2 Tbsp	30 mL
¼ cup	60 mL
⅓ cup	80 mL
½ cup	125 mL
⅔ cup	165 mL
¾ cup	185 mL
1 cup	250 mL
1¼ cups	310 mL
1⅓ cups	330 mL
1½ cups	375 mL
1⅔ cups	415 mL
1¾ cups	435 mL
2 cups	500 mL
2¼ cups	560 mL
2⅓ cups	580 mL
2½ cups	625 mL
2¾ cups	690 mL
3 cups	750 mL
4 cups/1 qt	1 L
5 cups	1.25 L
6 cups	1.5 L
7 cups	1.75 L
8 cups	2 L
12 cups	3 L

LIQUID MEASURES
(for alcohol)

IMPERIAL	METRIC
½ fl oz	15 mL
1 fl oz	30 mL
2 fl oz	60 mL
3 fl oz	90 mL
4 fl oz	120 mL

CANS AND JARS

IMPERIAL	METRIC
6 oz	170 g
14 oz	398 mL
19 oz	540 mL
28 oz	796 mL

WEIGHT

IMPERIAL	METRIC
½ oz	15 g
1 oz	30 g
2 oz	60 g
3 oz	85 g
4 oz (¼ lb)	115 g
5 oz	140 g
6 oz	170 g
7 oz	200 g
8 oz (½ lb)	225 g
9 oz	255 g
10 oz	285 g
11 oz	310 g
12 oz (¾ lb)	340 g
13 oz	370 g
14 oz	400 g
15 oz	425 g
16 oz (1 lb)	450 g
1¼ lbs	570 g
1½ lbs	670 g
2 lbs	900 g
3 lbs	1.4 kg
4 lbs	1.8 kg
5 lbs	2.3 kg
6 lbs	2.7 kg

LINEAR

IMPERIAL	METRIC
⅛ inch	3 mm
¼ inch	6 mm
½ inch	12 mm
¾ inch	2 cm
1 inch	2.5 cm
1¼ inches	3 cm
1½ inches	3.5 cm
1¾ inches	4.5 cm
2 inches	5 cm
2½ inches	6.5 cm
3 inches	7.5 cm
4 inches	10 cm
5 inches	12.5 cm
6 inches	15 cm
7 inches	18 cm
10 inches	25 cm
12 inches (1 foot)	30 cm
13 inches	33 cm
16 inches	41 cm
18 inches	46 cm
24 inches (2 feet)	60 cm
28 inches	70 cm
30 inches	75 cm
6 feet	1.8 m

TEMPERATURE

(For oven temperatures, see chart below)

IMPERIAL	METRIC
90°F	32°C
120°F	49°C
125°F	52°C
130°F	54°C
140°F	60°C
150°F	66°C
155°F	68°C
160°F	71°C
165°F	74°C
170°F	77°C
175°F	80°C
180°F	82°C
190°F	88°C
200°F	93°C
240°F	116°C
250°F	121°C
300°F	149°C
325°F	163°C
350°F	177°C
360°F	182°C
375°F	191°C

OVEN TEMPERATURE

IMPERIAL	METRIC
200°F	95°C
250°F	120°C
275°F	135°C
300°F	150°C
325°F	160°C
350°F	180°C
375°F	190°C
400°F	200°C
425°F	220°C
450°F	230°C
500°F	260°C
550°F	290°C

BAKING PANS

IMPERIAL	METRIC
5- × 9-inch loaf pan	2 L loaf pan
9- × 13-inch cake pan	4 L cake pan
11- × 17-inch baking sheet	30 × 45 cm baking sheet

Acknowledgements

MANY PEOPLE were involved in cooking up something as delicious and complex as this book, and that means many thanks are due.

It starts and ends, of course, with the chefs and bartenders in these pages. Vancouver is truly fortunate to have so many talented and passionate culinary professionals defining the city's cuisine, and it has been a real pleasure working with you all on this. Thank you for your time, your stories, your delicious food and your patience in answering all my questions.

Thank you, too, to the remarkable publicists and assistants and all those who deftly fielded requests and wrangled timetables and kept the chefs running on time, which is no easy task. You know who you are—all true professionals without whom I couldn't do my job.

On a personal note, I'd like to thank Amy Rosen for putting my name forward to Figure 1 in the first place, and Lionel Wild for bravely sampling all the recipes I tested, even the ones that didn't quite work out in the first round.

Working with Figure 1 has been a true delight, and how often do you hear that in the world of publishing? It never felt like anything but a real collaboration with senior editor Michelle Meade, who made the whole process seem easy and fun, and at the same time made my words sing. Even the copy edits were a pleasure, thanks to the thoughtful Grace Yaginuma. Because of her, we all know our fermented radishes now.

Diners taste first with their eyes, and this book is a sumptuous visual feast, thanks to photographer Kevin Clark, creative director Jessica Sullivan, art director Naomi MacDougall and prop stylist Issha Marie. Thanks, too, to the ceramicists, woodworkers and other creative folks who loaned us props for our epic shoot: Kelsey Kovacevich; Eikcam Ceramics; LISSU linen; the Wild Bunch; Don Asperin Woodworks; Union Wood Co.; Tina Kami; Anja Schulz; and Mitch Iburg Ceramics.

This book has truly been a labour of love, a culinary ode to a remarkable city that is redefining cuisine with its own unique flavour. I can't wait until you taste what we've created here!

Index

About the Author

JOANNE SASVARI is a journalist who covers food, drink and travel for *Vancouver Sun*, WestJet and Destination BC, among others. She is the editor of *Westcoast Homes & Design* magazine and former editor of *FLAVOURS* magazine. Certified by the Wine and Spirit Education Trust (WSET), she writes about spirits and cocktails for the *Alchemist* and *TASTE* magazines. She is also the author of *Paprika: A Spicy Memoir from Hungary*, *Frommer's EasyGuide to Vancouver and Victoria* and *The Wickaninnish Cookbook*. She currently lives in North Vancouver, where she is working on her next book.

JOANNE SASVARI